From E
Adoration to
Evangelization

From Eucharistic Adoration to Evangelization

Edited by

Alcuin Reid

burns & oates

Published by Burns & Oates International

A Continuum Imprint
The Tower Building, 11 York Road, London SE1 7NX
80 Maiden Lane, Suite 704, New York NY 10038

www.continuumbooks.com

British Library Cataloguing-in-Publication Data
A catalogue record for this book is available from the British Library

ISBN: 978-1-4411-0227-0 (paperback)

Typeset by Newgen Imaging Systems Pvt Ltd, Chennai, India
Printed in India

Contents

Editor's Preface

Adoratio 2011 was more an event than a conference. It brought to Rome more than three hundred clergy, religious and laity from around the world not only to listen to eminent speakers, but to pray together in the Sacred Liturgy – daily in the solemn celebration of the Sacrifice of the Mass and of the Liturgy of the Hours – and throughout each night in solemn Adoration of the Blessed Sacrament.

This volume makes available the texts of all the conferences and homilies from *Adoratio 2011*. The organizers wished to make them available as soon as possible in order to ensure that the teaching and witness they contain will be available to those who could not be present in Rome as well as to assist all in the apostolate of the New Evangelization, which is fundamentally Eucharistic.

We are indebted to the speakers for providing their texts so readily, and to the many translators who have worked quickly to ensure the prompt publication of this book. To that end, the book's publication has not been delayed by an insistence upon rigorous academic referencing: the texts stand, by and large, as the authors presented them in Rome. It is to be hoped that the authors' sources are clear and easily accessible in English. The opinions they express herein remain their own.

The event that was *Adoratio 2011* encompassed something of the vitality and rich Catholic diversity of the Church united with and under Peter at the beginning of the third millennium. May the efforts of its speakers and its organizers bring forth an abundant harvest!

Dom Alcuin Reid

Welcome

Bishop Gino Reali
Bishop of Porto-Santa Rufina, Italy
Translated from Italian by E. Scott Borgman

At the beginning of this International Congress on Eucharistic Adoration, brought about by His Excellency Bishop Dominique Rey, Bishop of Fréjus-Toulon, France, and organized by the Missionaries of the Most Holy Eucharist, I am happy to offer you my most cordial greetings and to welcome each of you to this house belonging to the Sons of Don Bosco.

Along with this greeting to Bishop Rey, I give a fraternal welcome to the cardinals and bishops who will guide the reflections and prayers in the following days. Furthermore, welcome to the distinguished speakers and to all those who in their various responsibilities are contributing to the intense programme of work of this Congress in order that it may produce good fruit for our spiritual lives and for the ministry, which all of us are called to give to the Church and to the world.

I also hope to express the joy of welcoming into our diocese such an important initiative as this one, which has captured the attention of such a great number of participants. There are also great expectations attached to this most decisive part of our faith and pastoral mission, which is that of recognizing and adoring the Lord, Who is sacramentally present among His own, feeding and guiding them as He accompanies them on the paths of testifying and proclaiming the Gospel.

The Church of Porto-Santa Rufina, which welcomes you in these days is, along with the Church of Ostia, the oldest of the suburbicarian dioceses [dioceses surrounding Rome]. Tradition has it that St Peter evangelized this territory and founded the first Christian communities on this periphery of Rome. Located on the north-west side, between the city and the sea, this ancient Church, called 'Portuense', has grown enormously in population since the middle of the last century. This expansion continues to transform the entire territory of the diocese with the appearing of new neighbourhoods on the Roman side and of entire new cities on the coastal area. This surge in population requires additional generosity from the Christian community in its apostolic work and in its witness to holiness.

Indeed, this holiness of life in Christians is the most convincing and effective form of evangelization within the Christian proposal, as is proven in the history of our Church. The memory of the holy *Portuensi* martyrs and of the martyrs of the *Selva Candida*, who with their witness and with their blood irrigated our land, urges us to be coherent and courageous as we truly serve the Gospel.

The name of our Church conserves the name of the ancient settlements of the community: the gate of Rome, the mouth of the Tiber and the basilica of the Holy Martyrs *Rufina* and *Secunda*, on the *Via Boccea*, between the ancient consular roads, the *Aurelia* and the *Cassia*. These are well known to 'Roman' pilgrims and, therefore, our name conserves and proposes once again the special vocation of this Church which is that of being the *gate of Rome*, that of giving a brotherly welcome to those who are on the road towards the city of Peter and towards the tombs of the apostles. We intend to honour this vocation by growing evermore in our communion and faithfulness to the apostolic See and in the love toward the successor of Peter, sustaining daily with our prayers the ministry of the Holy Father, Pope Benedict XVI, to whom we want to offer today our filial congratulations for the sixtieth anniversary of his priestly ordination.

The same Pope Benedict XVI never tires of repeating to us that, in the life of the Christian, the harmony of two points of reference must be lived out. The first is the prioritizing and fundamental reference to Christ and to His friendship. The second is the reference to our fellow man and to the world – the place where this friendship with Christ must live itself out and expand until it reaches everyone. This model is evident when Jesus first calls the apostles to *be* with Him before sending them out into the world to preach (cf. Mk 3.14–15); furthermore, He also proposes this same path to the other disciples.

To place the Eucharist at the centre of the life of the Church and at the centre of our lives is to place the encounter with Christ before all else, to be with Him, identifying Him in that extraordinary sacramental presence which precedes and excels all other forms of the presence of the Lord. And the Eucharist transforms us. In particular, Eucharistic Adoration becomes union. The Pope was saying this to the youth gathered in Cologne in August of 2005, explaining the different meanings of the term *'Adoration'* in Greek and in Latin:

'*Proskynesis* . . . refers to the gesture of submission, the recognition of God as our true measure . . . The Latin word for adoration is *ad-oratio* – mouth to mouth contact, a kiss, an embrace, and hence, ultimately love. Submission becomes union, because he to whom we submit is Love' (Homily, 21 August 2005).

I truly hope that all of you may, through this Congress, deepen your experience of the love of Jesus, which sustains us, which calls us together, sends us into the world and saves us.

Thank you and may your work be profitable!

Introduction

Bishop Dominique Rey
Bishop of Fréjus-Toulon, France

Your Excellency, Bishop Reali, thank you for your welcome to the Diocese of Porto Santa Rufina, in which we are situated here at the Salesianum.

Your Excellencies, brother priests, dear deacons and religious men and women, ladies and gentlemen, it is a great privilege to stand before you and to welcome so many people from all parts of the world to the Salesianum here in Rome for *Adoratio 2011*.

At the very beginning I wish to thank Father Florian Racine, founder of the Missionaries of the Most Holy Eucharist, a new community in my diocese, and his team for all the preparations they have made for us. And I wish to thank all those who will help us throughout the conference with the many different practical arrangements, the translations into different languages, the liturgical celebrations, etc. Thank you, also, to the team here at the Salesianum who have already given us a warm welcome.

I wish to say at the outset that *Adoratio 2011* is not a conference. It is an event. It is an ecclesial event. Yes, there are important conferences to which we shall listen and that we shall discuss. But there is much more. During these days we will pray and adore Jesus Christ together as Catholics united in the faith of the Church. We will share our meals. In our conversations we shall share our hopes and experiences as fellow disciples of the Risen Lord. Then we will bring *Adoratio 2011* to a close as we stand and kneel and walk with our beloved Holy Father Pope Benedict XVI, in celebrating the feast of Corpus Domini.

My brothers and sisters, most people in the world do not share our faith in Jesus Christ and in His One, Holy, Catholic and Apostolic Church. They need to hear the Good News. They need to live the Gospel. They need to know that salvation comes through Jesus Christ in His Church. They need a New Evangelization.

The New Evangelization is a response to the spiritual and moral breathlessness of our society. It is born from the keen awareness of the Church's missionary identity and from a new spiritual hunger arising in the face of the economic upheaval and the social, cultural and ethical issues affecting us. 'The New Evangelization is the task that lies ahead', wrote Blessed John Paul II in *Ecclesia in Europa*. The history of the Church witnesses to this: missionary revivals are rooted in movements of Eucharistic renewal. 'An authentically Eucharistic Church is a missionary Church' (*Sacramentum caritatis*, 84). As we walk the path of the New Evangelization, Christ invites us to rediscover the place of Eucharistic Adoration as 'the source and summit' (*Lumen gentium*, 11) of the mission of the Church.

But the first condition for the New Evangelization is adoration. We, the Church, must regain the ability to adore Christ in the Most Holy Eucharist, in the Sacrifice of the Mass and in adoration of the Blessed Sacrament outside of the Mass if we are to bring the men and women of the twenty-first century to faith in Jesus Christ. This is one of the key themes of the pontificate of Pope Benedict XVI, and this is why we are here.

It is my hope, it is my wish, and it is my fervent prayer that each of us will leave Rome after these days, with hearts that have grown larger in love through our adoration of Jesus Christ, who offered Himself in sacrifice on the cross for the salvation of all, which sacrifice He continues to make present to us today in the Holy Mass. It is my hope that we will leave here with minds that have been stimulated and challenged by the eminent and excellent speakers who have so kindly agreed to make presentations to us. Above all, it is my desire that, because of our participation in this event, each of us, in our different vocations and states of life, will be stronger Apostles and evangelists for the world.

May Almighty God bless you for your presence at *Adoratio 2011*! May God the Holy Spirit inspire you during these days! And may Jesus Christ, the unique saviour of the world, reward you for all that you do in His name!

One

Adoration and the New Evangelization

Bishop Dominique Rey
Bishop of Fréjus-Toulon, France
Translated from French by Sean Davidson

Introduction – The Call to a New Evangelization

The New Evangelization is a spiritual, theological and pastoral challenge with which the Church finds herself faced. In fact, we find ourselves at the beginning of the third millennium in a new paradigm: that of post-modernity which requires us to 'begin again in Christ' with an Evangelization 'new in its ardour, methods and expression' (discourse of Blessed John Paul II at the 19th Plenary Assembly of CELAM, 9 March 1983).

The term 'New Evangelization' invented by Blessed John Paul II (and repeated by him, more than 300 times in his discourses) makes reference first of all to the Church's awareness of her missionary identity and second to the acknowledgement of the considerable economic, social, cultural and ethical upheavals in our society.

Blessed John Paul II, in the wake of what Pope Paul VI had already expressed in the Apostolic Exhortation, *Evangelii nuntiandi*, reminded the faithful in various ways of the need for a new missionary season for the whole People of God. At the dawn of the third millennium not only are there many peoples who do not yet know the Good News, but there are many Christians who need the Word of God to be re-announced to them in a persuasive manner so that they may concretely experience the power of the Gospel.

Many of our brothers and sisters are 'baptized, but insufficiently evangelized'. In a number of cases, nations once rich in faith and in vocations are losing their identity under the influence of a secularized culture . . . The Church, sure of her Lord's fidelity, never tires of proclaiming the Good News of the

Gospel and invites all Christians to discover anew the attraction of following Christ. (Benedict XVI, *Verbum Domini*, 96)

The history of Evangelization across the centuries witnesses that the great missionaries were also great people of prayer, more specifically that they were authentic adorers. Indeed, the Eucharist is 'the source and the summit of the Christian life' (*Lumen gentium*, 11), and the 'source and summit of all evangelisation' (*Presbyterorum ordinis*, 5).

Eucharistic Adoration is by its Nature Missionary

In his general audience of 21 June 2000, Blessed John Paul II underlined with force the missionary dimension of the Eucharist:

> The celebration of the Eucharist, the Sacrament of the Lord's Passover, *is in itself a missionary event,* which plants the fertile seed of new life in the world. This *missionary* aspect of the Eucharist is explicitly recalled by St Paul in the Letter to the Corinthians: 'As often as you eat this bread and drink this cup, you proclaim the Lord's death until He comes' (1 Cor. 11.26).

The Church repeats St Paul's words in the doxology after the Consecration. The Eucharist is a 'missionary' Sacrament not only because the grace of mission flows from it, but also because it contains in itself the principle and eternal source of salvation for all. The celebration of the Eucharistic Sacrifice is therefore the most effective missionary act that the Ecclesial Community can perform in the history of the world.

Pope Benedict XVI teaches:

> The Eucharist is thus the source and summit not only of the Church's life, but also of her mission: 'an authentically Eucharistic Church is a missionary Church'. We too must be able to tell our brothers and sisters with conviction: 'That which we have seen and heard we proclaim also to you, so that you may have fellowship with us' (1 Jn 1.3). Missionary outreach is thus an essential part of the Eucharistic form of the Christian life. (Benedict XVI, *Sacramentum caritatis*, 84)

The New Evangelization must therefore be anchored in a true Eucharistic renewal and in particular in a renewal of Eucharistic Adoration. This liturgical prayer which prolongs the Eucharistic celebration has specific dimensions which give structure to the missionary activity of the Church. The New Evangelization must assume and integrate all of these dimensions.

Eucharistic Adoration: To Make Salvation Visible

During the years which accompanied and followed the Council there developed a pastoral practice of obfuscation, a over-valuing of 'the world' as a theological reality. Are our societies not pervaded by and transformed from within by the Holy Spirit? Beginning from the seeds of truth, spoken of in *Gaudium et spes*, a pastoral strategy of listening and encounter was developed. The Church was seen as the bridge extended towards the world by Christ (cf. Discourse of Paul VI at the opening of the 3rd session of the Second Vatican Council, 1964).

This very positive approach to the world is not without doctrinal and spiritual truth. But it showed its limitations very quickly. Certain pastoral programmes, seeking to be too much one with the world, were diluted into a horizontal humanism. The obfuscation sometimes became a total disappearance. We witnessed an 'auto-secularization' of the Church as Cardinal Ratzinger observed, in the secular reductionism of the faith. The Gospel was thus emptied of its provocative force. Announcing the Gospel was replaced by a promotion of 'Gospel values'. Certain catechesis at times sought to make the faith consensual and acceptable for everybody. One forgot that the Christian faith transcends all supposed 'inclusivity' and that it is a refusal to remain enclosed within the immanence of the world. The Christian is not 'of the world' (in the Greek sense of the term), that is to say on the side of those who refuse to hear the voice of Christ (cf. 1 Jn 4.4–6). The Gospel because of its newness always finds itself removed from the 'world', which is old because of sin. The Church is not there to espouse the evolution of trends. She is not the hostage of fashions.

The end of the twentieth century has sounded the hour of 'disenchantment' (Marcel Gauchet). To the economic and social difficulties, often linked to globalization, were added the institutional crises (the state, schools, politics). The traditional systems of ethical reference have disintegrated. It is the failure of the great political utopias.

The New Evangelization is a response to the spiritual and moral lifelessness of our society. It responds to the insistent repeated appeals of Paul VI, Blessed John Paul II and Benedict XVI, who insist that the task of Evangelization is the most profound task in these times which are our own; and that 'the New Evangelisation is the duty which awaits you' (Blessed John Paul II, *Ecclesia in Europa*, 45).

Eucharistic Adoration underlines liturgically the transition from a pastoral practice of obfuscation to a pastoral practice of visibility and attestation. The hidden presence of Christ in the consecrated species is given in order to be seen and to enable one to see.

Eucharistic Adoration – the Primacy of Grace in all Apostolates

Blessed John Paul II teaches that:

> In order to realize an efficacious work of Evangelization, we must return to, seek inspiration from, the first apostolic model. This model, which is foundational and paradigmatic, we contemplate in the Cenacle: the Apostles are united to Mary and they persevere with her in waiting for the gift of the Holy Spirit. It is only with the outpouring of the Holy Spirit that the work of Evangelization begins. It is necessary therefore to commence evangelization by invoking the Holy Spirit and in searching where He blows (cf Jn 3.8). (Speech, 6th Symposium of the Episcopal Conferences of Europe, 11 October 1985)

Mission begins in the Cenacle with a Pentecostal experience. Without the Spirit who is the soul of all apostolate, Evangelization becomes proselytism, propaganda, recruiting or a publicity campaign.

Prayer is the Motor of Mission

> 'Jesus preached by day, by night He prayed'. With these few words, [the author] wished to say: Jesus had to acquire the disciples from God. The same is always true. We ourselves cannot gather men. We must acquire them by God for God. All methods are empty without the foundation of prayer. The word of the announcement must always be drenched in an intense life of prayer. (Joseph Cardinal Ratzinger, The New Evangelization, 10 December 2000)

Prayer commits us to radicalizing our relationship with Christ. All mission begins with a resignation, a gift of one's entire life to Christ as the only Lord and Saviour.

The missionary must remember, not only Pentecost, but also the Last Supper. His prayer is centred upon the contemplation of the sacrifice which Jesus makes of His own life. In the *tertia pars* of the *Summa theologiae* St Thomas Aquinas underlines that the Sacrament of the Eucharist 'commemorates the Passion of the Lord'. The Church remembers (anamnesis) the central and foundational event of faith which Jesus accomplished during the Last Supper.

Adoration is the Memorial of the Last Supper

Adoration places us in a 'Paschal situation'. It is an encounter with the infinite love of God revealed in Jesus Christ and which is made present under the consecrated species. God reveals Himself without condition. He leaves man helpless in the face of the marvel of His manifestation: an all-powerful God Who makes Himself so small, so poor, under the appearance of bread. From this point of view, the singularity of Eucharistic Adoration, compared to all other forms of prayer, comes from the fact that by the sacramental presence of Jesus the Host, God takes the initiative in coming to meet us. Christ precedes me in the response that the Father awaits. Cardinal Ratzinger says, 'the Eucharist means, God has answered: The Eucharist is God as an answer, as an answering presence'.[1] St John-Mary Vianney wrote: 'When God wanted to give a food to our soul which would sustain it in the pilgrimage of life, He cast His gaze over all of creation and found nothing which would be worthy of it. Thus He withdrew into Himself and resolved to give His Very Self to us'. The Eucharist actualizes this gift.

Eucharistic Adoration is a school of fervour. In contemplating the Eucharistic Jesus, given so that the world might have life, we are invited to give our own life in return, to Christ and to our brothers. The Eucharist heals us of indifference and of turning in upon ourselves. In plunging ourselves into Adoration we discover our consistency as Christians.

Eucharistic Adoration is also a prayer of reparation. Blessed John Paul II, in his Apostolic Letter for the Year of the Eucharist (2004–5), spoke of contemplating Jesus present in the Eucharist: 'to make reparation by our faith and love for the acts of carelessness and neglect, and even the insults which our Saviour must endure in many parts of the world' (*Mane nobiscum Domine*, 18). In 1980 he urged us 'to make reparation for the great faults and crimes of the world by our unceasing adoration' (Letter, *Dominicæ Cenæ*, 24 February 1980). It is in this way that Jesus addressed Himself in the seventeenth century to St Margaret-Mary in Paray-le-Monial. Christ invited the humble Visitation sister to prostrate herself before the Blessed Sacrament during the night from Thursday to Friday to accompany Him in His agony.

Eucharistic Adoration, Evangelization of Self

The first person encountered by mission is the missionary himself. He must let himself be evangelized by Christ, whom he will have the vocation to announce. The New Evangelization is a school of personal sanctification, but also of conversion and interior purification.

The world which rejects God or which doesn't recognize Him in the face of Jesus Christ, suffers from various sicknesses and

---

[1]   Joseph Cardinal Ratzinger, *God is Near Us*, San Francisco: Ignatius, 2003, p. 90.

knows many sufferings. Evangelization is the proclamation of the salvation brought by Christ, and the Eucharist, 'the source and summit of mission' is the Sacrament of healing and restoration.

In his homily for Corpus Christi 2008, Pope Benedict XVI taught:

> Adoring the God of Jesus Christ, who out of love made Himself bread broken, is the most effective and radical remedy against the idolatry of the past and of the present. Kneeling before the Eucharist is a profession of freedom: those who bow to Jesus cannot and must not prostrate themselves before any earthly authority, however powerful. We Christians kneel only before God or before the Most Blessed Sacrament.

For the Fathers of the Church, the Eucharist is considered as the medicine of eternity. It is a remedy. Jesus continues to touch the sick with His Eucharistic Body. St Thomas Aquinas understands the Eucharist as the bread of the soul: as bread sustains the body, the Eucharist sustains the soul. As bread repairs the body, the Eucharist repairs the soul. As bread increases the life of the body, the Eucharist increases the life of the soul. As bread gives joy to the body, the Eucharist gives joy to the life of the soul, sometimes even to the life of the body, as it is given to us to see.

In refusing to go and draw from the Eucharist the source of healing, many of our contemporaries are tempted to seek out pseudo-healings in false spiritualities.

What are the spiritual sicknesses which can afflict us and which find a remedy in the Eucharist? The Fathers of the Church respond: the Eucharist liberates us from ties to the Evil One; the Eucharist puts the devil to flight; the Eucharist liberates us from concupiscence; the Eucharist liberates us from the defilements of the heart; the Eucharist is a healing and therapeutic force against ignorance and darkening of the heart.

It was at the 'breaking of bread' that the disciples of Emmaus recognized the Risen Lord. Thus the understanding of the scriptures made them enter profoundly into the God's plan.

The Eucharist heals us from discouragement. The Eucharist, the bread of the strong, strengthens the heart of man (Ps. 104). The Eucharist is a strength which helps us to continue along the road to the Promised Land. Faced with the fear of death, ('who eats this Bread will never die', 'Who eats my flesh, I will raise him up on the last day' cf. Jn 6) the Eucharist is the Sacrament of Eternal Life.

The Eucharist is a place of fruitfulness. 'Abide in me, as I abide in you and thus you will bear much fruit' (cf. Jn 15.4–5). Eucharistic Adoration heals the Church of spiritual and missionary sterility.

The New Evangelization at the school of Eucharistic Adoration, must thus help Christians to enter upon a path of baptismal renewal, starting from a personal and living encounter with Christ, present in the Blessed Sacrament. Pope Benedict XVI states:

> Contemplation of the Eucharist must urge all the members of the Church, priests in the first place, ministers of the Eucharist, to revive their commitment of faithfulness . . . For lay persons too, Eucharistic spirituality must be the interior motor of every activity, and no dichotomy is acceptable between faith and life in their mission of spreading the spirit of Christianity in the world. (Homily, Conclusion of the 11th Ordinary General Assembly of the Synod of Bishops and the Year of the Eucharist, 23 October 2005)

Adoration christianizes our interiority, delivering it from subjectivism, from sentimentalism, from narcissism, so that it can unite itself to Christ in His work of salvation. It makes concrete the presence of Christ in His real and ongoing work of redemption.

Eucharistic Adoration is Thanksgiving for Mission

The Eucharist is thanksgiving (beraka), it is the gratitude of the believing people for the supreme gift they have received. Pierre de Bérulle says that God in creating us, has given us an instinct, a reflex towards Himself. This movement is inseparable from the creature, and will endure eternally. We must, in adoring God, give ourselves over to this universal movement which He has imprinted in the intimacy of the creature towards its Creator.

The community thus sends up its praise and glorification to the Father of Mercies, and this thanksgiving makes it missionary. 'How can I repay the Lord for his goodness to me?' sings the psalmist. 'I will lift the cup of salvation and call upon the name of the Lord' (Ps. 115).

Contemplating the Eucharistic Jesus, the adorer is invited to enter into a missionary dynamic: to give love for love. Eucharistic Adoration sustains, strengthens and renews the missionary dynamic. It makes us understand that Evangelization is owed to mankind. Evangelization is certainly 'owed' to God, but it equally concerns the work of God for man whom He wishes to save. Thus we must say that Evangelization is owed to mankind. The popes do not hesitate to say in relation to this that 'the multitudes have the right to know the riches of the mystery of Christ' (Blessed John Paul II, *Redemptoris missio*, 8). Or again, like Christ during the time of His preaching and the twelve on the morning of Pentecost, the Church also sees before her an immense crowd of souls who have need of the Gospel and who have the right to it, since God wills that 'all men be saved and come to the knowledge of the truth' (Paul VI, *Evangelii nuntiandi*, 53).

Certainly, those who do not know Christ also do not know their right to hear His love and His plans for them. Nonetheless this right is real: it is, we might say, intrinsic to their humanity which God wills to fulfil in Christ.

Some people are tempted to abstain from announcing Christ because they believe that by this they would show themselves to be more respectful of the human and spiritual values already present in the cultures and religions of the world. In reality this is to show respect for a partial value, rather than allowing that value to come to its definitive realization – which is what happens when it encounters the Gospel. It is on the contrary a lack of respect for the values present in the cultures and religions of the world, as well as those in whom those values are found, when, in silencing the Gospel, we deprive them of what would have brought them to fulfilment.

Evangelization is a sign of theological maturity. Mission is part of God's plan for man, for the Church and for the world. As the decree of the Second Vatican Council *Ad Gentes* explains: 'missionary activity comes from the will of God who desires that all men be saved and come to the knowledge of the truth' (*Ad Gentes* 7; 1 Tim. 2.45). The evangelist collaborates with the infinite love of God for men and the expression of this love in the work of salvation.

To evangelize is part of Christian identity itself. The gift of God in Christ is of such a superabundance that it cannot be fully welcomed without overflowing towards others.

Negatively, the weakening of evangelical dynamism can only signify a crisis in Christian identity, a difficulty in interiorizing the gift of God, in perceiving it and in living it to the full. St Paul expresses it when he speaks of Evangelization as a necessity which behoves him, and when he goes so far as to exclaim: 'Woe to me if I do not preach the gospel!' (1 Cor. 9.16). This necessity is part of the very nature of the gift received, from the Holy Spirit Himself, and from the manner in which he is called to increase and bear fruit. As Blessed John Paul II put it: 'This is why the Church's mission derives not only from the Lord's mandate but also from the profound demands of God's life within us' (*Redemptoris missio*, 11).

Eucharistic Adoration in the Missionary Struggle

The Council of Trent marks fundamental stage in the history of Eucharistic dogma. Faced with the Protestant interpretation according to which the presence of Christ is produced by faith, the Council Fathers affirm that in the Eucharist, Christ is not present because we believe, but that we believe because He is already present, and that He is not absent because we do not believe, but that He remains with us so that we can live in communion with Him (cf. Denzinger 1654). The Council of Trent puts the accent clearly on the affirmation of the Real Presence of Christ in the Eucharist. The expiatory end and the sacrificial character of the Eucharist mark, in a determining fashion, the theology of this sacrament.

The celebration of the Eucharist places us at the foot of the Cross. Eucharistic Adoration prolongs the contemplation of the redemptive sacrifice of Christ. Adoration 'fixes' Jesus in the situation of crisis, in that moment in which He pays for the salvation of all with His life, in that moment where He responds with the offering of love to the violence which strikes Him.

The adorer finds himself placed in intercession with Christ in respect of the fractures of humanity. His supplication embraces all the situations in which man has lost his dignity, his integrity, his resemblance to God. Adoration evangelizes by applying the salvation which starts from the Eucharistic Christ and passes through the Church and by the Church out into all of the situations in which man no longer responds to his vocation.

The Eucharist is the gage of the victory of Christ over death, hatred and sin. To contemplate Jesus present in the Blessed Sacrament of the Altar is to lean upon this victory won by Christ and which the Church proposes for our contemplation, so that in all of the difficulties we face in announcing the Gospel we may find the strength of the faith in the redemptive sacrifice of Christ.

The combats of the missionary are certainly found in the opposition the world poses to the faith. But the resistances are equally present within us, within the interior of the Church. The following are some of the pastoral obstacles to Evangelization:

Immobilism: It is easier to maintain the status quo, to let the machine continue to run, than to question the bureaucratic structures, the value of the manner of doing things inherited from the past, and to put in place a pastoral programme which goes beyond maintaining the current order and which puts in place a development that is truly missionary.

Secularism: Evangelization must assume the 'evangelical rupture', of being 'in the world' (incarnation) without being 'of the world' (distance). And this dissident position of spiritual resistance becomes the place of a prophetic call. From the interior of the Church, secularism is also at work: it seeks to unite itself to the world, to give itself to the world. This surrender annihilates all missionary activity. 'Christianity-lite', based on consensus is a denatured Christianity.

Functionalism: Our society obeys the logic of merchandizing, of consumerism. And this logic exports itself into the interior life of the Church. Just as one consumes entertainment, sport, etc., many would like her liturgical and sacramental services to be available as products to consume. They would have her become a religious supermarket! Functionalism is a degeneration of missionary life. Functionalism retains the channels, but it has forgotten the dynamism and the initial fervour.

Activism: In the context of a quest for efficiency and productivity, and equally in a context of crisis, one is quickly conquered by this dangerous temptation of activism, as though salvation depended upon us. The world of today is even more fascinated with activism so much so that it has lost the sense of contemplation. Activism makes us seek success and a sense of self-worth in adding up the results of our apostolic enterprises. But Evangelization depends first of all upon prayer and upon the primary initiative of God Who precedes our initiatives.

Individualism: In a culture of 'everyone for himself', the missionary will be tempted to work for his own ends, counting only upon his own abilities. The mission of the Church is not the sum total of individual initiatives, but the witness to the charity of Christ which lives on in the Church and which each member, united to the other members, has the vocation to manifest according to his own particular charism. It is the whole Church which is missionary.

Scepticism: A certain number of Christians are tired and discouraged. Overburdened, they do not see relief on the way. They find themselves confronted by new generations who have very little interest in the message for which they gave their lives. The pressures of contemporary media weigh heavily upon the Church, with their suspicion of priests and indeed of all Christians. Negative images of the Church are projected upon them. This scepticism is a disease attacking Hope.

In the face of all these battles, Adoration draws the strength of faith from the Pascal victory of Christ to overcome all of these challenges.

Eucharistic Adoration, Place of Spiritual and Pastoral Conversion

One of the fundamental givens of Eucharistic faith is to manifest a transformation, a transformation of the bread and wine. It is the principle of transubstantiation. The Lord takes hold of bread and wine to make them pass out of, so to speak, their own state of being, and to place them in a new order of being. Even if they remain unchanged to our physical eyes, they have become profoundly different. There, wherever Christ is made present, it is impossible that nothing has changed. There, wherever He lays His hand, a new reality has come to be. To adore is to consent to letting ourselves also be transformed, converted, evangelized, so as to access our true humanity. Adoration is not a 'spiritual device or accessory'. It is a 'transforming force' (cf. Blessed John Paul II, *Ecclesia de Eucharistia*, 62). It is a place of hope also – the world is transformable. It will be, in its totality, the New Jerusalem, the New Temple of God. 'How helpful the rediscovery of Eucharistic Adoration is for many Christians . . . How great is humanity's need today to rediscover the source of its hope in the Sacrament of the Eucharist!' (Benedict XVI, Address to the Plenary Assembly of the Pontifical Committee for the International Eucharistic Congresses, 9 November 2006). St Francis de Sales exhorts us: Believe me: if you adore the Beauty, the Goodness and the Purity present in this Sacrament, you will become beautiful, good and pure.

The *Lineamenta* for the 2012 Synod of Bishops on the New Evangelization speak in paragraph ten of a veritable pastoral conversion that is necessary: 'now is the time for the Church to call upon every Christian community to evaluate their pastoral practice on the basis of the missionary character of their programmes and activities'. This appeal is in line with the discourse of Pope Benedict XVI in Aparecida to the General Episcopal Conference of Latin America and the Caribbean (13 May 2007).

'This pastoral conversion consists of letting go of the atrophied projects in order to go there, where life begins, there where we see the fruits of life "in the Spirit" produced' (cf. Rom. 8) (Blessed John Paul II, Speech, 6th Symposium of the Episcopal Conferences of Europe, 11 October 1985).

Priests must adopt a 'new style of pastoral life', abandoning a pastoral approach of maintenance, in favour of a pastoral approach of proclamation and of begetting life. The lay faithful must recognize that their baptismal identity is first of all missionary and that they must deploy their proper charisms for the sanctification of the world. Families must discover that they are the primary agents of the transmission of the faith; youth that they must communicate to the new generations the joy of believing; the consecrated religious that the proclamation of the Kingdom is at the heart of the life of the Church, etc. It is about passing from a Christianity inherited from the past to a Christianity of personal adherence which leads us to

its proclamation. All these transformations find their source in the
Eucharist and in Eucharistic Adoration.

Eucharistic Adoration, Source of Missionary Communion

The history of the Eucharist attests to the fact that there is a connection between the celebration of the mysteries of Christ and the
building up of the community of the faithful: new faithful are united
to the Church by this Sacrament.

The Second Vatican Council, in several documents, strongly
accentuated the clear link that exists between the Eucharist and the
Church. We find this teaching in *Lumen gentium* at least three times
(cf. nn. 3, 11, 26): in being nourished by the Body of Christ in Holy
Communion the concrete unity of the People of God is manifested
'which in this Sacrament is fittingly signified (significatur) and mar-
vellously realised (efficitur)' (11). In *Sacrosanctum concilium*, it is said
that the Sacred Liturgy is the 'summit towards which all the action
of the Church must tend, and towards which all of her apostolic
work must be oriented' (10). Thus the Church manifests herself
fully, 'realizes' herself, in the Eucharistic Celebration.

'The Eucharist makes the Church and (in return) the Church
makes the Eucharist', said Henri de Lubac. 'Eucharistia facit
ecclesiam' teaches us that the Eucharist renews, in each Christian
community and in each Christian life, reconciliation and pardon.
But in her turn, the Church makes the Eucharist, 'Ecclesia facit
eucharistiam'. Thus the Eucharist has need of, for its realization,
the ministerial service of the Church. It is this ordained ministry
which gathers the faithful, proclaims the Word, breaks and shares
the bread of Life. The Eucharist is the source, the centre and the
summit of the life of the Church, the very heart of her communion
and her mission.

'The Eucharist founds the community and puts it at the service of
men', said the Synod of Bishops in 1971. 'As much as to make Jesus
present in the Host, the Eucharist is given to us to make Jesus present in the world'. The action and the accomplishment of the love of
Christ in this world, in all human history, is truly one of the fundamental objectives of the Eucharist in the life of the Church.

One can then rightly say that the Church and her mission exist in
order to bring the Salvific Body of Jesus, to all times and to all places
in the world. In this way all of humanity, in all nations and in all of
human history, can gather as one family, one community, around the
table of the Lord, until the end of time.

The Apostles, united around Peter, received the double mandate: 'Do this in memory of me' (1 Cor. 11.25), and also, 'Go into all
the world and preach the Gospel to all creation' (Mk 16.15). These

two mandates are inseparable. The Eucharist not only gathers the Church, but sends us out, renewed, to gather the whole world.

All Christians are thus called to welcome the living and active presence of the Crucified and Risen Lord into their hearts, and in leaving the holy table, to transmit this presence through charity and service, in all of the actions of their live daily life, so that the Ecclesial and Sacramental Body that is the Church can accomplish its destiny, which is to make of all humanity the Living Body of Christ in the world.

Evangelization is not just the proclamation of Christ but also a process of incorporation into the Church. From this comes the sacramental link between Evangelization and the Eucharist. The community constitutes itself, in its sacramentality, through the Eucharist and Eucharistic Adoration. As Blessed John Paul II teaches:

> Incorporation into Christ, which is brought about by Baptism, is constantly renewed and consolidated by sharing in the Eucharistic Sacrifice, especially by that full sharing which takes place in sacramental communion. We can say not only that *each of us receives Christ*, but also that *Christ receives each of us*. He enters into friendship with us: 'You are my friends' (Jn 15.14). Indeed, it is because of Him that we have life: 'He who eats me will live because of me' (Jn 6.57). Eucharistic communion brings about in a sublime way the mutual 'abiding' of Christ and each of His followers: 'Abide in me, and I in you' (Jn 15.4). (*Ecclesia de Eucharistia*, 22)

Adoration, Place of Missionary Hope

The Eucharist is an act instituted by Christ Himself, inscribing itself in the history of salvation, in this interval of time that unfolds between His death and His return at the Parousia. The eschatological awareness which accompanies this prayer is one of the distinctive traits which gives the Eucharist its proper nature, until the day when the Lord Jesus will accomplish the 'universal restoration' (cf. Acts 3.20). The 'until you come again', repeated after the Consecration, clearly attests the eschatological nature of the Eucharistic Banquet, as a confirmation and anticipation of the New Heaven and of the New Earth of the Kingdom of God.

In its eschatological dimension the Eucharist gives us the pledge and the means of this transfiguration. The Eucharist is a source of hope for our world as we await the return of Christ in glory, as we await the Wedding Feast of the Lamb. This hope is not just a form of waiting, it is a discovery of the real and actual presence of God here and now in the Eucharist, which already makes present that for which we wait. It is the Real Presence of Jesus hidden in the consecrated species.

One of the obstacles to the missionary awakening is a lack of hope and thus of spiritual enthusiasm. We have become fixated upon the failures, the resistance we find in the field, the negative signs coming from society, and all this can make us forget the spiritual needs of our times, and that there is the emergence of new generations of witnesses.

Paul VI held that the Christian lives in the world, but comes to it starting from its future. Christianity is an inheritance but also a promise. It is the future of humanity. And every Mass celebrates the coming of the Saviour and Messiah, whose glorious coming we await. To evangelize is to make an act of hope, to believe that the world can be changed because salvation has been given to us in the Lord.

Adoration converts our complaints and our scepticisms into filial confidence in the work of God which transforms the world, starting from the transubstantiation of matter. As Pope Benedict XVI has said, 'Before any activity, before the world can change there must be adoration' (Address to the Roman Curia, 22 December 2005), and 'How great is humanity's need today to rediscover the source of its hope in the Sacrament of the Eucharist!' (Address to the Plenary Assembly of the Pontifical Committee for the International Eucharistic Congresses, 9 November 2006).

Two

A Mystagogical Catechesis of Eucharistic Adoration

Dom Mark Daniel Kirby OSB
Prior of the Monastery of Our Lady of
the Cenacle, Tulsa, Oklahoma, USA

Ut, dum visibiliter Deum cognoscimus, per hunc, in invisibilium
amorem rapiamur

(Missale Romanum)

Introduction

The Year of the Eucharist proclaimed by Blessed John Paul II 7 years ago and fervently endorsed by Pope Benedict XVI on the day following his election (Message, 20 April 2005), was for many a pressing invitation to discover or rediscover Adoration of the Most Blessed Sacrament. I know of no more fitting expression of what happens during Adoration of the Most Blessed Sacrament, than that magnificent line of the Preface of the Nativity: 'Ut, dum visibiliter Deum cognoscimus, per hunc, in invisibilium amorem rapiamur' – 'So that, even as we know God visibly, we are, by this, ravished unto the love of what is invisible' (*Missale Romanum*).

There is nothing random about my choice of this particular liturgical text in relation to the mystery of the Most Holy Eucharist. With singular theological acuity the Missal of 1962 attributes to the feast of Corpus Christi and to Votive Masses of the Most Blessed Sacrament, the very Preface sung at Christmas in thanksgiving for the Mystery of the Incarnation. Thus does the Sacred Liturgy teach us that the Most Holy Eucharist prolongs the adorable Mystery of the Incarnation, and this until the end of time. 'Behold', says the Lord, 'I am with you all days, even to the consummation of the world' (Mt. 28.20).

Though hidden beneath the sacramental veil, the Sacred Humanity of Our Lord or, if you will, His 'Eucharistic Face', to use the expression coined by Blessed John Paul II (*Ecclesia de Eucharistia*, 7), becomes in Eucharistic Adoration that by which we know God visibly, and that by which we are ravished unto the love of what is invisible. The adorable Face of Christ hidden in the Sacrament of the Altar today remains, no less than in His earthly life, 'the brightness of the Father's glory, and the figure of His substance' (Heb. 1.3). 'No man has seen God at any time: the only begotten Son who is in the bosom of the Father, He has made Him known' (Jn 1.18), and continues to make Him known in the Sacrament of His Love. Thus was St Thomas Aquinas inspired to write in the last strophe of the *Adoro Te Devote*:

> *Iesu, quem velatum nunc aspicio,*
> *oro fiat illud quod tam sitio;*
> *ut te revelata cernens facie,*
> *visu sim beatus tuae gloriae.*

> Jesus, here your Face is hid, from my sight concealed,
> How I thirst to meet your gaze gloriously revealed!
> After life's obscurity, let me wake to see
> Beauty shining from your Face for eternity.

The mystery that the Preface of the Nativity proclaims in a lyrical mode is, of course, borne out in the daily experience of the saints. I am thinking, in particular of St Gaetano Catanoso, the humble priest whom Pope Benedict XVI quoted in the homily at the very first canonization ceremony of his pontificate on 23 October 2005: 'If we wish to adore the real Face of Jesus . . . we can find it in the divine Eucharist, where with the Body and Blood of Jesus Christ, the Face of Our Lord is hidden under the white veil of the Host'.

The Sacred Liturgy itself and, I would argue, only the Sacred Liturgy and the writings of the saints and mystics inspired by it, can provide us with words and sentiments adequate to Adoration of the Most Blessed Sacrament, even when Adoration unfolds and is prolonged in silence. In his Apostolic Letter for the Year of the Eucharist, *Mane nobiscum, Domine*, Blessed John Paul II said, 'Pastors should be committed to that mystagogical catechesis so dear to the Fathers of the Church, by which the faithful are helped to understand the meaning of the liturgy's words and actions, to pass from its signs to the mystery they contain, and to enter into that mystery in every aspect of their lives' (17). I propose to offer something in the way of a mystagogical catechesis of Eucharistic Adoration.

The magnificent Trinitarian Christocentrism of the Fathers that finds lyrical expression, for example, in the *Gloria* of the Mass, as well as in the *Te Deum* of the Divine Office, is the very breath of a Eucharistic Adoration carried out in union of heart and mind with the heart and mind of the Church.

The Christological movement of the *Gloria* shapes and inspires the Adoration of one who would adore the Most Blessed Sacrament with a sensibility that is fully and gloriously Catholic:

Lord Jesus Christ, Only Begotten Son,
Lord God, Lamb of God,
Son of the Father,
you take away the sins of the world,
have mercy on us;
you take away the sins of the world, receive our prayer;
you are seated at the right hand of the Father, have mercy on us.
For you alone are the Holy One,
you alone are the Lord,
you alone are the Most High, Jesus Christ, with the Holy Spirit,
in the glory of God the Father. Amen.[1]

The Word of God and the Most Holy Eucharist

Eucharistic Adoration is not static. It is, rather, a movement of ascent to the Kingdom, initiated by the proclamation and hearing of the Word of God. In Eucharistic Adoration as in all Christian prayer, the initiative is divine not human. It begins, as we will sing in the hymn at Lauds on the feast of Corpus Christi, with 'the heavenly Word proceeding forth, yet leaving not the Father's side'.[2] God reveals Himself in uttering His Word; the descending Word, proclaimed and received in the heart of the Church, becomes the Word through whom, with whom, and in whom we ascend to the Father in the unity of the Holy Spirit.

The Word by whom the Father redeems us, heals us, and raises us even to Himself, becomes in us, by the power of the Holy Spirit, the Word by whom we praise, bless, adore, and glorify the Father; the Word by whom we give Him thanks for His great glory and implore His mercy upon the world; the Word through whom we make reparation for the evil wrought by sin. Catherine de Bar, in

---

[1] Domine Fili unigenite, Iesu Christe, Domine Deus, Agnus Dei, Filius Patris, qui tollis peccata mundi, miserere nobis; qui tollis peccata mundi, suscipe deprecationem nostram. Qui sedes ad dexteram Patris, miserere nobis. Quoniam tu solus Sanctus, tu solus Dominus, tu solus Altissimus, Iesu Christe, cum Sancto Spiritu: in gloria Dei Patris. Amen (English translation: Third Edition of the Roman Missal, 2002).

[2] 'Verbum supernum prodiens, Nec Patris linquens dexteram', Hymn of St Thomas Aquinas, Lauds of the Solemnity of the Most Holy Body and Blood of Christ.

religion, Mother Mectilde du Saint-Sacrement, foundress of the Benedictines of Perpetual Adoration in 1653, puts it compellingly: 'Our Lord Jesus Christ alone can adore God perfectly in spirit and in truth, and we cannot do it apart from our union with Him'.[3]

Eucharistic Adoration is enkindled then, not only when the Sacred Host is withdrawn from the tabernacle and exposed to our gaze, but even before that, when the Word of God is proclaimed, repeated, prayed, and treasured in the heart. The seeds planted in the corporate *lectio divina* of the Sacred Liturgy – Holy Mass and the Divine Office – and in the solitary *lectio divina* that the Sacred Liturgy shapes and inspires come to fruition in silent Adoration before the Most Blessed Sacrament.[4] Eucharistic Adoration presupposes a long familiarity with the Word of God received and sung in the liturgical assembly, repeated and prayed in *lectio divina*, pondered and held in the heart.

This is why the Church recommends the reading of the Word of God as a source of Christian prayer, and at the same time exhorts all to discover the deep meaning of Sacred Scripture through prayer 'so that a dialogue takes place between God and man. For, 'we speak to Him when we pray; we listen to Him when we read the divine oracles'.[5]

The Divine Office and Eucharistic Adoration

The intuitions of numerous saintly founders and foundresses, among them Mother Mectilde du Saint–Sacrement, St Peter Julian Eymard, founder of the Congregation of the Blessed Sacrament, and Mother Marie-Adele Garnier, foundress of the Adorers of the Sacred Heart, of Tyburn, O.S.B. (1838–1924), bore fruit in the conjunction of the choral celebration of the Divine Office with Perpetual Adoration of the Most Blessed Sacrament. St Peter Julian Eymard, among others, insisted on the choral Office as the primary and highest corporate expression of Eucharistic Adoration.[6] The saint's particular grace was, in fact, the unified focus of his entire being, spirit, soul and body on the Divine

---

[3]   Catherine de Bar, 'Lettre n° 261 à Madame de Béthune, abbesse de Beaumont-les-Tours', in: *Adorer et adhérer*, Paris: Cerf 1994, p. 59.

[4]   The Mass and Liturgy of the Hours are the primary locus and daily expression of the Church's corporate *lectio divina*. It is in the Mass and in the choral celebration of the Divine Office that the Church proclaims the Word of God (*lectio*), listens to it and repeats it (*meditatio*), prays it (*oratio*), and abides in it (*contemplatio*). The *lectio divina* of the individual Christian is an appropriation and imitation of what the Church does corporately in her Liturgy.

[5]   Congregation for the Doctrine of the Faith, *Letter to the Bishops of the Catholic Church on Some Aspects of Christian Meditation*, 15 October 1989, 6.

[6]   See P. E. C. Núñez, S.S.S., *La spiritualité du P. Pierre–Julien Eymard*, Rome: Maison Généralice des Prêtres du T. S. Sacrement, 1956, pp. 359–63.

Person of Jesus Christ really, truly, and substantially present in the Blessed Sacrament. Understanding the choral Office in this light, he presented it as the solemn and collective glorification of Jesus in the Most Holy Sacrament of the Altar, the prayer of the redeemed to the Lamb, the prayer of the Mystical Body addressed to Christ the Head, the prayer of the bride addressed to Christ her Spouse. This being said, St Peter Julian Eymard in no way distanced himself from the Trinitarian character of all liturgical prayer. Rather, he applied to the choral Office in the presence of the Blessed Sacrament exposed what St Augustine wrote concerning the Psalms in general:

> When we speak with God in prayer we do not separate the Son from Him, and when the Body of the Son prays it does not separate its Head from itself: it is the one Saviour of His Body, Our Lord Jesus Christ, the Son of God, who prays for us and in us and is Himself the object of our prayers. He prays for us as our priest, He prays in us as our head, He is the object of our prayers as our God.[7]

Experienced on a daily basis, the Divine Office, personal *lectio divina*, and Eucharistic Adoration become an effective school of the prayer without ceasing to which Jesus calls His disciples.[8] The quality of the prayer of Eucharistic Adoration is moreover, in some way, proportionate to the quality of our exposure to and reception of the Word of God. One of the great adoring souls of the nineteenth century, Blessed Théodelinde Dubouché, foundress of the Congregation of the Adoration Réparatrice at Paris in 1848 illustrates this in writing:

> By a singular grace, for me who have not much of a memory, all the texts of the Gospel, and much from the Sacred Scriptures, came into my thought with no effort; and this nourishment was so abundant that even when I was not carried away by love, I was holding very real conversations with Our Lord . . . I have often understood, or rather sensed, that God is altogether there in the Scriptures, but that the full intelligence of them will be the occupation of eternity.[9]

---

[7] St Augustine, *En.* Ps. 85.1: CCL 39, 1176–7.

[8] And He told them a parable, to the effect that they ought always to pray and not lose heart (Lk. 18.1).

[9] Théodelinde Dubouché, *L'adoration au soleil de Dieu, fragments spirituals*, Paris: Les Sœurs de l'Adoration, 1995, pp. 80–1.

Two Gospel Paradigms of Eucharistic Adoration

St Luke's Gospel offers two paradigms of Christian worship that can be brought to bear upon Eucharistic Adoration. The first is his account of the feeding of the 5,000. '[Jesus took the Apostles] and withdrew apart to a city called Bethsaida. When the crowds learned it, they followed Him; and He welcomed them and spoke to them of the kingdom of God, and cured those who had need of healing' (Lk. 9.10–11).

If the crowds follow Jesus and seek Him out, it is because the Holy Spirit is already at work, assembling a body of believers, fashioning a community – a Church – hungry for the Word of God. 'No one can come to me, says Jesus, unless the Father who sent me draws him . . . It is written in the prophets, 'And they shall all be taught by God' Everyone who has heard and learned from the Father comes to me' (Jn 6.44–46). Jesus welcomed the crowds. He is the perfect expression of the Divine Hospitality, of the God Who, in the Most Holy Eucharist, makes Himself our shelter, food and drink.

'He spoke to them of the Kingdom of God' (Lk. 9.11). Our Lord's Word is efficacious and full of power. It sows the seeds of the Kingdom within us and causes the glory of the Kingdom to open over our heads and to unfold within our hearts. This is why the Gospel at Mass is heralded by alleluias, framed by acclamations addressed to Christ Himself – *Laus tibi, Christe! Gloria tibi, Domine!* – and proclaimed amidst clouds of incense. Christ speaks, unleashing the power of the kingdom and making whole those who are in need of healing. Flowing from the abundance of His Heart, the Word of Jesus held the attention of the crowds for a long period of time, until the day began to wear away (Lk. 9.12). Only then does Jesus pass from this protracted 'Liturgy of the Word' to the breaking of the bread.

Taking five loaves and two fish, 'He looked up to heaven, and blessed and broke them, and gave them to the disciples to set before the crowd' (Lk. 9.16). St Luke highlights the four verbs that constitute the very shape of the Eucharistic action: to take, to bless, to break, and to give. He *takes* bread. Then, with eyes raised to heaven, Jesus *blesses* His Father, praising Him and offering thanks over the bread. He *breaks* it for distribution to the many and finally, He *gives* the bread, or as St Luke says, gives it to the disciples 'to set before the crowd' (Lk. 9.16).

In Lk. 24.13–31, the foundational text of *Mane nobiscum, Domine*, Blessed John Paul II's Apostolic Letter for the Year of the Eucharist, we find a similar paradigm of Christian worship.

The image of the disciples on the road to Emmaus can serve as a fitting guide for a Year when the Church will be particularly engaged in living out the mystery of the Holy Eucharist. Amid our questions and difficulties, and even our bitter disappointments, the Divine Wayfarer continues to walk at our side, opening to us the Scriptures and leading us to a deeper understanding of the mysteries of God. When we meet him fully, we will pass from the light of the Word to the light streaming from the 'Bread of life', the supreme fulfilment of His promise to 'be with us always, to the end of the age' (cf. Mt. 28.20; *Mane nobiscum Domine*, 2).

The road to Emmaus is the scene of a peripatetic Liturgy of the Word. The Risen Jesus walks with two of His bereaved and downcast disciples. 'And beginning with Moses and all the prophets, He interpreted to them in all the scriptures the things concerning Himself' (Lk. 24.27). The experience of the Word of God in the power of the Holy Spirit allows the two to open themselves to communion with the mysterious third, the Divine Wayfarer. 'Stay with us, for it is toward evening and the day is now far spent' (Lk. 24.29).

The prayer of the disciples on the road to Emmaus is the prayer of the Church, repeated so often as she listens to the Word of God: *Mane nobiscum, Domine*, 'Stay with us, Lord'. The Liturgy of the Word calls for completion in the Liturgy of the Holy Sacrifice and in Holy Communion. What happens at the ambo is ordered to what happens at the Altar.[10] What happens at the Altar is prolonged in Eucharistic Adoration.

'So He went in to stay with them. When He was at table, He took the bread and blessed, and broke it, and gave it to them. And their eyes were opened and they recognized Him; and He vanished out of their sight' (Lk. 24.31).

Once again, we find the same significant sequence of four verbs. St Luke makes the recognition of Christ coincide with the disciples' partaking of the bread, adding, 'He vanished out of their sight' (Lk. 24.31). In vanishing from their sight, the Risen Christ does not withdraw His presence. Rather, in a way wonderful beyond all imagining, He answers and fulfils the prayer inspired by the Holy Spirit, 'Stay with us, Lord' (Lk. 24.29). In her pilgrimage towards the kingdom, the Church prays again and again, 'Stay with us', and again and again, her Bridegroom and Lord replies, 'This is my Body which is given for you. Do this in remembrance of me' (Lk. 22.19). Set as an icon over the portal of the Year of the Eucharist by Blessed John Paul II, the Liturgy enacted by Christ on the way to Emmaus became, by the same token, an icon of Eucharistic Adoration.

---

[10] The movement from ambo to altar determines to a great extent the content and form of liturgical preaching. The homily is in every Mass a bridge into the mystery of the Eucharistic Sacrifice. All preaching has a Eucharistic finality.

From Word to Sacrament

In the light of these two Lucan paradigms of Christian worship we see that the inspired impulse of Eucharistic Adoration must necessarily be traced back to the hearing of the Word, 'beginning with Moses and all the prophets' (Lk. 24.27). The Word, made fruitful by the Holy Spirit, quickens those who hear it, causing the four ends of the Holy Sacrifice, as defined by the Venerable Pope Pius XII in *Mediator Dei*, to rise in the hearts of the faithful: the first of these is to give glory to the Heavenly Father; the second end is duly to give thanks to God; the third is that of expiation, propitiation and reconciliation; the fourth is that of impetration or supplication.[11] It is with these four ends in view that the priest ascends to the Altar, there to offer the Holy Sacrifice. It is with these four ends in view that the faithful unite themselves to the words and actions of the priest. It is with these same four ends in view that St Peter Julian Eymard would have those intent on learning Adoration at his school take their place before the Blessed Sacrament exposed in the monstrance.[12]

The Liturgy of the Word sets in motion an irrecusable ascent to the Altar and to the rites of the Offertory, canon of the Mass, and Holy Communion. The Liturgy of the Word, in some way, remains incomplete or suspended without the Sacrifice and Communion to which it is ordered. 'What shall I render to the Lord, for all the things He has rendered unto me? I will take the chalice of salvation; and I will call upon the name of the Lord . . . I will sacrifice to You the sacrifice of praise' (Ps. 115.12–13, 17). Eucharistic Adoration is situated in the prolongation of this same sacrifice of praise. Adoration becomes, effectively, perpetual in the soul of the adorer who, having been nourished by the Word of God and by the Sacrament of Our Lord's Body and Blood, abides in Him. Thus was Mother Mectilde du Saint–Sacrement able to say in 1679 to her Benedictines of Perpetual Adoration of the Most Blessed Sacrament:

> Live not except from the love, the praise, the glory, and the Adoration that you will ceaselessly render to the majesty of the triune God . . . And just as Jesus Christ must be your glory and your praise to His Divine Father, abide in Him to praise Him, adore Him, and love with Him. The Holy Spirit will tell you the rest.[13]

---

[11] Pius XII, Encyclical *Mediator Dei*, 1947, 71–4.
[12] Cf. Núñez, op. cit., 'La méthode des quatre fins du sacrifice', pp. 196–202.
[13] Catherine de Bar, op. cit., p. 32.

Eucharistic Adoration and the Holy Sacrifice of the Mass

Eucharistic Adoration outside Mass is 'strictly linked to the celebration of the Eucharistic Sacrifice' (*Ecclesia de Eucharistia*, 25). Holy Mass,
then, provides the liturgical and theological context for the prayer of
Eucharistic Adoration; it shapes it and determines its content.

Adoration of the Most Blessed Sacrament is always, in a very
real sense, situated between the Consecration and Holy Communion, even when this Communion takes place outside of Mass as, for
example, in the case of Viaticum. Ultimately, the Body of Christ, be
it reserved in a ciborium or exposed in the monstrance, waits for the
hand of the priest to place it on the tongue of a communicant. Out of
this liturgical contextualization emerges a theological and spiritual
approach to Eucharistic Adoration generated by the Holy Sacrifice of
the Mass, and leading to the extension of its influence into all of life.

Our Lord Jesus Christ handed over the mystery of the Most Holy
Eucharist to His spouse, the Church, so that she, obedient to His
command, 'Do this in remembrance of me' (Lk. 22.19), might 'continually experience within herself the fruit of His redemption'.[14] The
Venerable Pope Pius XII, treating of this in *Mediator Dei*, writes:

> The august sacrifice of the altar is, as it were, the supreme
> instrument whereby the merits won by the divine Redeemer
> upon the cross are distributed to the faithful: 'as often as this
> commemorative sacrifice is offered, there is wrought the work
> of our Redemption'. This, however, so far from lessening the
> dignity of the actual sacrifice on Calvary, rather proclaims
> and renders more manifest its greatness and its necessity, as
> the Council of Trent declares. Its daily immolation reminds
> us that there is no salvation except in the cross of Our Lord
> Jesus Christ and that God Himself wishes that there should be
> a continuation of this sacrifice 'from the rising of the sun till
> the going down thereof,' so that there may be no cessation of
> the hymn of praise and thanksgiving which man owes to God,
> seeing that he requires His help continually and has need of
> the Blood of the Redeemer to remit the sin which challenges
> God's justice.[15]

The Mass, in other words, makes present the whole mystery of Our
Lord's *magnum pietatis opus*.[16] It is the Sacrifice of the Cross presented

---

[14] Cf., Collect of the Solemnity of the Most Holy Body and Blood of Christ.
[15] Pius XII, *Mediator Dei*, 79.
[16] *O magnum pietatis opus*, First Antiphon at Lauds in the Office of 14 September,
      Exaltation of the Holy Cross, *Antiphonale Monasticum*, Solesmes 1934, p. 1040.

to the Father in an unbloody manner. 'For the victim', teaches the Council of Trent, 'is one and the same, the same now offering by the ministry of priests who then offered Himself on the cross, the manner alone of offering being different'.[17] 'So decisive is this sacrifice for the salvation of the human race', wrote Blessed John Paul II, 'that Jesus Christ offered it and returned to the Father only after He had left us a means of sharing in it as if we had been present there. Each member of the faithful can thus take part in it and inexhaustibly gain its fruits' (*Ecclesia de Eucharistia*, 11).

Eucharistic Adoration and *Actuosa Participatio*

Just how the faithful take part in the Sacrifice of Christ, renewed in Holy Mass, poses a question that, ultimately comes to bear upon our understanding of Eucharistic Adoration. Over the past forty years the *actuosa participatio* of The Constitution on the Sacred Liturgy, *Sacrosanctum concilium*, article 14, has been variously understood, misunderstood, and misrepresented. Had the conciliar text been read in the context of its source in *Mediator Dei* and interpreted in its light, its implementation would have been, I think, more serene and more fruitful. The Venerable Pope Pius XII writes:

> The faithful should be aware that to participate in the Eucharistic Sacrifice is their chief duty and supreme dignity, and that not in an inert and negligent fashion, giving way to distractions and day-dreaming, but with such earnestness and concentration that they may be united as closely as possible with the High Priest, according to the Apostle, 'Let this mind be in you which was also in Christ Jesus.' And together with Him and through Him let them make their oblation, and in union with Him let them offer up themselves.[18]

Eucharistic Adoration is, in the modalities proper to it, an authentic expression of *actuosa participatio* in the Sacrifice of Christ, which is, as Alcuin Reid has argued, 'essentially contemplative'.[19] Adoration dilates and prolongs the graces of a fruitful participation in the Holy Sacrifice of the Mass culminating in reception of the Body and Blood Christ. Our Lord Jesus Christ is in the Sacrament of the Altar and in the soul of the communicant, just as He is the heavenly sanctuary beyond the veil: the

---

[17] Ibid.
[18] Pius XII, *Mediator Dei*, art. 80.
[19] Alcuin Reid, 'Looking Again at the Liturgical Reform: Some General and Monastic Considerations' in: *The Downside Review*, vol. 124, no. 437, October 2006, p. 248.

hostia perpetua, the Victim ceaselessly offering Himself to the Father; the immolated Lamb who lives forever in the Father's sight; the 'pure victim, the holy victim, the spotless victim' of the Roman canon.[20]

Writing in 1697 to her spiritual daughters, the Benedictines of Perpetual Adoration of the Most Blessed Sacrament, Mother Mectilde du Saint–Sacrement said that if they wished 'to understand the spirit of their vocation, they had to keep themselves at every moment in the state of a victim in His holy Presence'.[21] Perseverance in Eucharistic Adoration leads, inexorably, to a mystic identification with Christ, Priest and Victim, that is, with Christ offering and with Christ offered. In this way, the sacrificial movement of the Mass *ad Patrem* is extended and prolonged in the souls of communicants become adorers and, thereby, participants in the perpetual exercise of Our Lord's victimal priesthood in heaven and in the Most Holy Sacrament of the Altar.

The Reservation and Exposition of the Most Blessed Sacrament

Eucharistic Adoration, outside of Holy Mass, depends necessarily on the reservation of the Most Blessed Sacrament in the tabernacle. The reservation of Sacred Hosts in the ciborium for Holy Viaticum and Communion outside of Mass illustrates that, in instituting the Most Holy Eucharist on the night before He suffered, Our Lord left His Church the means of incorporation into Himself: the Sacrament of Unity, by which the members of the Church – many though they be, wherever they may be, and in all the circumstances of human life, including sickness, imprisonment, old age, and the hour of death – can be united to Christ and, through Christ, among themselves, so as to form a single Body.

The reservation of a large Sacred Host suitable for exposition in the monstrance, suggests that in instituting the Most Holy Eucharist, Our Lord desired not only to perpetuate the Sacrifice of the Cross until the end of time, and not only to unite the members of His Mystical Body among themselves and to Himself as a single oblation to the Father in the Holy Spirit, but also that He might abide in the tabernacles of the world until the end of time, offering souls the consolation of His Divine Friendship. Exposed and lifted up in the monstrance, Our Lord draws us to Himself, offering to our eyes

---

[20] Unde et mémores, Dómine, nos servi tui, sed et plebs tua sancta, ejústdem Christi Fílii tui Dómini nostri tam beátæ passiónis necnon et ab ínferis resurrectiónis, sed et in cælos gloriósæ ascensiónis: offérimus præcláræ majestáti tuæ de tuis donis, ac datis, hóstiam + puram, hóstiam + sanctam, hóstiam + immaculátem, Panem + sanctum vitæ ætérnæ, et Cálicem + salútis perpétuæ.

[21] Catherine de Bar, *Document Biographique, Écrits spirituals*, Rouen: Bénédictines du Saint-Sacrement, 1973, p. 127.

the contemplation of His Eucharistic Face and to our hearts the companionship of His Heart.

From at least the eleventh century onward in the West, the reserved Blessed Sacrament became a kind of spiritual hearth from which the faithful rekindled both fire and light. At the same time a growing desire to gaze upon the Sacred Host gave rise to an elevation after the consecration in addition to the more ancient showing of the Sacred Species to the people immediately before Holy Communion. In time, this elevation came to be practiced as a kind of ocular communion, a contemplation of 'the Eucharistic Face of Christ', and a peak moment of Adoration and desire within the Mass. The desire of the faithful to fix their gaze on the Body of Christ represented a spiritual instinct that was, at the deepest level, a hunger for the Bread of Life. Resourceful sacristans were quick to discover that a reliquary designed to hold a fragment of the Cross or the bone of a saint could be easily adapted to hold the Sacred Host thereby permitting a prolonged and aesthetically pleasing elevation outside of the Mass itself.

The emergence of a popular desire for prolonged 'showings' of the Sacred Host led in time to exposition of the Most Blessed Sacrament in the monstrance. This form of Adoration fills a particular need at present when, in spite of frequent Communion, many hearts have grown cold and the spiritual eyes of many grown dim. 'Seeing, they do not perceive, and hearing, they fail to understand' (Mt. 13.13). The remedy for this spiritual insensibility born of routine and minimalism is Eucharistic Adoration.[22] Pope Benedict XVI wrote:

> Communion and contemplation belong together: a person cannot communicate with another person without knowing him . . .

---

[22] The Eastern Churches, untouched by the controversies that Berengarius of Tours aroused in the West, developed a profoundly expressive worship of the holy and life-giving mysteries of Christ's Body and Blood within the margins of the liturgical action itself. At the Liturgy of the Pre-sanctified, the reserved Blessed Sacrament is adored with profound bows and prostrations. The Eastern Churches express what Blessed John Paul II called Eucharistic 'amazement' (*Ecclesia de Eucharistia*, 6), not by exposing the Sacred Species but by veiling the Sacrament in mystery and by approaching it with awe and holy dread. Only the chalice containing the Body and Blood of Christ is exposed to the gaze of the faithful immediately before and after Holy Communion. The cult of holy icons in the East, predating the development of the cult of the Most Blessed Sacrament in the West, in some way, addresses the same fundamental desire to engage the sense of sight in Adoration and contemplation of the Face of Christ. The contemplation of the Face of Christ depicted in holy icons prepares and prolongs in its own way sacramental participation in the Mysteries of His Body and Blood.

Communicating with Christ therefore demands that we gaze on Him, allow Him to gaze on us, listen to Him, get to know Him. Adoration is simply the personal aspect of Communion.[23]

A Theological Orientation of Adoration Derived from the Mass

Like the impetuous stream that gladdens the City of God, Eucharistic Adoration carries us along in the same direction as the Mass itself: to the Father, through the Son, in the Holy Spirit. Adoration presupposes a prayer of desire, a prayer of hunger, of readiness, and of waiting. It is the Church's response to the 'still, small voice' (I Kings 19.12) of the Holy Spirit inviting us to the Eucharistic Heart of the Son, and through His open Heart into the bosom of the Father and the glory of the kingdom. Just as the Sacred Liturgy is Trinitarian, doxological, and eschatological, so too is Eucharistic Adoration, for it springs from the Liturgy and returns to it.

Trinitarian Adoration

A 1989 instruction of the Congregation for the Doctrine of the Faith entitled, *Letter to the Bishops of the Catholic Church on Some Aspects of Christian Meditation* affirms that all Christian prayer 'has to be inserted into the Trinitarian movement of God'.[24] Adoration of the Most Blessed Sacrament, though it be experienced as an obscure contemplation of the Eucharistic Face of Jesus, or as a drawing near to His pierced Heart, is nonetheless Trinitarian. 'No one comes to the Father', says Jesus, 'but by me' (Jn 14.6). I would inscribe Eucharistic Adoration within the great circular movement of the Sacred Liturgy articulated by Dom Cipriano Vagaggini: from the Father, through His Son, Jesus Christ, in the Holy Spirit, to the Father. Every good thing comes to us from the Father, through the mediation of His incarnate Son, Jesus Christ, by means of the presence in us of the Holy Spirit; and likewise, it is by means of the presence of the Holy Spirit, through the mediation of the incarnate Son, Jesus Christ, that everything returns to the Father.[25]

---

[23] Joseph Cardinal Ratzinger, *God is Near Us, The Eucharist, the Heart of Life*, San Francisco: Ignatius, 2003, p. 97.

[24] Congregation for the Doctrine of the Faith, *Letter to the Bishops of the Catholic Church on Some Aspects of Christian Meditation*, 15 October 1989, p. 7.

[25] The 'recapitulatory formula': 'A Patre, per Filium eius, Iesum Christum, in Spiritu Sancto, ad Patrem'. See Cipriano Vagaggini, O.S.B., *The Theological Dimensions of the Liturgy*, Collegeville: Liturgical Press, 1976, p. 198.

Mother Mectilde du Saint–Sacrement, speaking out of her own mystical experience of Perpetual Adoration in the seventeenth century, applies this same grand theological principle to the interior life of her Benedictines, saying: 'We must then enter within ourselves and, from there, pass into Jesus Christ so as to be, as St Paul says, hidden with Him in God. This will be by the operation of the Holy Spirit'.[26] In another place, she writes:

> To adore always it is not necessary to say, 'My God, I adore Thee.' It is sufficient that we should have a certain interior attention to God present, a profound respect in homage to His greatness, believing that He is in you, as in truth He is: the Holy Trinity making His dwelling there; the Father acting and operating by His power; the Son by His wisdom; the Holy Spirit by His goodness. It is therefore in the secret of your soul where this God of majesty resides, that you must continually adore Him.[27]

Some would contend that Eucharistic Adoration detracts from the full development of the interior life by objectifying the presence of Jesus outside the soul in the Most Holy Sacrament of the Altar to the detriment of the higher states of prayer, or by minimizing the soul's attention to indwelling Trinity. Such critics would do well to familiarize themselves with the writings of those saints whose spiritual experience was predominantly marked by Eucharistic Adoration. In every case, they will find devotion to real presence of Our Lord in the Sacrament of His Love leads to an increased awareness of the soul's interior participation in the life of the Three Divine Persons.

Eschatological Adoration

Eucharistic Adoration is an eschatological prayer, a prayer that desires, prepares, and hastens the advent of the Kingdom. The adorer grows in awareness of the dawning fulfilment of the prophecy in the psalm intoned by Jesus from the cross:

> The poor shall eat and shall be filled,
> and they shall praise the Lord those who seek Him. . . .
> All the ends of the earth shall remember,
> and shall be converted to the Lord;
> and all the families of the nations shall adore in His sight (Ps.
>   21.27–28).

---

[26] Catherine de Bar, *Adorer et adhérer*, p. 35.
[27] Ibid., p. 64.

Made in this spirit, Eucharistic Adoration delivers the soul from a narrow preoccupation with self and, by stretching it to Catholic dimensions, inflames it with the apostolic zeal of the Heart of Christ. 'I came to cast fire upon the earth; and would that it were already kindled' (Lk. 12.49).[28]

'After this I looked, and lo, in heaven an open door! And the first voice, which I heard speaking to me like a trumpet, said, "Come up hither" ' (Apoc. 4.1). Adoration is at once the open door and the invitation. It is faith's response to the promise made by Christ to the one who conquers: 'I will grant to him to sit with me on my throne, as I myself conquered and sat down with my Father on His throne' (cf. Apoc. 3.21).

Praying before the Most Blessed Sacrament exposed in the monstrance, the adorer, 'with unveiled face, beholding the glory of the Lord, is changed into His likeness from one degree of glory to another' (2 Cor. 3.18), in anticipation of complete transfiguration in the Kingdom of God. A glimpse of the glory that lies 'beyond the veil' (Heb. 6.19) is given us already in the mystery of the Most Holy Eucharist. The experience of the saints through the ages attests to this.[29] In the Magnificat Antiphon at Second Vespers of Corpus Christi we sing that the Most Blessed Sacrament is 'a pledge of future glory'.[30] Adoration seeks 'the light of the knowledge of the glory of God' (2 Cor. 4.6) in the 'Eucharistic Face of Christ'.

Doxological Adoration

Eucharistic Adoration is like a sustained note prolonging and echoing the doxology that concludes the canon of the Mass: 'Through Him, and with Him, and in Him, to you, O God, almighty Father, in the unity of the Holy Spirit, is all honour and glory, for ever and ever. Amen'. Like the Sacred Liturgy itself, Eucharistic Adoration is a doxological prayer, a prayer suffused already *here-and-now*, with the jubilation, praise, and thanksgiving of the glorious *there-and-then*. In the Apocalypse St John describes theological climate of Eucharistic Adoration:

---

[28] Magnificat Antiphon, First Vespers of the Solemnity of the Sacred Heart of Jesus.

[29] 'We have before us the example of the Saints, who in the Eucharist found nourishment on their journey towards perfection. How many times did they shed tears of profound emotion in the presence of this great mystery, or experience hours of inexpressible 'spousal' joy before the Sacrament of the Altar'. Blessed John Paul II, *Mane nobiscum, Domine*, art. 31.

[30] Magnificat Antiphon, Second Vespers of the Solemnity of the Most Holy Body and Blood of Christ.

After this I looked, and behold, a great multitude which no man
could number, from every nation, from all tribes and peoples
and tongues, standing before the Lamb, clothed in white robes,
with palm branches in their hands, and crying out with a loud
voice, 'Salvation belongs to our God who sits upon the throne,
and to the Lamb!' And all the angels stood round the throne
and round the elders and the four living creatures, and they
fell on their faces before the throne and worshiped God, saying,
'Amen! Blessing and glory and wisdom and thanksgiving and
honour and power and might be to our God forever and ever.
Amen'. (Apoc. 7.9–12)

Adoration: Between the Consecration and the Communion

The Sacred Host, be it reserved in the tabernacle or exposed to our
gaze in the monstrance was bread taken and set apart for the Holy
Sacrifice at the Offertory of the Mass, bread over which the priest, lend-
ing his voice to Christ, the Eternal High Priest, pronounced the words
of Consecration. Thus is mere bread transubstantiated into the adorable
Body of Christ, the Sacrament of Unity. 'The Bread of Angels' becomes,
as we will sing in the Sequence of the Mass on Corpus Christi, 'the food
of mortal wayfarers'.[31] Eucharistic Adoration is then, in every instance,
situated both liturgically and theologically, between the Consecration
of the Mass and the reception of Holy Communion.

What then should our prayer of Adoration be before the Most
Blessed Sacrament reserved in the tabernacle or exposed in the
monstrance? The question is perhaps best answered by referring,
with St Peter Julian Eymard, and with the Venerable Pope Pius XII
in *Mediator Dei*, to the four ends of the Mass itself. This approach in
no way limits the personal prayer of the adorer but rather shapes it
and gives it a certain objective direction derived from the Liturgy
and leading back into it.

The Four Ends of the Holy Sacrifice of the Mass and of Eucharistic Adoration

Applying the four ends of the Sacrifice of the Mass to Eucharistic
Adoration, it is evident that the first of these, the glorification of the
Father, is fulfilled in the prayer of the adorer who, united by charity
to Christ Jesus in the Sacrament of the Altar, enters with Him, by

---

[31] *Ecce panis angelorum, factus cibus viatorum.* Sequence of the Mass of Corpus
Christi (*Lauda Sion*).

faith, 'beyond the veil' (Heb. 6.19). There he adores the Father 'in spirit and in truth' (Jn 4.24) by participating, through the Spirit of filial adoption, in Christ's own love of the Father, and in the exercise of His eternal priesthood, the true and perfect fulfilment of the Old Dispensation's foreshadowings and figures.

The second end of the Holy Sacrifice and, therefore, of Eucharistic Adoration is to give thanks to God. Eucharistic Adoration is an ongoing response to the great cry of the Preface Dialogue: *Gratias agamus Domino Deo nostro* – 'Let us give thanks to the Lord our God'. The adorer, by taking his place before the Blessed Sacrament, responds with his entire being, *Dignum et iustum est* – 'It is right and just'. The adorer thanks the Father for the ineffable gift of the Body and Blood of the Son, offered in sacrifice and given in Holy Communion from the rising of the sun to its setting (Mal. 1.11). The adorer thanks the Son for the consolation of His Real Presence in this valley of tears, for the largesse of His Eucharistic Hospitality, for the grace of being able to converse with God 'face to face as a man is wont to speak to his friend' (Exod. 33.11), and for the glorious wound in His side from which flows a stream of living water, the Holy Spirit, Lord and Giver of Life.

I would note, in passing, that this second end of the Holy Sacrifice exercised so powerful an attraction on yet another adorer of nineteenth century France, Virginie Danion (1819–1900), that in 1884, with the encouragement of St Peter Julian Eymard, she founded the *Congrégation de l'Action de Grâces* vowed, as its name indicates, to Eucharistic Adoration in a spirit of perpetual thanksgiving.

The third end of the Holy Sacrifice, and therefore of Eucharistic Adoration, is that of propitiation, reparation, and reconciliation.[32] The adorer kneeling in Adoration before the Blessed Sacrament will, if he offers no resistance, be drawn sooner or later into the mystery of the Lamb immolated in expiation for the sins of the world. Among the noteworthy adorers of the Blessed Sacrament considered thus far, no one more fully grasped the implications of this mystical identification with the Victim Christ than the foundress of the Benedictines of Perpetual Adoration of the Most Blessed Sacrament, Mother Mectilde du Saint–Sacrement.

The two imperatives of the Mectildian-Benedictine charism are reparation and the Perpetual Adoration of the Most Blessed Sacrament. For Mother Mectilde, the first imperative – reparation – rose out of a lucid consciousness of her own sin and of the devastation wrought by sin in the world around her; it arose, at the same time,

---

[32] For a magisterial treatment of reparation, see the Encyclical of Pope Pius XI on Reparation to the Sacred Heart of Jesus, *Miserentissimus Redemptor*, 8 May 1928.

out of her awareness of the boundless love of Christ scorned, forsaken, and reviled, even in the Most Holy Sacrament of the Altar. The second imperative – Perpetual Adoration – arose out of Mother Mectilde's conviction that reparation, renewal, and reconciliation could not be attained apart from a total incorporation into and identification with the Eucharistic Christ. The Mectildian-Benedictine Perpetual Adoration is an adherence, without compromise and at every moment, to Christ in the Sacrament of His Love and in all the saving mysteries it contains.

The fourth end of the Holy Sacrifice and, therefore, of Eucharistic Adoration is supplication or impetration. 'In the days of his flesh', Christ the Eternal High Priest, 'with a strong cry and tears, offering up prayers and supplications to Him that was able to save Him from death, was heard for his reverence' (Heb. 5.7). Having entered 'into heaven itself that He may appear now in the presence of God for us . . . He is able also to save for ever them that come to God by Him; always living to make intercession for us' (Heb. 9.24; 7.25). Our Lord's priestly intercession from the Cross and His glorious intercession in the sight of the Divine Majesty in heaven are brought close to the Church on earth in the Holy Sacrament of the Altar where He continues to exercise His mediation on our behalf, so that, as the Roman canon asks, we may be filled with every grace and heavenly blessing. For one called to a life of Eucharistic Adoration the perfection of intercessory prayer consists in an unconditional adherence to the intentions and desires of Our Lord, and to the priestly intercession that, at every moment, ascends, like a fragrant incense, from His Eucharistic Heart.

The Liturgical Preparation for Holy Communion: A Model of the Prayer of Eucharistic Adoration

It remains for us now to consider the liturgical preparation for Holy Communion, beginning with the *Agnus Dei* of the Mass, as a norm and model of Eucharistic Adoration. In the chant of the *Agnus Dei*, the Church addresses Jesus Christ, the Lamb of God Who takes away the sins of the world; the petitions for mercy and peace are made by the whole Church in the context of a world disfigured and fragmented by sin.

By granting His mercy and peace the Lamb of God repairs and heals every wound and brokenness; it is this that inspires Adoration made in the spirit of reparation. In his 2010 *Pastoral Letter to the Catholics of Ireland*, Pope Benedict XVI called specifically for Eucharistic Adoration in a spirit of reparation:

> Particular attention should be given to Eucharistic Adoration, and in every diocese there should be churches or chapels specifically devoted to this purpose. I ask parishes, seminaries,

religious houses and monasteries to organize periods of Eucharistic Adoration so that all have an opportunity to take part. Through intense prayer before the real presence of the Lord, you can make reparation for the sins of abuse that have done so much harm, at the same time imploring the grace of renewed strength and a deeper sense of mission on the part of all bishops, priests, religious, and lay faithful. (19 March 2010)

Even as the adorer enters into the 'ascending' reparation made by the Lamb of God to the Father, he opens himself to the 'descending' reparation by which the Lamb of God restores likeness to the image of God in souls disfigured by sin. Christ presents Himself in the Most Holy Eucharist as the spotless Victim come to repair sinners, restoring wholeness and beauty to souls. At the same time He is the Priest who offers perfect reparation to the Father by restoring all things to Him 'whether in heaven or on earth, making peace by the Blood of His cross' (Col. 1.20). Blessed Elizabeth of the Trinity (1880–1906) understood this. In her prayer to the Holy Trinity the Carmelite addresses Christ, saying, 'Come into me as Adorer, as Restorer (*Réparateur*), as Saviour'.[33]

The Most Holy Eucharist is the mystery of Christ offering Himself to us as the immolated Lamb; it is the mystery of the Blood and water gushing from His side (cf. Jn 19.34). The litanic form of the *Agnus Dei* invites to the contemplation of the Crucified evoked by St John: 'They shall look on Him whom they have pierced' (Jn 19.37). Pope Benedict XVI, writing on the Heart of Christ, suggests that Eucharistic Adoration allows us 'to recognize our sins, to recognize how we have struck Him, how we have wounded our brethren and thereby wounded Him; to look upon Him and, at the same time, to take hope, because He whom we have wounded is He who loves us; to look upon Him and to receive the way of life'.[34]

Oriented by the *Agnus Dei* of the Mass, Eucharistic Adoration becomes a prolonged contemplation of the pierced Heart of the Lamb. In the obscurity of faith the eyes of the adorer begin to read on the 'Eucharistic Face of Christ' the 'thoughts of His Heart to all generations: to deliver their souls from death and feed them in time of famine'.[35]

---

[33] Élisabeth de la Trinité, *J'ai trouvé Dieu. Œuvres complètes*, Paris: Tome I/A, Cerf,1980, p. 200; Elizabeth of the Trinity: *The Complete Works*, Vol. 1, trans. Sr. Aletheia Kane, O.C.D., Washington, DC: ICS, 1984, p. 183.

[34] Joseph Cardinal Ratzinger, *A New Song for the Lord, Faith in Christ and Liturgy Today*, New York: Crossroad, 1997, p. 145.

[35] Ps. 32:11, 19, Entrance Antiphon, Mass of the Solemnity of the Sacred Heart of Jesus.

The Prayers of Preparation for Communion

The Roman Missal contains two prayers recited quietly by the priest, that express his personal sentiments before receiving the Body and Blood of Christ. In these prayers, we find yet another perspective on the content and orientation of Eucharistic Adoration. Whereas the *Agnus Dei* invites to an ecclesial prayer that is immense in scope, the prayers of the priest before Communion address the individual's need for a more personal and intimate exchange with Christ present in the Most Holy Sacrament.

> Lord Jesus Christ, Son of the Living God, who by the will of the Father and the work of the Holy Spirit, through your death gave life to the world; free me by this your most holy Body and Blood from all my sins and from every evil; keep me always faithful to your commandments, and never let me be parted from you.

The prayer addresses Christ in the words of St Peter, 'You are the Christ, the Son of the Living God' (Mt. 16.16). In a concise Trinitarian formula it admirably expresses the economy of salvation: 'who by the will of the Father and the work of the Holy Spirit, through your death gave life to the world'. The adorer kneeling before the Blessed Sacrament, like the communicant receiving it, is drawn into the mystery of the Trinity.

'Free me by this your most holy Body and Blood from all my iniquities and from every evil'. Eucharistic Adoration prolongs and strengthens the liberation from evil that is effect of Holy Communion. 'Make me always cling to your commandments, and never let me be separated from you'. The Church, by clinging to the Eucharistic commandment of Christ, 'Do this in remembrance in me' (Lk. 22.19), makes possible obedience to all the commandments of Him who said, 'Apart from me you can do nothing' (Jn 15.5). 'If you keep my commandments, you will abide in my love, just as I have kept my Father's commandments and abide in His love' (Jn 15.10). The adorer kneeling before the Most Blessed Sacrament sees more clearly that obedience to the commandments of Christ, a fruit of Holy Communion, is the path of personal liberation from every evil.

'Never let me be separated from you'. With the Body of Christ before his eyes, the adorer cannot but repeat the words of the Apostle, 'Who shall separate us from the love of Christ?' (Rom. 8.35). The Eucharist given in Holy Communion and exposed in the monstrance is the epiphany of the Heart of Jesus offering an undying love and seeking not to be separated from sinners, but rather united to them for their healing. It is in Eucharistic Adoration that one realizes the words of Jesus: 'Those who are well have no need of a physician, but those who are sick. Go and learn what this means, 'I desire mercy, and not sacrifice'. For I came not to call the righteous, but sinners' (Mt. 9.12–13).

> May the receiving of your Body and Blood, Lord Jesus Christ, not bring me to judgment and condemnation, but through your loving mercy be for me protection in mind and body, and a healing remedy.

The second prayer before the Communion of the priest invites the adorer to consider the St Paul's teaching on worthy reception of the Body and Blood of Christ:

> Whoever . . . eats the bread or drinks the cup of the Lord in an unworthy manner will be guilty of profaning the Body and Blood of the Lord. Let a man examine himself, and so eat of the bread and drink of the cup. For anyone who eats and drinks without discerning the body eats and drinks judgment upon himself. (1 Cor. 11.27–29)

Eucharistic Adoration is the discernment of one's own heart as well as the discernment of the Body of Christ. In the presence of the 'Eucharistic Face of Christ', the adorer realizes the import of the psalmist's words: 'You have set our iniquities before You, our secret sins in the light of Your countenance' (Ps. 89.8). Adoration becomes, in this way, a school of purity of heart.

At the same time, Adoration is a discernment of the Body of Christ. This is the very discernment expressed in the *Ave, Verum Corpus*:

> Hail, true Body born of the Virgin Mary!
> The same that suffered upon the Cross,
> immolated there for man,
> the Body from whose pierced side
> flowed the water and the blood.[36]

In discerning both his own sinful heart *and* the spotless Flesh of the Lamb immolated for the salvation of the world, the adorer is spared the 'judgment and condemnation' of those who 'eat and drink' (1 Cor. 11.29) without examining themselves and without recognizing the

---

[36] Ave Verum Corpus natum de Maria Virgine: Vere passum, immolatum in cruce pro homine. Cuius latus perforatum fluxit aqua et sanguine. Esto nobis praegustatum mortis in examine. O Iesu dulcis! O Iesu pie! O Iesu fili Mariae!

Body of the Lord. Even more, the adorer comes to contemplate and to experience the Eucharist as 'protection in mind and body, and a healing remedy'.[37]

Behold the Lamb of God

The *Agnus Dei* and the priest's personal prayers of preparation for Holy Communion are followed by a showing of the Sacred Host and, in the Missal of 1970, by this invitation: 'Behold the Lamb of God! Behold Him who takes away the sins of the world! Blessed are those who have been called to the Supper of the Lamb!'

The invitation to Holy Communion is composed of three exclamations. The first, 'Behold the Lamb of God', is a call to awareness, a cry to gaze upon and recognize Christ who comes veiled in the Sacred Species. The liturgical text is drawn from Jn 1:29. Speaking of John the Baptist, the Evangelist writes, 'He saw Jesus coming toward Him, and said, 'Behold, the Lamb of God, who takes away the sin of the world'. Christ adored in the Eucharist is, at every moment, coming towards us. This is the mission of 'the living Bread which came down from heaven' (Jn 6.51): not to remain in the tabernacle or in the monstrance, but to come towards us.

Preaching for the first time on the Solemnity of Corpus Christi as Bishop of Rome (2005), Pope Benedict XVI said that, 'in this Sacrament the Lord is always en route toward the world'.[38] Eucharistic Adoration welcomes Jesus coming towards us. It prolongs the jubilant cry of the *Sanctus*, 'Blessed is He who comes in the name of the Lord' (Mk 11.9), and poises the adorer in the eschatological hope of the whole Church. 'Behold, He says, I am coming soon' (Apoc. 22.12).

Further in the same Gospel we discover that the Baptist also identifies Jesus as the one upon whom the Spirit descended and remained (Jn 1.32) and as the Son of God (Jn 1.34). St John the Baptist's confession of the Christ is Trinitarian. The invitation to fix our gaze upon the Lamb of God is also an invitation to confess Him in His relationship to the Father and the Holy Spirit.

'Behold Him who takes away the sins of the world'. The invitation's second exclamation invites us to contemplate the Lamb of God in relationship to the world redeemed by the Blood of His Sacrifice. Here Christ is confessed as the Paschal Lamb provided by God in fulfilment of Abraham's words to Isaac, 'God Himself will provide the lamb, my son' (Gen. 22.8). Isaiah says, 'He was oppressed and He was afflicted, yet He opened not His mouth; like a lamb that is led

---

[37] Second Prayer before the Communion of the Priest, Roman Missal.
[38] 'In questo Sacramento, il Signore è sempre in cammino verso il mondo'. Homily, Basilica of St John Lateran, 26 May 2005.

to the slaughter' (Isa. 53.7). Eucharistic Adoration becomes, in the light of the second exclamation, an ongoing response to the jubilant cry of the Apostle: 'Christ, our Paschal Lamb has been sacrificed. Let us, therefore, celebrate the festival' (1 Cor. 5.7).[39] Adoration extends the festive joy of Christ's Passover, the mystery sung in every Holy Mass and tasted in every Holy Communion, and expands that joy into silence.

'Blessed are those who are called to the Supper of the Lamb' (Apoc. 19.9). The third and final exclamation calls *beati*, blessed, those who will receive the Body and Blood of Christ. The text is lifted from the description of the glorious heavenly Liturgy in the nineteenth chapter of the Apocalypse. The little phrase, 'Supper of the Lamb', evokes the glory of the kingdom in all its splendour. The 'Supper of the Lamb' is the unending communion of the Father and the Son and the Holy Spirit into which the Church is assumed in every Holy Mass. 'Behold, I stand at the door and knock; if any one hears my voice and opens the door, I will come in to him and eat with him, and he with me' (Apoc. 3.20).

It is in the silence of Adoration that the promises made by the Lord through the mouth of the prophet Isaiah attain their fullest interior resonance. 'Behold, my servants shall eat . . . behold, my servants shall drink . . . behold, my servants shall rejoice . . . behold, my servants shall sing for gladness of heart' (Isa. 65.13–14).

The Body of Christ. Amen

Having looked to the Mass itself for the internal structure of the prayer of Eucharistic Adoration, there remains, in the Missal of 1970, a single phrase: the words addressed personally to each communicant: 'The Body of Christ'. The Missal of 1962 preserves a fuller expression of the same: 'May the Body of Our Lord Jesus Christ preserve your soul unto life everlasting. Amen.' Herein lies the essence of prayer before the Eucharist: the Body of Christ shown and offered as food 'for the life of the world' (cf. Jn 6.33), the Body of Christ eliciting the 'Amen' of a faith that is silent and adores. 'May words cease', wrote Blessed John Paul II, 'and Adoration endure' (Homily, Mass of the Lord's Supper, 1 April 1999), *Tacere et adorare.*

'The Body of Christ'. The phrase remains suspended, as it were, waiting for the 'Amen' of the dying man or woman, of the sick child, of the elderly shut-in, of the person to whom the Body of Christ reserved in this particular tabernacle or exposed in this particular monstrance will ultimately be given as heavenly food and healing

---

[39] Alleluia Verse, *Pascha nostrum immolatus est Christus*, Mass of Easter Day.

remedy. Cardinal Ratzinger calls Eucharistic Adoration 'an education in sensitizing our conscience'.[40] The Eucharistic Body of Christ cannot be separated from the Mystical Body, which it nourishes, heals and perfects.

Adoration of the Most Blessed Sacrament implies no lessening of the social and ethical implications of the Eucharistic Sacrifice, nor of the missionary mandate of the Church. On the contrary, as we grow in awareness of the Divine Hospitality revealed in the Blessed Sacrament we are transformed into the humble servants of that hospitality extended to 'the poor, the maimed, the lame, and the blind' (Lk. 14.13), servants sent out by the Giver of the Great Banquet. 'Go out to the highways and hedges, and compel people to come in, that my house may be filled' (Lk. 14.23).

Conclusion

Eucharistic Adoration, practiced in the school of the Sacred Liturgy, and in the company of the Blessed Virgin Mary and the saints, has a transfiguring effect not only on individuals but also on communities and, in a very real sense, on the whole Church, and this because, as the Preface of the Nativity sings, 'even as we know God visibly, we are, by this, ravished unto the love of what is invisible'. The pierced Heart of Jesus living and present in the Most Blessed Sacrament repairs with an inexhaustible torrent of love the brokenness caused by sin, and to the adorer who perseveres in seeking His Eucharistic Face, Christ restores wholeness and beauty. A soul, a community, a Church faithful to Eucharistic Adoration will be 'ravished unto the love of what is invisible', through which, according to St Benedict, 'our hearts are opened wide and the way of God's commandments is run in a sweetness of love that is beyond words'.[41]

---

[40] Joseph Cardinal Ratzinger, *God is Near Us*, p. 98.
[41] *Rule of St Benedict*, Prologue: 49.

Three

Loving Jesus in the Eucharist with Mary: The Foundation of Religious Life

Mother Adela Galindo

Foundress, Servants of the Pierced Hearts of Jesus and Mary,
Miami, Florida, USA

Since the topic of my conference begins with the call to love Jesus, I would like to speak briefly about the vocation to love that is engraved in our human hearts. Love is our essence, our vocation, our greatest dignity, our greatest gift, and our most sublime task.

We are Capable of Loving

In his book *Love and Responsibility*, Karol Cardinal Wojtyla reminded us of a truth somehow forgotten in our post-modern era, a truth that reveals the essence of our identity and vocation: 'Love is exclusively the portion of human persons'.[1] It is a capacity 'inherent in human beings and is bound up with their freedom and will'.[2] Love is a capacity given to the human heart. Only the human person can make choices of love and for love. We were created out of love, and we were created to know love, to live by love, to be capable of choosing love, to give ourselves for love, to make of our lives a free and sincere gift of self, to freely and generously communicate love in such a powerful way that it will beget life. As St Maximilian Kolbe always said, 'Only love creates'.

We are capable of loving because we are capable of God; we, created in His image and likeness, are capable of freely choosing to live according to our dignity as children of God. As St John tells us: 'God is love, and he who abides in love abides in God, and God abides in Him' (1 Jn 4.16). 'These words from the First Letter of John', taught

---

[1] K. Wojtyla, *Love and Responsibility,* San Francisco: Ignatius, 1993, p. 28.
[2] Ibid.

our Holy Father Pope Benedict XVI in his first encyclical, *Deus caritas est*, 'express with remarkable clarity the heart of the Christian faith: the Christian image of God and the resulting image of mankind and its destiny. In the same verse, St John also offers a kind of summary of the Christian life: 'We have come to know and to believe in the love God has for us' (*Deus caritas est*, 1). This simple verse of Sacred Scripture is a fundamental expression of our hearts:

> We have come to believe in God's love: in these words the Christian can express the fundamental decision of his life. Being Christian is not the result of an ethical choice or a lofty idea, but the encounter with an event, a person, which gives life a new horizon and a decisive direction. (1)

This is the definition of a vocation! A vocation is an encounter with God's love, which gives a new horizon and a decisive direction to one's life. A vocation is a concrete path of loving, a concrete and fundamental response, a choice of love, of making the sincere gift of self. It is the way we are to beget – to generate life, to give abundant fruit – as Jesus calls us in the Gospel of St John, chapter 15.

Therefore, a vocation is always an orientation of the human heart to find the fullness of love and to dedicate oneself to the service of love. A vocation will always imply the free and total response to love, the total giving and surrender of self for the cause of the beloved and to find the full realization of self in this free and total donation of self. Love is a fundamental decision. Love is our vocation, our dignity, our gift, and our task. 'Love is now no longer a mere command, it is the response to the gift of love with which God draws near to us' (*Deus caritas est*, 1).

Women's Vocation to Love

'The dignity of women can only be measured by the order of love' (Blessed John Paul II, *Mulieris dignitatem*, 29). Men also have the vocation to love, proper to the manly characteristics of their masculine genius. But it is women who, in a certain sense, have the vocation and mission to teach men to discover, understand and put into practice the vocation to love. In the Apostolic Letter *Mulieris dignitatem*, Blessed John Paul II told us: 'In God's eternal plan, woman is the one in whom the order of love in the created world of persons takes first root' (29). Yes, the loving plan of God and His communication of love is able to firmly take root first in the heart of woman, thus making her heart a special place where love can grow, be manifested and become fruitful. Women have the particular vocation to reveal and to remind others of the primacy of love – to be a living memory – and to enable others to see in the order and logic of love, and by the gift of their complementarity to call forth men to put their love into action. What a calling! What a dignity! What a Marian gift to the life of the Church and to humanity! What a Marian gift to the Petrine principle of the Church! As Blessed John Paul II taught, 'From the beginning, woman inserts humanity in the order of love' (7), and the Church, being a 'she' – as Cardinal Ratzinger explained – 'that is not an apparatus, nor a social institution. The Church is a She . . . She is a person. The Church is a woman. She is a Mother. She is alive'.[3] She inserts humanity in the order of love. As Blessed John Paul II taught us in *Mulieris dignitatem*, 'the Church's structure is totally ordered to the holiness of Christ's members, and holiness is measured according to the great mystery in which the Bride responds with the gift of love to the gift of the Bridegroom' (27). The first member of the Church to respond and the only one to do so perfectly – without sin and with all of her being filled with the Holy Spirit – is Mary. As the Catechism of the Catholic Church states, referring to Blessed John Paul's II teaching, 'This is why the "Marian" dimension of the Church precedes the "Petrine"'.[4]

Women, therefore, and religious women in particular are called to be living images, living witnesses, and active builders of the civilization of love, to choose and to form hearts in the order of love, to call forth love in the heart of the Church and in the heart of the world through their feminine, spousal, and maternal capacity to love and to dedicate themselves to love, to choose abnegated love and to generate life and to guard it, nourish it, educate it for love. The hearts of women are capable of calling forth love in the Petrine principle. Women are uniquely capable of understanding the science and logic of love – with their Marian gaze and wisdom – and of building the civilization of love in the heart of the Church and in the heart of the world!

Religious Life: A Gift in the Heart of the Church

In *Vita consecrata* Blessed John Paul II teaches that religious life is 'a gift of the Father to the Church' (1). For this reason:

> The consecrated life is at the very heart of the Church as a decisive element for her mission, since it 'manifests the inner nature of the Christian calling' and the striving of the whole

---

[3]   Joseph Cardinal Ratzinger, 'The Ecclesiology of the Second Vatican Council', in: *Church, Ecumenism and Politics*, San Francisco: Ignatius, 2008, p. 28.

[4]   *Catechism of the Catholic Church*, 773; cf. Blessed John Paul II, *Mulieris dignitatem* 27, fn 55.

Church as Bride toward union with her one Spouse . . . it is also a precious and necessary gift, since it is an intimate part of her life, her holiness and her mission . . . it is a choice which finds expression in a radical gift of self for love of the Lord Jesus, and in him, of every member of the human family'. (*Vita consecrata*, 3)

On 19 October 1997, Blessed John Paul II proclaimed St Thérèse of the Child Jesus and the Holy Face, virgin, a religious woman, to be the youngest Doctor of the Universal Church: 'an outstanding recognition which raises her in the esteem of the entire Christian community far beyond any academic title',[5] simply because she understood the science of love. She understood that love is the heart of the Church and that all vocations can reach their fullness as far as they are moved by the power of love.

I know that the Church has a heart and that this heart is burning with love. I understood that love alone makes the Church members act. That love was everything comprises all vocations and that embraces all times and places. Oh Jesus, my love! I have found my place in the Church, and it is You who has given me this place. I have found my vocation: in the heart of My Mother, the Church, I would be love![6]

St Thérèse understood her vocation to love as a Bride of Christ. Jesus Himself gave her the place she has in the Church: she is the Church's heart! Because the heart of the Church is love, and because St Thérèse vocation was to love Jesus with the love of a Bride and, therefore, to communicate love to all the members of His Mystical Body with an all embracing Marian motherhood, embracing in her own oblation (victimhood) of love to Christ all the vocations in the life of the Church. Blessed John Paul II very simply expressed the most profound truth of the religious vocation of St Thérèse in the homily of her proclamation as Doctor: 'She knew Jesus, loved him and made him loved with the passion of a Bride. She penetrated the mysteries of his infancy, the words of his Gospel, the passion of the suffering Servant engraved on his holy Face, in the splendour of his glorious life, in his Eucharistic Presence'.[7]

---

[5]   Blessed John Paul II, Homily, 19 October 1997.
[6]   St Thérèse of the Child Jesus, *Spiritual Canticle*, Prologue, 3.
[7]   Blessed John Paul II, Homily, 19 October 1997.

The Primacy of Love in the Heart of the Church

The primacy of love as the essence, nature, vocation, heart, path and destiny, and authentic force for the life and mission of the Church, as the potent force that moves her through history and through the challenges of every generation, and today as the force that leads the Church into the ocean of the new millennium with the task of the New Evangelization for the building of a new civilization, has been clearly and strongly highlighted by the most recent Pontiffs. The same Pope, Blessed John Paul II – the Petrine heart who elevated St Therese, a Marian heart, to be a Doctor of the Church – expressed his vision of the centrality of love in his own life and mission: 'Love explained everything to me. Love solved everything for me, that is why I admire love wherever it is found. Only love has been able to overcome all obstacles, only love has persevered to the end, only love generates love in others. Only love can guard love, only love is stronger that death (Song 8.6)'.[8]

Our Holy Father, Pope Benedict XVI, whose first encyclical was dedicated to theme of God's love and was written with the purpose of calling forth in the world a renewed energy and commitment in the human response to God's love (cf. *Deus caritas est*, 1), told us in his homily during the Celebration of Vespers in his apostolic visit to Pavia, Italy, to venerate the remains of St Augustine:

> Love is the soul of the Church's life and of her pastoral action. Serving Christ is first of all a question of love. Dear brothers and sisters, your membership in the Church and your apostolate always shine forth through freedom from any individual interest and through adherence without reserve to Christ's love. The first pastoral goal is to lead people to Christian maturity. The Church is not a mere organization of group events. The Church is a community of people who believe in the God of Jesus Christ and commit themselves to live in the world the commandment of love that He bequeathed to us. Thus, she is a community where one is taught to love, and this education happens not despite but through the events of life. This is how it was for Peter, for Augustine and for all the saints. So it is for us. (Homily, 22 April 2007)

---

[8] As quoted from the poem 'The Shores of Silence' written by Karol Wojtyla and very beautifully quoted in the movie, *Karol: The Man Who Became Pope* (Universal Studios, 2006), at the moment after his election as Successor of Peter in the room of tears.

In this homily the Holy Father, also exhorted us to mature in our 'ability to read and interpret the present time in the light of the Gospel in order to respond to the Lord's call and to progress in your personal and communal witness to active love' (Homily, 22 April 2007).

We can humbly and gratefully contemplate how the Holy Spirit has been guiding us to recognize – in so many ways – that to proclaim, teach and witness to God's love and to respond to His love by living it with authenticity is the path and the task of the Church of the third millennium and also our particular mission: we are being called to be witnesses to potency and fecundity of love, heroic love, love to the extreme, formed by the luminous splendour of truth. This potency and fecundity of self-giving, oblative love in the life of the Church is contemplated, received, and communicated in the Eucharist, in the gift of Jesus' self-oblation to give us life, abundant life. The new civilization of love can only be built by its witnesses, and the witnesses to love are formed in the School of the Eucharistic Heart, the School of the Sacrament of Love, the school of the generous, oblative, sincere, and pure gift of self for the good of the beloved. We religious women are called to witness to the primacy of Eucharistic love in the heart of the Church, and we must witness it to the world. We must witness to love by loving Jesus in the Eucharist with the heart of a bride, and we must witness to Eucharistic love by freely and generously giving to many the fruitfulness of this spousal communion. We must witness to His Eucharistic love by giving life through our apostolic mission, by going across the mountains of humanity as Our Lady went out in haste filled with the life of Christ (cf. Lk. 1.39). 'Those who have drunk from the fountain of God's love become in their turn a fountain from which flow rivers of living water in the mists of a thirsting world' (Benedict XVI, *Deus caritas est*, 42). We religious are called to love the Eucharist with spousal love to proclaim with all of our being that the Eucharistic Lord is our life, is the centre of our life.

The Eucharist is the Centre of My Life!

In his book *Gift and Mystery* published in 1996 on the occasion of his fiftieth anniversary of priestly ordination, Blessed John Paul II gave us a personal testimony on the splendour of the gift and mystery of the priestly vocation: a sublime gift, freely given by the Father, a great mystery which infinitely transcends the person who receives it. Because it is a gift and a mystery of divine election, he also understood the priesthood to be his most sublime task, his response of love, of responsible love, because the greatest treasure of the Church, the Eucharist, was entrusted to his hands. Blessed John Paul II gave us a testimony of love, he opened his priestly and Petrine heart to relate – above and beyond the external events – what belonged to his deepest being, to his innermost experience,[9] and from his own experience he wrote to all priests with deep and powerful simplicity: 'The Eucharist is the most important moment of the priest´s day, the centre of his life'.[10] And many times throughout his pontificate, we heard him exclaim: 'The Eucharist is my life! The Eucharist is the absolute centre of my life and of everyday of my life!'

Blessed John Paul II desired that his witness to the gift and mystery of his priestly vocation, his profession of faith and love for the Eucharistic Jesus, be a gift for the whole Church, for his brother priests, for religious and consecrated persons, and for lay people, and offered it to the Virgin Mary as a homage of his filial love – another luminous witness to the fruits of the maternal mediation of Our Lady in his life and of the formation he had received in the School of Mary's Heart: to be totally and unconditionally given to Christ and to the Church, as Jesus has given Himself up for the good of His Bride, the Church.[11]

Blessed John Paul II learned oblative love and life-giving purity in the School of Our Lady, Mother of the Church, Mother of priests, Mother of the Eucharist. In the School of Our Lady´s Heart and in the School of the Eucharistic Heart, Blessed John Paul II learned to be a witness to love at all times and at all cost: he learned to be always ready to give his life, to offer himself, to make of his life a gift, a sincere gift of self for Christ who has first loved us, who has first given himself for us, who has loved us to the extreme giving us 'a model to follow' (Jn 13.15). As he said in *Gift and Mystery*:

> I was spared much of the immense and horrible drama of the Second World War. I could have been arrested any day, at home, in the stone quarry, in the plant, and taken away to a concentration camp. I would ask myself: so many young people of my own age were losing their lives, why not me? . . . Amid the overwhelming evil, everything in my own personal life was tending towards the good of my vocation . . . In the face of the spread of evil and the atrocities of the war, the meaning of the priesthood and its mission in the world became much clearer to me.[12]

In the midst of great evils, he opened his heart to respond to a call from Christ´s Heart to love, to give himself totally at the service of

---

[9]   Cf. Blessed John Paul II, *Gift and Mystery*, New York: Doubleday, 1999, p. 2.
[10]   Ibid., p. 75.
[11]   Ibid., p. 99.
[12]   Ibid., pp. 34, 36.

the Kingdom of God, at the service of the Church and of humanity . . . to choose heroic love. He understood himself to have been
preserved simply to be given . . . and to be freely given with the
totality of his personal I, making of his life a sincere gift of self,
through the vocation to the priesthood. He laid down his life for the
good of the Church, for the good of humanity and he found in this
choice the greatest fulfilment and realization of his heart as we read
in the Constitution *Gaudium et spes*, 24: 'man can fully discover his
true self only in a sincere giving of himself'.

The Church Lives from the Eucharist

The same *'totus tuus'* Pope who would exclaim 'The Eucharist is my
life . . . the most sacred moment of my journey, the centre of my life!'
would also teach that 'the Eucharist is the living heart of the Church'.[13]
On Holy Thursday 2003, during the year of the Rosary and the twenty-
fifth year of his Petrine ministry, Blessed John Paul II gave to the
Church the encyclical *Ecclesia de Eucharistia*: 'The Church lives from
the Eucharist!' Blessed John Paul II gave us this gift with the intention
of shedding light on the mystery of the Eucharist in its indispensable
and vital relationship to the life of the Church. We can sense in the
title of this encyclical, the same movement of his heart calling us out
of love for the Eucharist to make the Eucharist the centre of our life,
the treasure of our hearts, the pledge of the fulfilment for which our
hearts long, the love that can quench the thirst of the restless heart, the
strength for our journey, the nourishment of our lives, the light in our
dark valleys, the love that conquers our hearts and leads us to choose
in all things what is true, what is good, and what is beautiful.

A Journey into the Eucharistic Heart Through the Heart of Mary

In the last five years of Blessed John Paul II's pontificate, we can
clearly and evidently see how he was leading the Church with a
pedagogy of renewed love for the Eucharistic Lord that can only be
a fruit of profound contemplation. First, the Great Jubilee of the year
2000, a year of grace and mercy, that he intended to be 'intensely
Eucharistic' (*Tertio millennio adveniente*, 55; cf. *Novo millennio ine-
unte*, 6), since the real presence had to be at the centre of the Holy
Year dedicated to the Incarnation of the Word. In the Great Jubilee
Year the whole Church was called to contemplate, to fix our gaze on,
the luminous face of Christ and also to make his face shine before
the generations of the new millennium. Then, on 16 October 2002, the
Holy Father surprised the whole Church by proclaiming the Year of

---

[13]   Ibid., p. 85.

the Rosary, to culminate the Great Jubilee Year with a Marian crown and, as an exhortation to all of us, to contemplate the face of Christ in union with, and at the School of the Blessed Mother (cf. *Rosarium Virginis Mariæ*, 1). It had hardly been a year since the conclusion of the Year of the Rosary and we received yet again another initiative of the Holy Father: The Year of the Eucharist (October 2004–5), a year to rediscover the mystery of the real presence of Christ at the School of the inner dispositions of the Heart of Mary, *the* 'woman of the Eucharist' (*Ecclesia de Eucharistia*, 53) in her whole life. This *'totus tuus'* Pope who exclaimed 'the Eucharist is my life' and 'the Church lives from the Eucharist' passed away on the Vigil of Divine Mercy Sunday during the year of the Eucharist.

Yes, the Pope who exclaimed 'the Eucharist is my life!' called us at the beginning of the third millennium by the proclamation of the year of the Eucharist and through his Apostolic Letter for the Eucharistic year, *Mane nobiscum Domine* (Remain with us Lord), to build a 'Eucharistic culture':

> For the Eucharist is a mode of being, which passes from Jesus into each Christian, through whose testimony it is meant to spread throughout society and culture. For this to happen, each member of the faithful must assimilate, through personal and communal meditation, the values which the Eucharist expresses, the attitudes it inspires, the resolutions to which it gives rise. Can we not see here a special charge which could emerge from this Year of the Eucharist? (25)

Blessed John Paul II called the whole Church to be renewed in our Eucharistic spirituality, by proclaiming in words, actions, and choices that the Church lives from the Eucharist. For this Eucharistic culture and Eucharistic spirituality to be renewed in the heart of the Church, he directed our eyes to Mary, 'woman of the Eucharist':

> If we wish to rediscover in all its richness the profound relationship between the Church and the Eucharist, we cannot neglect Mary, Mother and model of the Church. Mary can guide us towards this Most Holy Sacrament, because she herself has a profound relationship with it. Mary is the 'woman of the Eucharist' in her whole life. (*Ecclesia de Eucharistia*, 53)

The Woman of the Eucharist in Her Whole Life!

What a coherent, authentic and luminous definition of the truth and beauty of the vocation of consecrated religious women is enclosed in this title given to Our Lady in *Ecclesia de Eucharistia*. Yes, we religious sisters are to be recognized by our love for our Eucharistic Jesus, our Bridegroom. How beautiful would be if what is said of Our Lady was said of us: Women of the Eucharist in their whole lives! Women of intrepid, self-giving, oblative and fruitful love! All that is Marian is all who we are. All that is Marian is all that we religious women are to be, since we are the Marian image and presence of Our Lady through history, a continuation in history of her spousal love, her prayer, her contemplation, her feminine receptivity, her total fiat, her humble and dedicated service, her trusting and filial obedience, her total availability to cooperate in the Father's plan. 'The Mystery of Mary spreads out in history, transcending time, through the Church, bride and mother', our Holy Father Pope Benedict XVI tells us in his second volume of *Jesus of Nazareth*.[14]

Our total consecration to Christ – of intimate spousal communion with His Heart, of profound prayer, contemplation and Eucharistic Adoration, of treasuring and keeping His Word, of unreservedly serving His designs of love, of placing our feminine genius at the service of the Church and humanity – is a Marian gift in the life of the Church. We are to be Marian! We are to be women of God, we are to be women of the Word, women of the Eucharist in our whole life! We are to be women of love, of truth, of light to illumine, like Our Lady, the oceans that the Church of the third millennium is to go out into, and to conquer. We must be women of the Eucharist, women who love the Eucharistic Heart of Jesus undivided and totally, unconditionally and permanently. We must learn to love Him in the School of the Heart of Mary!

The Marian Identity of Religious Life
Mary's presence in the Church should be mirrored by members of the consecrated life (cf. Blessed John Paul II, *Redemptoris Mater*, 19, 24, 28, 48). Our Lady is the first consecrated woman, the woman who made of her life a gift and a response of love to the One who loved her first. She assented to His calling and to His will, in love and for love, and for the cause of God's redeeming love, by giving her total, unconditional, unreserved, and perpetual fiat, her loving obedience of faith. In the Encyclical *Redemptoris Mater* we read:

> As the Council teaches, "The obedience of faith" (Rom. 16.26; cf. Rom. 1.5; 2 Cor. 10.5–6) must be given to God who reveals, an obedience by which man entrusts his whole self freely to

---

14   Pope Benedict XVI, *Jesus of Nazareth – Holy Week: From the Entrance into Jerusalem to the Resurrection*, San Francisco: Ignatius, 2011, p. 22.

God.' Indeed, at the Annunciation Mary entrusted herself to God completely, with the 'full submission of intellect and will', manifesting 'the obedience of faith' to him who spoke to her through his messenger. She responded, therefore, with all her human and feminine 'I', and this response of faith included both perfect cooperation with 'the grace of God that precedes and assists' and perfect openness to the action of the Holy Spirit, who 'constantly brings faith to completion by his gifts'. (13; quoting *Dei verbum*, 5; cf. *Lumen gentium*, 56)

This description of Our Lady's obedience of faith to God Who called her to be His, to cooperate with Him in the work of redemption, to place herself totally in her personal, human, feminine 'I', at the service of His plan of love – to give the gift of herself, to make of her life a sincere gift of self, to place the truth, beauty and goodness of her feminine genius (all her feminine potentialities), with a spousal undivided love for God and with an oblative maternal dedication and Marian fecundity – I consider it to be the most luminous, elevated description and dignity of women, and in a particular way, of religious consecrated women. In the Apostolic Letter *Mulieris dignitatem* he taught us that:

The 'fullness of time' manifests the extraordinary dignity of the 'woman'. In one hand, this dignity consists in the supernatural elevation to union with God in Jesus Christ to which the 'woman' is the representative and the archetype of the whole human race. On the other hand, however, the event at Nazareth highlights a form of union with the living God which can only belong to the 'woman'. (4)

A Form of Union which Can Only Belong to Women, to Her Feminine, Spousal Heart

Blessed John Paul II was convinced of and affirmed that the vocation of woman is one, and it is her greatest calling: to love with the genius of her feminine heart. Woman, in her feminine being (body, soul and psychology), has inscribed in her heart a special calling of self-giving, of self-donation: to love with the great capacity of self-sacrifice, of self-oblation for others to have life. In *Vita consecrata* he spoke of consecrated life as the living image of the Church as Bride:

In the consecrated life, particular importance attaches to the spousal meaning, which recalls the Church's duty to be completely and exclusively devoted to her Spouse, from whom she receives every good thing. This spousal dimension, which is part of all consecrated life, has a particular meaning for women, who find therein their feminine identity and as it were discover the special genius of their relationship with the Lord. (34)

We, religious women, in our undivided and virginal love for Christ become spiritual mothers of many hearts. We cannot give Christ to others as mothers until we first receive Him interiorly. The primacy of our vocation as religious is prayer, Eucharistic Adoration and contemplation. Our primary mission is an interior one, one of total receptivity before Christ's presence, to receive Him so that we may be able to conceive spiritual life in our hearts and go across the mountains of our missions to give His life to others. This power of the religious, spousal heart is potently manifested in her communication of spiritual life, which is motherhood.

> We can see [in consecrated life] a vivid image of the Church as Bride, fully attentive to her Bridegroom and ready to accept his gift. In Mary the aspect of spousal receptivity is particularly clear; it is under this aspect that the Church, through her perfect virginal life, brings divine life to fruition within herself. (*Vita consecrata*, 34)

This Marian receptivity and Marian openness to the Lord calls forth in the history of the Church many gifts, much new life, new charisms, new families in the heart of the Church. The Marian heart is always a gift to the life of the Church. 'Mary, you are a response . . . a living response to the action of the Holy Spirit to the dramatic challenges at the end of the Millennium' (Blessed John Paul II, *Homily for the Vigil of Pentecost 1998*).

In September 2010, His Holiness Pope Benedict XVI began a series of 18 general audiences dedicated to women saints and mystics who have contributed – and played a precious role – with their feminine hearts and genius in the life of the Church. The Holy Father said, citing *Mulieris dignitatem*, n. 31, at the beginning of the series: 'The Church gives thanks for all the fruits of feminine holiness' (Audience, 1 September 2010). These women were filled with spiritual wisdom and holiness who lived virtuous lives, who had great capacities in exercising the ministry of authority and great competency in organizational aspects in their religious communities, who had a profound Marian gazing and understanding of the mysteries of Christ and of the meaning of the Sacred Scriptures, of the Liturgy and Tradition. These women were great teachers who ardently lived and taught the values of evangelical radicalism and who had an ardent apostolic zeal for humanity. These women mystics did not spare any sacrifices, penances or sufferings, and with courageous love followed the Lamb wherever He would take them. They lived their spousal love for Christ and so reached high levels of communion with their beloved and were entrusted with the secrets of His Heart. These women saints and mystics, these Marian charisms in the life of the Church were all Eucharistic women! Each was a woman of the Eucharist in her whole life!

In a particular way I would like to mention St Clare of Assisi, a woman of the Eucharist whose love for her Beloved was manifested in the oblative and sacrificial love of her daily life for Jesus and her daughters. St Clare – who spent hours contemplating the Mystery of love of the Eucharistic Heart and who lived and taught her sisters to give themselves totally to Christ as He has given Himself up for us – was a Marian vocation in the life of the Church. St Francis would call her many times: Woman made Church! In fact:

> St Francis placed the vocation of St Clare and the Poor Sisters in the aura of the Virgin Mary, the humble handmaid of the Lord who, overshadowed by the Holy Spirit, became the Mother of God. The humble servant of the Lord is the prototype of the Church: Virgin, Spouse and Mother. Clare perceived her vocation as a call to follow the example of Mary, who offered her own virginity to the action of the Holy Spirit to become the Mother of Christ and of His Mystical Body. The figure of Mary accompanied the vocational walk of the Saint of Assisi until the end of her life. According to a noteworthy testimony given at the Process of Canonization, Our Lady approached St Clare on her deathbed, bending over her, whose life was a radiant image of Her own. (Blessed John Paul II, Message for the 750th anniversary of the Death of St Clare, 9 August 2003)

St Clare, a charism who mirrors the Marian heart of love and contemplation for the Eucharist and who is known for her total spousal trust and faith in the real presence of Christ, is a witness to the power of the Eucharistic Lord to protect His brides. She is a witness in the heart of the Church of love for the Eucharist, of the love of the Bride of Christ for His Eucharistic Presence, for the Sacrament of Love. As Pope Benedict XVI said in the general audience dedicated to St Clare: 'The entire Church through the mystical nuptial vocation of consecrated virgins, appears what she will be forever: a pure and beautiful bride of Christ' (15 September 2010). In the message mentioned above Blessed John Paul II said to the spiritual daughters of St Clare: 'Her whole life was a Eucharist! She gazed and remained fixed on the Son of God to the end, in ceaseless contemplation of His mysteries. Hers was the loving gaze of the spouse, filled with the desire of an ever more complete sharing in His life'. St Clare always exhorted the sisters to: 'Gaze upon Him, consider Him, contemplate Him, as you desire to imitate Him'.

To Learn to Gaze, Contemplate Jesus in the Eucharistic with the Heart of Mary

The Immaculate Heart of Mary is the *School of Love* for Christ. It is a school where we learn to contemplate, to gaze with our hearts – with pure and undivided love and with feminine depth – to ponder and reflect carefully the Mysteries of the Eucharistic Heart 'Mary can guide us towards this Most Holy Sacrament, because *she herself has a profound relationship with it'* (Blessed John Paul II, *Ecclesia de Eucharistia*, 53; emphasis added).

Who can teach us better than Mary to know and to love Christ? To enter in to the School of Mary is *'to put ourselves in living communion with Jesus through the heart of his Mother'* (Blessed John Paul II, *Rosarium Virginis Mariae*, 2; emphasis added). The Heart of Mary is the greatest school to learn about the mysteries of Christ. Who better than her can teach us about Jesus?

> Christ is the supreme Teacher, the revealer and the one revealed. It is not just a question of learning what he taught but of 'learning him'. In this regard could we have any better teacher than Mary? From the divine standpoint, the Spirit is the interior teacher who leads us to the full truth of Christ (cf. Jn 14.26; 15.26; 16.13). But among creatures no one knows Christ better than Mary; no one can introduce us to a profound knowledge of his mystery better than his Mother'. (Blessed John Paul II, *Rosarium Virginis Mariae*, 14)

St Luke tells us repeatedly that the Virgin Mary *kept all things* in her heart and even says that she did it: *carefully* (cf. Lk. 2.19, 51). She pondered lovingly and carefully all things about Christ. The Blessed Mother is not only a careful guardian and custodian of the Body of her Son, but also of His words, His life, mysteries, actions, and gestures. In Her Heart the treasure was kept. Because she kept and pondered everything in Her Heart, Our Lady is the Marian memory of the Church:

> Mary's memory is first of all a retention of the events in remembrance, but it is more than that, it is an interior conversation with all that has happened. Thanks to this inner dialogue,

she penetrates into the interior dimension, she sees the events in their inter-connectedness and she learns to understand them.[15]

If we enter into the School of her Heart, we enter into her profound dialogue, pondering, memory and understanding of the Mysteries of Jesus.

In Mary's Heart We Learn to Contemplate the Mysteries of Love of the Eucharist

'The Christian people sit at the School of Mary and are led to contemplate the beauty of the face of Christ and to experience the depths of his love' (Blessed John Paul II, *Rosarium Virginis Mariae*, 1).

The Blessed Mother teaches us the *art of love which is contemplation, which is to gaze* with the heart, to gaze with love, to penetrate mysteries of love and to learn to enflesh them, to make them a way of life for us. We must learn to gaze, to contemplate Christ, His Eucharistic face, His Eucharistic Heart so that we may become what we contemplate. We must learn in the Heart of Mary to gaze, to penetrate, to ponder and keep, to enflesh and to actualize the mysteries we contemplate.

We must be pure of heart, to grow in purity of love, purity in the eyes of our hearts, so we can see God, as Jesus taught us in the Sermon on the Mount. To contemplate Christ, to see His Eucharistic face and to learn the mysteries of love of His Eucharistic Heart, our gaze must be purified and elevated by the Immaculate Heart (her immaculate love) and by the Immaculate gaze of Mary (her undivided, pure contemplation). Blessed John Paul II taught in *Rosarium Virginis Mariae,* that 'the contemplation of Christ has an incomparable model in Mary' (10). Because no one has ever devoted all her life to the contemplation of the face of Christ and the Heart of Christ as faithfully and lovingly as Mary.

To Gaze with Our Lady's Heart

We must learn to gaze as Our Lady gazes. She gazes with Her Heart, with the purity of Her Love. She gazes and contemplates all things through God's love, finding God's face and presence, His Will in everything. She gazes with a pure heart. She gazes and keeps in her heart all the treasures that are entrusted to her. She gazes with love and responsibility – with responsible love.

---

[15]   Joseph Ratzinger, *Jesus of Nazareth – From the Baptism in the Jordan to the Transfiguration,* New York: Doubleday, 2007, p. 234.

'Mary lived with her eyes fixed on Christ' taught Blessed John Paul II in his Apostolic Exhortation on the Holy Rosary (11). We must learn to live like her with our eyes fixed on Christ. She always gazed at Jesus. We must learn to gaze with the eyes of her Heart! As Blessed John Paul II taught us in this Apostolic Exhortation:

> The eyes of her heart already turned to Him at the Annunciation, when she conceived Him by the power of the Holy Spirit. [Then through her *interior gaze*] . . . in the months that followed she began to *sense and live in his presence and to picture his features.* When at last she gave birth to Him in Bethlehem, *her eyes gazed tenderly on the face of Her Son,* as she [held him in her arms] and 'wrapped him in swaddling clothes and laid him in a manger'. (Lk. 2.7). Thereafter, Mary's gaze, ever filled with adoration and wonder, would never leave Him. (10; emphases added)

We must learn to gaze with the eyes of Her Heart!

> [Her gaze as in the presentation was one of deep silence before the mystery.] At times, Our Lady gazed at Jesus, with a *questioning look,* as in the episode of the finding in the Temple . . . it would always be a *penetrating gaze,* one capable of deeply understanding Jesus, even to the point of *perceiving his hidden feeling and anticipating his decisions,* as at Cana. (cf. Jn 2.5) (10; emphases added)

Let us learn to gaze through the eyes of Her Heart!

> At other times *it would be a look of deep sorrow,* especially beneath the Cross, where her vision would still also be filled of suffering and at the same time, that of a mother giving birth . . . for Mary not only shared the passion and death of her Son, she also received the new son given to Her in the beloved disciple (cf. Jn 19.26–27) [and in him, received us all]. On the morning of Easter hers would be *a gaze of radiant joy of the Resurrection.* (10; emphases added)

The joy of contemplating that Life has conquered death! We must learn to gaze with the eyes of Her Heart!

> And on the day of Pentecost, *she gazed filled with fire,* it was an ardent gaze with the outpouring of the Holy Spirit. (10; emphasis added)

And, how did she gaze at the Eucharist? Can we imagine the contemplation of the Blessed Virgin Mary when the Eucharistic Jesus was elevated before her eyes?

> What must the Blessed Mother have felt as she heard from the mouth of John, Peter, James and the other Apostles the words spoken at the Last Supper: 'This is my Body . . . this is my Blood' (cf. Lk. 22.19–20)? The body given up for us and made present under sacramental signs was the same body which she had conceived in her womb! For Mary, receiving the Eucharist must have somehow meant welcoming once more into her womb that heart which had beat in unison with hers and reliving what she had experienced at the foot of the Cross. (Blessed John Paul II, *Ecclesia de Eucharistia*, 56)

Can we try to understand the love and Adoration of the Heart of Mary for Her Eucharistic Son? The Son she carried for nine months in her womb, the Son she held in her arms as a child, the Son she saw on the Cross offering Himself, the dead son she held in her arms and later contemplated resurrected and radiant? And now, her Son in the profound humility of the Eucharist? How she must have kept Her Heart and eyes fixed on Him!

And in Heaven, Our Lady keeps gazing immersed in the contemplation of the Blessed Trinity, gazing as a beloved daughter of the Father, as Mother of the Son and as Spouse of the Holy Spirit, gazing at the Blessed Trinity and gazing at the Church, gazing at us, at her children! That is why we pray in the Hail Holy Queen, 'Turn then, most gracious Advocate, thine eyes of mercy toward us, and after this our exile, show unto us the blessed fruit of thy womb, Jesus'. Not only after but during our pilgrimage on earth: show us the blessed fruit of your womb, Jesus, in the Eucharist!

Let us learn, to gaze, to contemplate Jesus in the Eucharist with the eyes of Our Lady's Heart, for no one has devoted herself so intensely and so constantly to the contemplation of the face of Christ, of the Heart of Christ, of His Words, actions and gestures, more than she, who was given the incomparable grace of being immaculate: totally pure and undivided in love, totally poor and dispossessed of her own will, totally obedient and available to the designs of God's love. Her gazing was penetrating and piercing, because she gazed with the luminosity of her immaculate love. Let us learn to see the mysteries of God and the realities of humanity, the signs of our times, with the piercing gaze and with the profound reading of history of the Blessed Mother's Heart.

Religious Women, Let Us be Women of the Eucharist in All of Our Lives!

May our gaze of the Eucharistic Heart be impregnated by the gaze of Our Lady´s. May our eyes also be fixed on Jesus, on His love, attentive to His face, His Heart and His Words. May we be transformed by His love. May we be healed, restored and elevated by love, and, thus, in the power of the Love of the Eucharist, may we become ardent witnesses to the power and fecundity of love to build a new civilization – a new culture of love. This task is a particular responsibility of women, of religious women. Religious women, Marian hearts in the heart of the Church, let us be women of the Eucharist! Let us exclaim with ardent love: the Eucharist is my life!

The time has come for us to enflesh the Petrine desire of Blessed John Paul II, whose priestly heart and life were totally given for the elevation of the Church in her Marian splendour:

> Let us take our place, at the school of the saints, who are the great interpreters of true Eucharistic piety. In them the theology of the Eucharist takes on all the splendour of a lived reality; it becomes 'contagious' and, in a manner of speaking, it 'warms our hearts'. Above all, let us listen to Mary Most Holy, in whom the mystery of the Eucharist appears, more than in anyone else, as a mystery of light. Gazing upon Mary, we come to know the transforming power present in the Eucharist. In her we see the world renewed in love. (*Ecclesia de Eucharistia*, 62)

Let us be women of the Eucharist in all of our lives! Let us love Jesus in the Eucharist with a Marian Heart! Let us be ardent witness to the power of Eucharistic love. Let us, from the Eucharist, go out into the deep taking our place in the mission of the Church at the beginning of the third millennium: the New Evangelization. Let us build the new civilization of love by being intrepid and zealous witnesses to the power and fecundity of the Eucharist in our religious lives and in the life of the Church.

Four

Eucharistic Adoration as a Way of Life: A Pastoral Perspective

Bishop Giovanni D'Ercole
Auxiliary Bishop of L'Aquila, Italy
Translated from Italian by E. Scott Borgman

A Look at the Current Situation in the World and the Church's Efforts in the New Evangelization

Our time is full of contrasts: there is light and shadow in the landscape of the world. Some positive elements nourish hope. In the 1990 Encyclical *Redemptoris missio* Blessed John Paul II spoke of the progressive convergence of peoples towards ideals and evangelical values. He enunciated some of them: the refusal of violence and war, the respect of the person and of his rights, the desire for liberty, for justice and for fraternity, the tendency to overcome racism, the affirmation of the dignity and value of women, ideals which are often heard even today. But there is mostly evidence of the widespread nostalgia for the Absolute which takes the place of the triumphant atheistic affirmation of one time. The need for spirituality is felt, even if it is often confused.

If positive examples are readily available, the negative ones are numerous and worrisome: indifference, agnosticism, a practical more than a theoretical atheism. Relativism has conquered large portions of society where the practice of faith is often scarce. In some places there is evidence of the silent apostasy of many believers.

A look at the mass media reveals a society which is post-Christian and passively secularized. The abandonment of the faith is no longer big news, but a religious practice. A culture is being created which is dangerous for the moral life, especially for youth. Ethical relativism and the predominant culture reduce man, and therefore reduce reason's capacity to reach truth.

It is still valid to ask: Why is there a lack of faith? Why, after receiving a religious education as children, do people find themselves on the paths of agnosticism, atheism and indifference? No one is a believer because they are good or no one is an atheist because they are bad. Today, the attack goes right to the heart of the faith. For the Russian writer Fyodor Dostoevsky, the first cause of disbelief is ignorance regarding the 'substance' of Christ; the lack of knowing Christ 'in his substance', in other words, lack of knowing the depths of Christ: He in whom is manifested the fullness of humanity and of divinity. Dostoevsky writes: 'Many believe that it is sufficient to believe in the morals of Christ to be Christian. It is not the morals of Christ, nor the teachings of Christ which will save the world, but precisely the faith in the Word which was made flesh' (The Demons).

Today, many seem to follow a Christianity without Christ. There is talk of Christian values independent of Christ. This leads to a 'self-service' Christian faith where each person feels authorized to take what they want and to leave aside that which they don't want (Christ yes, but no to the Church! Faith yes, but no to Christian morality as it concerns life, sexuality, family, etc.).

The second cause of disbelief is superficiality, which is an appendage of ignorance and feeds upon the cultural dilettantism. This superficiality emerges because of the way one confronts the great ethical questions. Not taking care carefully to understand issues and problems results in slogans and cultural approximations giving life to a subculture where details prevail over the essential.

The third cause is impurity of the mind and of the heart. The Russian author alludes here to intellectual prejudices, to the presumption of understanding and defining everything, while a lack of interior light caused by sin hinders seeing and understanding. It cannot be denied, as it is often said, that today there is a strong tendency to devalue the idea of sin, this when it is not altogether ignored. But this has produced an increase in the sense of guilt with dramatic consequences.

In order more clearly to understand the question it is good to specify certain theological truths.

Faith is a gift from God with its source in His saving love. Therefore, faith is not the work of the intelligence, nor of man's will.

The primacy of grace in faith does not destroy man's freedom. Faith is always subject to man's freedom.

Consequently, there are two elements which are obstacles to the development of the life of faith: a darkness within the mind and heaviness of heart. Often today the level of religious education for adults has remained at the elementary level. They have also created their own faith, based on polluted and superficial sources. More often than not, religious ignorance leads to the building of a God in one's own image and likeness. Paul VI wrote: 'The drama of our time is the separation between the Gospel and life'. Saint Augustine used to say: 'Intellige ut credas', in other words, force yourself to discover through deeper study the value and the strength of reasons to believe; be less dependent on sociological conditioning and external psychologies.

The second element is the heaviness of heart, that is to say, immorality in its widespread form. To believe does not mean mainly to adhere to an ensemble of truths, but to adhere to Christ, founding the truth upon Him. Faith is a personal relationship between Christ and man: a bond which is free, loving and filial. Sin interrupts this bond. Sin 'distresses, closes and blinds the eye of the heart with which one sees God' (St Augustine). It is necessary therefore to keep this eye healthy and free of what might distress it: greed, avarice and lust.

In our permissive and libertarian society, permeated with eroticism, greedy for power and possessions, there is no room for faith because faith flowers on humility of heart and on openness of the soul to Grace. The sense of sin has been lost; transgression is exalted – denying sin, forgetting prayer. In a culture such as this, God is a stranger, an inconvenience that must be eliminated. But 'a conscience without God is frightening and can lose itself all the way to committing the most immoral things'. 'In the West – observes Dostoevsky – they have lost Christ . . . and, because of this, the West is failing, only for this reason'.

I don't want to appear pessimistic. It's true that atheism and de-Christianization appear widespread and arrogant, but it is also true that religious sentiment and the nostalgia for the Gospel are making a comeback as they cause souls to blossom.

Things could not be otherwise, because atheism is anti-human. God is as necessary for us as is the air we breathe. Without Him, we cannot live very long, or live with very much dignity.

To be able to bow before God and Christ is the deepest need for man and also his greatest strength. Idols before which the humanity of the twentieth century bowed have crumbled. If they are still being worshiped, it is through blindness, laziness and cowardice. These have left paths which lead to emptiness, solitude and desperation. Can one live in desperation? Dostoevsky writes: 'Faith or the fire!' Therefore, here we have a new challenge and possibility for the New Evangelization, for a pastoral mission which knows how to welcome the demands of post-modernity. It is a commitment which involves all of us; a commitment which is arduous and exalting. Arduous because of the barrier of secularism and of indifference is thick; exalting because today the 'temptation of God', that is, the nostalgia for the truth and for peace is strongly present and widespread. The mission of the Church is to help man, although he has often lost his way, to feel the consoling and resolving presence of God Who, through Jesus Christ, has entirely given Himself to men. But what are we to do?

God is Present Among Us in the Eucharistic Mystery

There is a truth which today needs to be proclaimed strongly: God is not hidden or eclipsed! He is present in the Eucharist. And the Church has the grand mission of guarding, defending and adoring Him. The Church has the task of presenting Him to the world as the only salvation of humanity.

There is an historical coincidence which I would like to point out. At the end of his pontificate, Blessed John Paul II wanted to declare a Year of the Eucharist. His successor, Benedict XVI, opened his pontificate with the Synod of Bishops which had as its theme: 'The Eucharist, source and summit of the life and mission of the Church'. The Eucharist and the Church: the Church lives this dynamic. The Church returns to and departs from the Eucharist.

I will not pause at length on the theological, biblical and liturgical aspects of the Eucharistic miracle. I would simply like to consider some questions which come up spontaneously and which are tied to our existence and to the history of the world.

Why is the Eucharist the central act of transformation which is capable of renewing the world? Because – responds Benedict XVI – here violence is transformed into love, death into life. It is like a 'nuclear fission' in the most intimate part of the being; it is the victory of love over hate and the victory of love over death. In the Eucharist there is found the secret of the renewal of the universe: it is the explosion of good which conquers evil and thus triggers the transformations which change the world. Christ has redeemed the world: by His death and resurrection the essential has been accomplished, at this time it is our turn to enter into this dynamic nature of salvation in order to access His mystery and to be nourished by His Body and by His Blood.

In the Eucharist, in the Bread and the wine, Christ has left us His passion, His offering, His life which is love without end. When we come to the Eucharist, we become one people in which the love of God is circulated. We need to let the Eucharist transform our lives!

Benedict XVI notes:

Today in vast parts of the world there exists a strange forgetfulness regarding God. It would seem that everything is going fine without Him. But at the same time, there also exists a feeling of frustration, of dissatisfaction with everything and in everyone. One is inclined to exclaim: It's not possible that this could be life!

One asks oneself: how to evangelize this society which is deaf and apparently vaccinated against the Gospel?

Even religion almost becomes a product of consumerism. It is necessary, therefore, to discover the star which can guide us: and the only star which can guide us to the truth and to life is Jesus Christ, the Way, the Truth and the Life.

For this reason, we need the Eucharist as our starting point.

Eucharistic Adoration: Personal Experiences

If we want to bring men and women in the twenty-first century to faith in Jesus Christ, we need to recapture the ability to adore Christ in the Blessed Sacrament. This is one of the basic tenants of Benedict XVI's magisterium.

We hear of the New Evangelization often, but nothing is valid or effective without it being centred on Christ, truly present in the Eucharist.

I remember distinctly World Youth Day in Cologne, just a few months after the election of Cardinal Ratzinger as Supreme Pontiff, and later in Sydney, Australia. The Eucharistic vigil was an incredible experience of prayerful silence in the night. Thousands and thousands of young people from every part of the world gathered around the Successor of Peter in Adoration of Christ, truly present in the Eucharistic Sacrament.

In that night, I can testify that there were many conversions. Youths who came only out of curiosity, found a light which illuminated their lives. Young men and women, before the presence of Christ, came to see their vocations with clarity. And they chose to follow Him in the vocation of the priestly and religious life. When one listens to Jesus, creating the necessary conditions for opening the heart to divine Grace, authentic miracles occur and hearts are opened to the power of the Holy Spirit.

Going back in time, I remember my experience with the young missionaries in Cote d'Ivoire and how the Eucharist was the secret to the spiritual and pastoral renewal of the parish.

I remember also my visit to Korea in 1994 and the first contacts with Perpetual Adoration and the testimony of the archbishop in a large archdiocese in the south. Eucharistic Adoration was the secret of a vast spiritual, pastoral and vocational renewal in the diocese. I think of the missions which were carried out by youth from *Jeunesse et lumière*, the sentinels of the morning, lights in the darkness, who adored the Eucharist throughout the entire night. How many young people were approached on the beach or in the street and were taken to the feet of Jesus in the Eucharist!

And how much we can say about Perpetual Adoration! Wherever Perpetual Adoration begins, the parish blooms. A bit of courage is necessary in the beginning, but then everything moves forward by itself. The Lord works, converting hearts and changing the face of the parish community. It only takes a trial run in order to be convinced of the effectiveness of Eucharistic Adoration. The experience confirms how the Eucharist makes Christians, Christians make the Eucharist and how the Eucharist constitutes the Church. Moreover, it is becoming more important to educate the people in how to live the Eucharistic mystery through participation at the Sacred Liturgy and how to prolong the celebration of Mass into their whole lives with devotion and faith. Saints are those who continue to live the Mass throughout the day.

However, often today our faith in the Eucharist is sick: we find deserted churches, weekday Masses attended by very few people, shabby Liturgy, careless celebrations of Holy Mass, cobwebs in tabernacles, lack of respect for the presence of Christ, and even profanation. And yet, the Eucharist is the most sublime act of love Jesus gives us; it is the gift, par excellence: how much more could Jesus have given than His death? St Thomas affirms: 'The Eucharist is the greatest of all the wonders performed by Christ, the admirable testament of His immense love for men'. Perpetual Adoration helps to reveal this.

It is necessary to revive our 'Eucharistic sensitivity' in order to understand, appreciate and respond to the gift of Christ. How do we do this?

First, we need to move from understanding the Eucharist as an object to the Eucharist as a person (The Eucharist isn't a very holy thing, but a Person).

Secondly, we need to move from a Eucharistic formalism to a living relationship.

Thirdly, we need to update our formation on and appreciation of the Eucharist through the biblical texts, theology and spirituality, lives of the saints. It is important to renew the catechesis which helps us to understand the meaning of different terms: Mass, Feast of our Lord, Holy Eucharist, Eucharistic Sacrifice, Eucharistic Adoration.

Lastly, it is necessary to make some practical decisions: We must never receive the Eucharist without proper preparation (at least having read the Word of God); never approach the Eucharist with empty hands (we should have a concrete intention of conversion, we should carry to the Eucharist the great needs of the Church and of the world); we can permeate our day with 'Eucharistic stops' which are brief visits to a church or a chapel or recalling the Eucharistic Christ to the mind and to the heart. This is the very context in which Perpetual Adoration takes on its spiritual richness and its value. We could add many other reflections, but I think that at this conference there will be the possibility to hear other very interesting testimonies.

Mary, Eucharistic Woman: Model and Teacher

Jesus recalls Mary; the Eucharist recalls Mary. We need to place ourselves at the school of Mary, the Eucharistic woman. Blessed John Paul II inserted into the mysteries of the Rosary the institution of the Eucharist. Mary guides us toward this Supreme Sacrament. Mary is present at the Cenacle and is present at the first Eucharistic celebrations.

Mary is the model of Eucharistic faith throughout her life. There is a significant analogy to be had between her 'fiat' and the 'Amen' which we say when we receive the Eucharist.

Mary is the model of Adoration which becomes apostolate. In the Eucharist, God is within us and we are within Him. The dynamic pierces us and needs to be diffused through us unto the entire world because His love transforms the world. The term Adoration derives from the Greek *proskenesis*: submission, abandon to God, norm to follow; and from the Latin *ad-oratio*: kiss, submission which becomes love, freed from our will and to be completely guided by the love of Christ.

Mary is the first tabernacle in history. She visits Elizabeth. If the Eucharist becomes the centre of our lives, we enter into the process of transformation which the Lord has in mind. Who finds Jesus has to carry others to Him. Joy does not fold in on itself within us. If we participate in the same Bread, then we are all one and this has to manifest itself in life: capacity to forgive, availability to welcome and to share, commitment to others and service to others.

Mary is the model which made the sacrificial dimension of the Eucharist its own: participation in the sufferings of Christ.

Mary, Eucharistic 'gift'. In the words of Jesus: 'Do this in remembrance of me' everything that Jesus accomplished is present; so too is the gift of Mary as Mother. To celebrate the Eucharist is to take Mary with us and to conform ourselves to Christ, allowing Mary to shape us. Blessed John Paul II affirms: 'If the Church and the Eucharist are inseparable, then we can say the same of Mary and the Eucharist'. And: 'The Eucharist is given to us because our life, just as Mary's life, is entirely a *magnificat!*'

Conclusion

I would like to close with a consideration of Blessed John Paul II: 'Teaching the Sacred Scriptures, particularly the Gospel to the people . . . and to make them familiar with this Sacred Book, is like the Alpha of all the activities of a bishop and of his priests'. The Omega – if you permit me this analogy from the Book of Revelation – is represented by the Chalice, blessed at our altar daily. The two realities go together: 'the Word of Jesus and the Blood of Jesus'.

In Perpetual Adoration the Bible and the Eucharist are united concretely. Because of this, the promotion of Perpetual Adoration is a permanent school of listening and prayer, of Christian life and of pastoral action.

Five

Homily for the Solemn Mass of St Aloysius Gonzaga

Mauro Cardinal Piacenza
Prefect of the Congregation for the Clergy
Translated from Italian by James R. DeViese

Praised be Jesus Christ!
    Dear brothers and friends,

I am delighted to preside over this celebration of the Eucharist on the liturgical memorial of St Aloysius Gonzaga during your important conference: 'From Adoration to Evangelization'. May the Lord bless your work and have it bear fruit in abundance.

In his first letter, Saint John the Evangelist poses to us a crucial question which fits well into the theological and missionary dynamic of these days of reflection. He says: 'And who is he that overcomes the world, if not he who believes that Jesus is the Son of God?' The 'victory over the world', in this context, is certainly to be interpreted in the usual Johannine sense of the victory over evil, over limitations and over sin. The world, whether it be around us or even more so within us, is all that is opposed to Christ and to the expansion of the Kingdom of God.

The Evangelist is well aware that only One has conquered the world: Jesus Christ, died and risen! His is the singular victory, definitive and universal. He has conquered the world, coming into the world and taking upon Himself all the sin of the world! For this reason, the Baptist was able to say: 'Behold the Lamb of God' (Jn 1.36). And the Liturgy adds: 'Who takes away the sins of the world'.

The great leap forward which this Johannine passage urges us to take, is the acknowledgement that this victory of Christ over the world is shared by all who believe that Jesus is the Son of God. 'Who is he that overcomes the world, if not he who believes that Jesus is the Son of God?'

This is such a wonderful announcement, and it is extraordinary to hear that we, poor mortal men, by virtue of our faith in Jesus Christ, by virtue of our belief that Jesus is the Son of God, are made partakers of His victory over the world.

As the victory of Christ over sin and death was established by His resurrection, so over time and even today, His victory over the world is represented again, is witnessed to, and occurs anew in all those who believe that Jesus is the Son of God.

The centrality of the Faith in the lives of men, of the Church and of society, with the absolute primacy of God that flows from it, is the very condition by which the world recognizes those who believe that Jesus is the Son of God.

With this in mind, as has been emphasized since the start of the Year for Priests (2009–10), Eucharistic Adoration represents an indispensable horizon of reference, looking toward Him in Whom it is possible to establish the authentic and lasting reform of the Church and, therein, the hoped-for reform of the clergy.

The dynamic 'from Adoration to Evangelization' represents, in fact, the only real and possible path for an authentic witness which is capable of knowing how to 'overcome the world'.

An Evangelization which is not born from an authentic, prolonged, faithful and intimate relationship with God will bear fruit only with difficultly. Even more difficult still will be its ability to captivate the men of this age.

Not infrequently in recent decades has a correct approach to the circumstances of man been confused, springing forth from an authentic pastoral charity but with empty activity, entirely anthropocentric and philanthropic, forgetting the indispensable truth according to which the root and the origin of all love is only to be found in the Eternal Love.

Not only do strength and courage flow forth from Eucharistic Adoration, but so, too, does true creativity in Evangelization, from the rediscovery that any time spent with the Lord is, in reality, freely given to our brothers and is, in itself, Evangelization!

I think that in the correct dynamic between love for God and love for one's neighbour that even the Gospel has reminded us: 'Teacher, which is the greatest commandment in the Law? . . . You shall love the Lord your God with all your heart and with all your soul and with all your mind . . . And you shall love your neighbour as yourself' (Mt. 22.37a–39b). I believe that it is not only necessary to recover the absolute primacy of love for God, of prayer, and of Adoration, but that it can and must be taken a step further. Evangelization is not something 'to do' after we have adored; it is not something to do after Adoration ends. Evangelization *already happens in Adoration*: to adore is already to evangelize! It is so not only in the dimension of the visible witness which Adoration always involves, but also, and above all, in that hidden co-operation with God's work, in which he who adores is always called to participate.

Overcoming the *before* of Evangelization and the *after* of Adoration, we are called to rediscover the profound unity of these two dimensions, through which one evangelizes while adoring, and must continue to adore while evangelizing. There is not a something *before* Evangelization which is represented by Adoration, nor a something *after* Adoration represented by Evangelization. There is only the absolute primacy of God: 'Thou shalt love the Lord thy God . . . This is the greatest and first commandment' (Mt. 22.37b–38).

Paraphrasing what the Apostle John writes to us, we could say that Adoration conquers the world! The absolute primacy of God, recognized, adored and witnessed, conquers the world.

How are those who believe that Jesus is the Son of God called today to overcome the world? By what means? By living which 'methodology of Evangelization?' Looking at the gentle and forthright example of the strong-willed St Aloysius Gonzaga, whom we commemorate today, we must recognize that there is only one way to conquer the world: to captivate the world!

In history, the method used by God and lived for centuries by the Church, in its most complete expression, has always been this: Conquer the world by captivating the world.

In this context, of course, to captivate obviously does not mean to flatter, nor to acquiesce to the conditions of the world. Rather 'to captivate the world' means to show with joyful certainty all of the beauty, novelty, renewed life and reasonableness of Christianity, of our being those who believe 'that Jesus is the Son of God'.

The Father, after all, has captivated the hardened hearts of men, loving them, sending His only Son, Who gave His life for us, while we were yet sinners (Rom. 5.6). Only love is truly credible; only love captivates man and thereby conquers the world in Him and around Him.

As the Holy Father Pope Benedict XVI has mentioned so often, both in his Encyclical *Deus caritas est* and in *Caritas in veritate*, the witness of love has always been experienced, from the very beginning of Christianity, as essential to Evangelization. The Church makes a single gesture: in loving God, she loves His children; in loving His children, she loves God; and by loving Him, she evangelizes.

In this context of clarity about the absolute primacy of God, whether from the theological point of view or from the methodological point of view, there emerges every appropriate indication as to the authentic and ever-necessary reform of the Church and of her Ministers. 'From this, we know that we love the children of God when we love God and obey His commandments' (1 Jn 5.2).

The reform of the Church begins from the altar! It begins from the Eucharist, celebrated as the Church asks that it be celebrated, and adored in the true, real and substantial Presence in the world of the Risen One! The reform of the Church begins at the altar and from the ministers of the altar! How often it happens that one seeks to love God's children, while forgetting first to love God and above all to keep His Commandments!

Holy priests throughout history constantly remind us that authentic pastoral charity, which knows neither scheduled hours nor restraints, springs uniquely from an extraordinarily profound relationship with God. 'From Adoration to Evangelization', then, is also the horizon of what we call 'the New Evangelization'. So that it may not remain merely an empty slogan, it is urgent and necessary to go forth from the altar in order to open one's heart to the whole world, and then, with a heart changed by grace, to lead the brethren back to the altar, whereupon lies the true expansion of the Kingdom of God.

The altar conquers the world! The Eucharist conquers the world! A holy priest conquers the world! This victory is not the outcome of a battle always being fought, but one that comes through a compelling witness which bears fruit.

We must return to showing forth the full beauty of God, of His only begotten Son who has died and is risen, of the Eucharist and of the Sacred Ministry, firmly believing that such beauty captivates the world and, therefore, ultimately conquers it. It conquers it and saves it.

May she who is All Beautiful – *Tota pulchra es Maria!* – she in whom is the victory of Christ, appear in all her splendour. May the Blessed Virgin Mary, who first adored the Divine Presence in her womb, the first tabernacle and first monstrance in history, she who was the first to be evangelized and the first evangelizer, obtain for us that perennial reform which we so greatly need. As we gaze upon her, may she obtain for us that holiness which so captivates us!

Six

Celebrating the Feast of *Corpus Christi*

Monsignor Guido Marini
Master of Pontifical Liturgical Celebrations, Vatican City
Translated from Italian

When the title of this presentation was given to me, I immediately
thought back to a famous homily given by Pope Benedict XVI in 2008,
for the celebration of the Solemnity of *Corpus Christi* in Rome.

I shall deal with three great truths connected with the celebration
of *Corpus Christi*, at the same time seeking to draw out some important implications which particularly affect our liturgical life.

Standing in the Presence of the Lord

In the ancient Church, 'standing in the presence of the Lord' was
expressed by the term *'statio'* Let us try to understand something
more of the weighty significance of this term.

When Christianity spread beyond the confines of the Jewish
world, the Apostles and their immediate successors had one over-
riding concern: that in every city there would be only one bishop
and one altar. Why such a concern? The unity of the bishop and altar
was to give expression to the unity of the Church, beyond the many
differences, present in those who became members of the Church
by virtue of Baptism.

In the unity thus expressed, we find the most profound sense of the
Eucharist: by receiving the one Bread, we become a living organism –
the one Body of the Lord. And thus the Apostle Paul could exclaim:
'Here there cannot be Greek and Jew, circumcised and uncircumcised,
barbarian, Scythian, slave, free man, but Christ is all, and in all' (Col. 3.11).

Participation in the Eucharist implied, however, that one would
find people coming together from very different situations: man
and woman, rich and poor, nobleman and slave, intellectual and
ignorant, the ascetic and the sinner converted from a dissolute life.
Access to the Eucharistic celebration became, also visibly, entrance
into the one Body of the Lord, the Church.

Somewhat later, when the number of Christians began to increase,
it was not possible to maintain this external form, expressive of

the Church's unity. At Rome, titular churches were erected; in time, they evolved into the parishes. In this new context, it was necessary to give a new form to express the visible unity that existed earlier. And that happened with the institution of the *statio* (stational church). The Pope as Bishop of Rome, especially during Lent, celebrated the Sacred Liturgy in the various titular churches, where all the Christians of the City gathered. In this way, even if in a new way, the experience of the former time was renewed: all those joined by the same faith found themselves together, in the same place, in the presence of the Lord.

The feast of *Corpus Christi* retrieves that original intent. This feast is actually presented as the *statio urbis* (the station of the City). The doors of the churches, parishes, groups of our dioceses open and all find themselves together in the presence of the Lord to be one with Him, the source of their unity. Thus, it is He, the Lord present in the Most Holy Eucharist, Who makes us one Body and makes it possible that the multitude come together in the unity of the Church.

Entering into the 'We' of the Church

The celebration of *Corpus Christi*, then, teaches us every time to enter into the 'we' of the Church at prayer. This 'we' speaks to us of a reality, which is the Church, which goes beyond individuals, communities and groups. This 'we' reminds us that the Church, even when present in a local or particular dimension, is always universal; it reaches all times and places, and crosses the threshold of time to allow us to enter into eternity; she safeguards and transmits the mystery of Christ, the ultimate and definitive answer to the question of meaning present in the heart of every man.

It follows, then, that in celebrating *Corpus Christi*, we are recalled to some typical and undeniable dimensions of the Liturgy. Above all, I am referring to the dimension of catholicity, which is constitutive of the Church from the very beginning. In that quality of catholicity, unity and diversity come together in such harmony as to form one substantially unified reality, albeit in a legitimate diversity of forms. And then comes the dimension of historical continuity, in virtue of that auspicious development appears to be that of a living organism which does not deny its own past, even while passing through the present and orienting itself towards the future. And then, the dimension of participation in the Liturgy of Heaven, for which it is now more than ever appropriate to speak of the Liturgy of the Church as that human and spiritual space in which Heaven manifests itself on earth. One need only think of an example of this coming from the First Eucharistic Prayer: 'command that these gifts be borne by the hands of your holy Angel to your altar on high . . .'

And, finally, the dimension of the 'non-arbitrary', which avoids consigning to the subjectivity of an individual or group that which belongs to all as a treasure received – to be safeguarded and transmitted. The Liturgy is not some sort of entertainment, where each person can think he has the right to remove and add according to his own taste and his own greater or lesser happy inventive capacity. The Liturgy is not a feast in which one always has to find something new to hold the interest of the participants. The Liturgy is the celebration of the mystery of Christ, given to the Church, in which we are called to enter with always greater intensity, also in virtue of the ever-new and providential repetitiousness of the rite.

Entering into the 'we' of the Church beginning with the Eucharist signifies also letting oneself be transformed into the logic of that catholicity which is charity, which is openness of the heart, according to the measure of the Heart of Christ: it embraces everyone, bends its own ego to the exigencies of true love, is ready to give its own life without reservations. The Eucharist is the true source of the charity of the Church and in the heart of everyone. From the Eucharist our daily life of charity takes its form, which is the evangelical style of life to which we are all called.

Song and Language
Recently the Holy Father, in a letter written on the occasion of the hundredth anniversary of the foundation of the Pontifical Institute of Sacred Music, returned to the theme of the universality of language, because it pertains to Sacred Music.

The celebration of *Corpus Christi* in its being the root and expression of catholicity, calls our attention to the universality of the music proper to the Liturgy and to the necessity of being educated and of educating in that sense. Thus Pope Benedict XVI writes:

> Sometimes, in fact, these elements that are found in *Sacrosanctum concilium*, such as, precisely, the value of the great ecclesial patrimony of Sacred Music or the universality that is characteristic of Gregorian chant, have been held to express a concept which corresponds with a past that needs to be superseded and set aside because it is supposed to limit the freedom and creativity of the individual and of communities. Yet we must always ask ourselves anew: who or what is the authentic subject of the Liturgy? The answer is simple: the Church. It is not the individual person or group which is celebrating the Liturgy, but is first and foremost God's action through the Church which has her own history, her rich tradition and her creativity.

The Liturgy, and consequently Sacred Music, 'lives on a correct and constant relationship between healthy traditio and legitima progressio,' keeping constantly in mind the fact that these two concepts – which the Council Fathers clearly underlined – merge since 'tradition is a living reality, which therefore includes in itself the principle of development, of progress'. (Letter, 13 May 2011)

Universality, that is typical of Gregorian chant, is constantly recalled by the Magisterium, among the notes characterizing the musical expression that wants justly to be considered sacred and liturgical. In this universality we are able to understand the vital relationship between liturgical music and the mystery being celebrated. Concerning that mystery, which is universal because it is destined for all, music cannot be anything but a faithful interpreter and exegesis. Music or song that would only be an expression of subjectivity, or superficial and fleeting emotion, or of the current fashion would be too poor to have a place in the Liturgy. In the Liturgy, in fact, all must remain in a listening mode and participate in a universal language and, consequently, in music and song that open hearts to the mystery of the Lord.

Music and song in the Liturgy must maintain a privileged reference to the Word of God and to that word which the great spiritual tradition has handed down to us, as an echo and interpretation of the mystery of Christ. Only thus do music and song remain faithful to their innate vocation as the means of access to the Christian reality which is life-saving.

The celebration of *Corpus Christi*, the *statio urbis*, the sign of the universality of the Church gathered together around the Eucharistic Mystery, is a reminder also not to forget the element of catholicity that always must make itself present in liturgical music.

Walking Towards the Lord and with the Lord

Standing in the presence of the Lord has brought about, from the very beginning, walking towards the Lord and with the Lord.

This 'walking towards', this proceeding that has become a procession, can be better understood if we remember the experience of Israel, when the Israelites wandered for a long time across the desert. The ancient People of God were able to find a land and were successful in surviving even when losing the land because it did not live on bread alone but was nourished by the Word of the Lord. This 'Word' was the strength that sustained an arduous and tiring journey that reinvigorated the Israelites in desolation and trial, and that imbued them with courage when every human effort to cling to hope seemed to fail.

The experience of ancient Israel is a sign and a permanent reference for the life of the Church and for each one of us. If we are able to carry the load of a pilgrimage across the spectrum of history and its contradictions, we owe it to the fact that we walk towards the Lord and that, on the walk, He is with us.

In this way, the feast of *Corpus Christi* signifies walking towards the Lord and with the Lord and, consequently, celebrating the authentic sense of life: this act of walking is not wandering aimlessly without a goal in the solitude of spaces without boundaries. The life of man has a very precise direction. The direction is Christ, the Lord of time and history, the Saviour of all; and while we proceed in this direction, He, Who is the goal, is also the faithful companion along the road, the one who sustains our pilgrimage. 'Bone pastor, panis vere, Jesu, nostri miserére: Tu nos pasce, nos tuére. Tu nos bona fac vidére. In terra vivéntium', sings the Sequence for the liturgical Solemnity of *Corpus Christi* (Jesu, shepherd of the sheep: Thou thy flock in safety keep, Living bread, thy life supply: Strengthen us, or else we die. Fill us with celestial grace).

That which the Christian community lives by celebrating *Corpus Christi* does not live alone. It lives this experience of *Corpus Christi* through all of us: through those who remain outside of the Church, who have left the Church, or who have never even known her. The public processing of Christians through the streets of the City of Man towards the Lord and with the Lord is the visible witness of a new way of understanding life and history, a new way that has been given to us through grace and that must be transmitted to all. It is the new way of hope that flows from faith in Jesus Christ, the Incarnate God, Who becomes the Eucharist, Who shows us the way to take, accompanying the steps of our journey.

The Orientation of the Cosmos and History Towards Christ

The celebration of *Corpus Christi* helps us, therefore, to find again an orientation of everything towards Christ, because everything has been thought of and made 'through Him and for Him' (Col. 1.16).

Our personal artistic knowledge, together with very serious recent studies, remind us that one of the typical characteristics of the Christian Liturgy, from the beginning, was that of celebrating facing East.

Already in the term 'turned towards the east', there exists the entire significance of how the Christians, gathered together for the celebration of the divine mysteries, turned east in prayer. The churches were constructed facing east, because from there the sun rises (cosmic symbol of the coming of the Lord), a remembrance evermore expressive of the Sun of life, the Risen One. Christians at prayer turned their face towards the rising sun and thus oriented their heart to the Lord of history, beginning and end of creation.

When, in the course of time, it was no longer possible, for different reasons, to construct churches with an eastern orientation, a substitute was a large crucifix on the altar or in the apse – richly decorated and featuring pictures of the image of the Saviour. Thus, despite the absence of the eastern orientation of the actual churches, the orientation of prayer remained very clear, to which the gathered assembly was invited during the liturgical celebration.

Unfortunately, in our times, we run the risk of losing the orientation of prayer, with the consequences of running the risk of losing the orientation of life and of history. The recuperation of the centrality of the cross, as the Holy Father Benedict XVI invites us to do with the example of the Liturgy over which he presides, is not a marginal detail. In fact, it deals with an essential element of the liturgical action, of a sign that leads one's gaze and heart to the Lord, Who is the centre of our prayer, Who re-presents before the pilgrimage of our history the true goal towards which we are directed.

Here is the thought of the Pope:

> The idea that priest and people at prayer ought to look at each other comes exclusively from modern Christianity and is completely foreign to antiquity. Priest and people surely do not pray toward each other but toward the one Lord. Therefore, at prayer they face the same direction: either facing east as the cosmic symbol of the Lord Who is coming or, where this is not possible, toward an image of Christ in the apse, toward a cross, or simply towards Heaven, as the Lord did in His priestly prayer the night before His Passion (cf. Jn 17.1). Meanwhile, I am pleased that the proposal I made at the end of the chapter in question of my work, *The Spirit of the Liturgy*,[1] is advancing – not by way of new transformations but simply by placing a cross at the centre of the altar, toward which all (priest and faithful) can look, so as to be guided toward the Lord, Whom all beseech together'.[2]

The Christian Liturgy – and this is one of the fundamental truths – expresses in its own proper signs, the unbreakable bond between

---

[1]   Romano Guardini, *The Spirit of the Liturgy*, San Francisco: Ignatius, 2000; cf. pp. 74–84.

[2]   Joseph Ratzinger, Preface, *Gesammelte Schriften: Theologie der Liturgie*, Freiburg: Herder, 2008.

creation and covenant, between cosmic order and historic order of revelation. Thus must it always be.

Here is how the Holy Father expressed it in a homily for this year's Easter Vigil:

> Now, one might ask: is it really important to speak also of creation during the Easter Vigil? Could we not begin with the events in which God calls man, forms a people for himself and creates his history with men upon the earth? The answer has to be: no. To omit the creation would be to misunderstand the very history of God with men, to diminish it, to lose sight of its true order of greatness. The sweep of history established by God reaches back to the origins, back to creation. Our profession of faith begins with the words: 'We believe in God, the Father Almighty, Creator of heaven and earth.' If we omit the beginning of the Credo, the whole history of salvation becomes too limited and too small. (Homily, 23 April 2011)

Carrying within itself all the newness of salvation in Christ, the rite of the Church preserves and gathers together every expression of that cosmic Liturgy that has characterized the life of peoples in search of God through the prism of creation. In the Eucharist, all the ancient cultural expressions find a 'landing-place' of salvation. It is ever more significant, even from this point of view, that the First Eucharistic Prayer or Roman canon, refers us to 'the gifts of your servant Abel the just, the sacrifice of Abraham, our Father in faith, and the offering of your high priest Melchizedek'.

In this passage from the ancient prayer of the Church, we find a reference to ancient sacrifices, to cosmic worship and related to creation that now, in Christian Liturgy, is not only not denied, but rather assumed into the new and eternal sacrifice of Christ the Saviour.

On the other hand, in this same perspective, one must look at the many signs and symbols of the covenant used to give form to the new Christian worship. One thinks of light and darkness, wind and fire, water and earth, the tree and its fruits. One deals with that material universe in which man is called to make evident the traces of God. And one thinks equally of the signs and symbols of social life: washing and anointing, breaking the bread and sharing the chalice.

Everything, therefore, in the liturgical rite, finds its authentic orientation, its proper direction, its most intimate truth.

How beautiful it is, therefore, to look towards the Lord and those visible signs which render it easier to turn towards Him with the countenance of one's heart! The fact that a crucifix could take away some visibility between the celebrant and the assembly should not be a cause for wonderment. That visibility is not what counts most in prayer. We should moreover marvel at the absence of eloquent signs that guarantee and favour such a turning to Christ, considering that only by turning to Christ are we able to see clearly the road we are to travel and the true nature of our destination.

Thus must it be for us, every time we participate in the celebration of the divine mysteries. Turned to Christ in prayer, we rediscover the direction of our existence, we become capable of interpreting the cosmos and history in the light of the Risen One, we re-enter into our daily lives ready to bear witness to the new hope that has been given to us. And the Solemnity of *Corpus Christi* helps us remember exactly this, by bringing us back to the essential truth of Christian Liturgy and life.

Kneeling in the Presence of the Lord

From the moment that the Lord Himself is present in the Eucharist (for the Eucharist is in fact the Lord), Eucharistic Adoration has also always been involved.

We know that in its solemn form Eucharistic Adoration developed during the Middle Ages. Nevertheless, that was not an unwarranted change or one of decadence. Eucharistic Adoration emerges in a more evident way in that historical period as a truth that was already present from Christian antiquity. Or, if the Lord gives us Himself, His own Body and Blood, receiving Him cannot but call for kneeling, adoring Him, and glorifying Him.

One thinks of the Gospel accounts of the gesture of Stephen (Acts 7.60), of Peter (Acts 9.40), and Paul (Acts 20.36), who prayed while kneeling. It is also worthwhile to recall the Christological hymn of the Epistle to the Phil. (2.6–11) that presents the cosmic Liturgy as a kneeling at the mention of Jesus' Name (Phil. 2.10) and to see in that text the fulfilment of Isaiah's prophecy (Isa. 45.23) concerning the lordship of the God of Israel with respect to the world. Kneeling before the Lord, the Church fulfils the truth, rendering homage to Him Who is the victor because He gave Himself up even unto death, death on a cross.

If the celebration of *Corpus Christi* is realized by standing before the Lord and in journeying towards His presence, this same celebration also finds an expression ever more rich with significance in the act of Adoration.

In this manner, the Church affirms the truth of things and, together, her greatest freedom. Only one who bends the knee and the heart before God can have true freedom – freedom from the powers of the world, from ancient forms of slavery, and from the new forms of slavery of the present age.

Refusing the Lord Adoration goes against man, who then becomes capable of every degrading submission. Where God disappears, man remains entrapped in the slavery of various forms of idolatries. Adoring Jesus Christ, true God and true Man, present in the Eucharist, means celebrating true human freedom and, therefore, affirming man's greatest dignity. The dignity of a son, the son of a God Who created Him, and Who loved Him, and Who loves Him even to the point of a total gift of Self.

On the other hand, the act of Adoration also involves the act of adhesion, which is agreement or devotion. True Adoration, in fact, is giving oneself to God and to other men. Authentic Adoration is love, conformity to the Beloved, Who returns truth to our life and recreates our heart. There cannot be true Adoration without generous adhesion.

The Church who bends her knee before the Lord, also bends her heart to His will. And in her we all find such a spiritual experience: we kneel with our body because our thoughts, sentiments, affections, behaviour are also bent towards God's plan. Thus, in the act of Adoration is present already the figure of the new world, renewed by the power and love of God in Christ, also become the history of all of us through the Church.

The Language of Adoration

The celebration of *Corpus Christi* introduces us, therefore, into the prayerful language of Adoration. The feast of the Body and Blood of the Lord helps us keep such language with care, in the context of the liturgical celebration.

I am glad, in this context, to recall a fundamental element of this language. I am referring to sacred silence.

The Liturgy, when it is celebrated well, must envision a felicitous alternation between silence and the spoken word, where silence animates the spoken word, permitting the voice to sound again in harmony with the heart, maintaining every vocal and bodily expression in a proper climate of recollection.

Where there would be a unilateral predominance of the spoken word, an authentic language of the Liturgy would not resound. Therefore, the courage is needed to educate people to interiorization, which is the capacity to learn again the art of silence – that silence in which we learn the only Word that can save us from piling up vain words and empty, theatrical gestures.

Liturgical silence is sacred. It is not in fact a pause between a celebrating moment and the next moment. It is, moreover, a truly ritual moment, in a vital and reciprocal relationship to the word, vocal prayer, song, gesture, by means of which we live out the celebration of the mystery of Christ.

Moments of silence, which the Liturgy envisions and which are necessary to safeguard with attention, are important in and of themselves, but they also help in living the entire liturgical celebration in a climate of recollection and of prayer, recuperating silence, which is an integral element of the liturgical act. Thus it is possible to anchor to the Liturgy of silence as a true expression of a prayer of Adoration.

From this point of view, we can understand better why, during the Eucharistic Liturgy and, in particular, the canon, the praying People of God follow in silence the prayer of the priest-celebrant. That silence does not signify inactivity or lack of participation. That silence tends to allow everyone to enter into the significance of that ritual moment which re-presents, in the reality of the sacrament, the act of love with which Jesus offers Himself to the Father on the cross for the salvation of the world. That silence, truly sacred, is the liturgical space in which to say 'yes', with all the strength of our being, to the action of Christ, so that it becomes also our action in daily life.

Liturgical silence, then, is sacred because it is the spiritual place in which to realize the adhesion of our whole life to the life of the Lord; it is the space of the prolonged 'Amen' of the heart that surrenders to the love of God and embraces it as the new criterion of one's own life. It is precisely this stupendous significance of the final 'Amen' of the doxology at the conclusion of the Eucharistic Prayer, in which all say aloud what we have said for such a long time in the silence of a praying heart.

The Relationship Between Celebration and Adoration

The Solemnity of *Corpus Christi*, with the contemporaneous presence of celebration and Adoration, likewise has the capacity to make us live in healthy harmony the vital relationship between these two Eucharistic moments. In the context of a convention such as this one, it is worthwhile perhaps to spend some time considering the value of Adoration in relation to the Eucharistic celebration.

In fact, as the Magisterium of the Church always reminds – even of late – the act of Eucharistic Adoration follows on the celebration, as its prolongation. And, on the other hand, Adoration can help preserve in the heart the fruit of the celebration, grounding it in the heart of the person praying.

The mystery of salvation, of Christ dead and risen for us, that in the Eucharistic celebration is always rendered present again, in Adoration is completed and, in a manner of speaking, assimilated, in such a way that little by little it becomes ever more vital.

From this point of view, Adoration brings to fulfilment what is already implied in the Eucharistic celebration. In effect, what is definitive for the Liturgy is that those who participate in it might pray to share the same sacrifice of the Lord, His act of Adoration, becoming a single entity with Him, the true Body of Christ that is the Church. In other words, what is essential is that in the end the difference between Christ's action and our action is overcome, so that there would be a progressive harmonization between His life and ours, between His adoring sacrifice and ours, so that there would be only one action, at one and the same time, His action and ours. What Saint Paul affirmed is nothing other than what is the necessary consequence of the liturgical celebration: 'I have been crucified with Christ; it is no longer I who live but Christ who lives in me' (Gal. 2.20). And this is the goal of Eucharistic Adoration.

As an additional affirmation of what St Paul teaches, let us listen to the Holy Father in a passage from his Apostolic Exhortation, *Sacramentum caritatis*:

> As St Augustine put it: 'nemo autem illam carnem manducat, nisi prius adoraverit; peccemus non adorando – no one eats that flesh without first adoring it; we should sin were we not to adore it.' In the Eucharist, the Son of God comes to meet us and desires to become one with us; Eucharistic Adoration is simply the natural consequence of the Eucharistic celebration, which is itself the Church's supreme act of Adoration. Receiving the Eucharist means adoring him whom we receive. Only in this way do we become one with him, and are given, as it were, a foretaste of the beauty of the heavenly Liturgy. The act of Adoration outside Mass prolongs and intensifies all that takes place during the liturgical celebration itself. Indeed, 'only in adoration can a profound and genuine reception mature. And it is precisely this personal encounter with the Lord that then strengthens the social mission contained in the Eucharist, which seeks to break down not only the walls that separate the Lord and ourselves, but also and especially the walls that separate us from one another. (n. 66)

Standing, walking, adoring. In these three verbs and in what they signify, is found the truth of the celebration of *Corpus Christi*, to which we must always return. We must remember that returning to such a truth bears with it every time the stupendous and joyous rediscovery of the heart, of the centre, of the treasure of the Church and her Liturgy.

For this reason, in the sequence for the Solemnity of *Corpus Christi*, we sing: 'Sit laus plena, sit sonora, sit iucunda, sit decora, mentis iubilatio' (Let the praise be loud and high: Sweet and tranquil be the joy, felt today in every breast).

Seven

Adoration and the Sacred Liturgy

Bishop Athanasius Schneider
Auxiliary Bishop of Maria Santissima in Astana, Kazakhstan
Translated from Italian by Magdalen Ross

The Incarnation and Adoration

Adoration of the Most Holy Eucharist has as its source and its full justification in the truth of faith in the Incarnation of the Son of God, Second Person of the Most Holy Trinity. The immediate source of Eucharistic Adoration is the Sacrament of the Eucharist, and, more concretely, the Eucharistic sacrifice, which constitutes the most sublime act of divine worship. Holy Mass is, in itself, the supreme act of Adoration, says Pope Benedict XVI in the Apostolic Exhortation *Sacramentum caritatis* (66).

The Incarnation of God, the redemptive sacrifice of the Cross, and their perpetuation in the Eucharistic Sacrifice and in Eucharistic Adoration are inseparably connected: one presupposes the other, and the one is founded upon the other. The Venerable Pope Pius XII wrote in the encyclical *Mediator Dei*:

> No sooner, in fact, 'is the Word made flesh' than he shows Himself to the world vested with a priestly office, making to the Eternal Father an act of submission which will continue uninterruptedly as long as He lives: 'When He cometh into the world he saith . . . "behold I come . . . to do Thy Will" '. This act He was to consummate admirably in the bloody Sacrifice of the Cross: 'It is in this will we are sanctified by the oblation of the Body of Jesus Christ once'. He plans His active life among men with no other purpose in view . . . At the Last Supper He celebrates a new Pasch with solemn rite and ceremonial, and provides for its continuance through the divine institution of the Eucharist. On the morrow, lifted up between heaven and earth, He offers the saving sacrifice of His life, and pours forth,

as it were, from His pierced Heart the sacraments destined to impart the treasures of redemption to the souls of men. All this He does with but a single aim: the glory of His Father and man's ever greater sanctification. (17)

The Sacrifice of the Cross and Adoration

The Son of God came into this world to glorify the Father and this glorification is realized in the most perfect way when Jesus offered Himself in the sacrifice of the Cross with immense filial love to the Father and at the same with redemptive love for men. The sacrifice of the Cross comes to be described in Sacred Scripture with the symbolic expression, 'pleasing fragrance'. The fragrance [of this sacrifice] is the most pleasing perfume, the most holy, the most salvific and the most beautiful; beyond this it has no other end than to embrace in itself time and eternity, being offered by Christ through the Holy Spirit, as in the letter to the Hebrews. (9.14). St Paul teaches us that: 'Christ loved us and gave himself up for us as a fragrant offering and sacrifice to God' (*Christus dilexit nos, et tradidit semetipsum pro nobis oblationem et hostiam Deo in odorem suavitatis*) (Eph. 5.2).

The sacrifice of the cross, before being the act of redemption of the human race, contains the glorification of the Father by the Son and the glorification of the Son by the Father, as Jesus Himself has revealed to us: 'For this purpose I came to this hour. 'Father, glorify your name'. Then a voice came out of heaven: 'I have both glorified it, and will glorify it again' (Jn 12.27–28). In His priestly prayer, referring to the sacrifice of His life, Jesus prayed in these words: 'Father, the time has come. Glorify your Son, that your Son may glorify you. And now, Father, glorify me in your presence with the glory I had with you before the world began' (Jn 17.1, 5).

In the heavenly Jerusalem the sacrifice of the cross, the supreme act of love and Adoration, is forever present and perdures in the wounds of the Body of the Risen Christ. The symbol of this reality is the Lamb who having been immolated [now] stands alive, as the book of Revelation shows us (cf. Rev. 5.6): this is the living Christ who bears the signs of His immolation on the cross. The Sacred Liturgy proclaims this truth in one of the prefaces of the Easter season: 'Qui se pro nobis offere non desinit, qui immolatus iam non moritur, sed semper vivit occisus' (*Missale Romanum*, Praefatio paschalis III).

St Gaudentius of Brescia said: 'In the Sacrament of the Eucharist we have before our eyes each day the living re-presentation of the Passion of Christ' (*exemplar passionis Christi ante oculos habentes cotidie*), 'which we can hold in our hands and receive in our mouth and in our heart' (*ore etiam sumentes ac pectore*); (cf. *Tractatus*, 2, 31).

St Ephrem utilizes an expression which synthesizes in a doctrinally precise and spiritually profound way the Eucharistic mystery, saying: 'The Eucharist is Christ, the immaculate spouse in His Sacred Banquet. The faithful soul when it participates in the Eucharistic mystery must see with the eyes of faith Christ, the spouse of the soul, who is immolated in his banquet' (*quis vidit sponsum in convivio suo immolatum*); (cf. *Inno 37, 9, De ecclesia et virginitate*). St Paulinus of Nola explained the sacrificial character of holy communion thus: 'The Cross has produced the food of life for mortals. On the Cross is fixed the flesh with which they are fed. From the Cross flows that Blood in which life is drunk and the heart is cleansed' (*ep. 32, 7*). St Gregory the Great said that one receives by mouth the sacrament of the Passion of Christ (*sacramentum passionis Illius ore sumitur*); (cf. *In Ev. Hom. 2, 7*).

The Eucharistic Sacrifice and Adoration

The Servant of God Pope Pius XII has left us this wonderful teaching about Eucharistic Adoration and its intimate connection with the sacrifice of the Cross and the Eucharistic Sacrifice:

> The Eucharistic food contains, as everyone knows, 'truly, really, and substantially the Body and Blood together with the Soul and Divinity of Our Lord Jesus Christ'; therefore do not marvel that the Church, from its origins, has adored the Body of Christ under the Eucharistic species, as it appears in the same august Sacrifice, which requires of sacred ministers to adore the Most Holy Sacrament with genuflections and profound inclinations. The Sacred Councils teach that, from the beginning of its life, the Church must honour 'with one unique adoration God the Incarnate Word and His own flesh' . . . The Eucharist, then, is a sacrifice and also a Sacrament; and differs from the other Sacraments in that not only does it produce grace, but contains in a permanent way the Author of grace Himself . . . For this worship the Church, over the course of time, has introduced various forms, each time more beautiful and salvific: for example, devout and daily visits to the divine tabernacles; Benediction with the Most Holy Sacrament; solemn processions, especially at the time of Eucharistic Congress, which pass through cities and villages; and adoration of the Blessed Sacrament publicly exposed. Sometimes these public acts of adoration are of short duration. Sometimes they last for one, several and even for forty hours. In certain places they continue in turn in different churches throughout the year, while elsewhere adoration is perpetual, day and night, under the care

of religious communities, and the faithful quite often take part in them. These exercises of piety have brought a wonderful increase in faith and supernatural life to the Church militant upon earth and they are re-echoed to a certain extent by the Church triumphant in heaven which sings continually a hymn of praise to God and to the Lamb 'who was slain.'

Wherefore, the Church not merely approves these pious practices, which in the course of centuries have spread everywhere throughout the world, but makes them her own, as it were, and by her authority commends them. They spring from the inspiration of the liturgy and if they are performed with due propriety and with faith and piety, as the liturgical rules of the Church require, they are undoubtedly of the very greatest assistance in living the life of the liturgy. Nor is it to be admitted that by this Eucharistic cult men falsely confound the historical Christ, as they say, who once lived on earth, with the Christ who is present in the august Sacrament of the Altar, and who reigns glorious and triumphant in heaven and bestows supernatural favours. On the contrary, it can be claimed that by this devotion the faithful bear witness to and solemnly avow the faith of the Church that the Word of God is identical with the Son of the Virgin Mary, who suffered on the cross, who is present in a hidden manner in the Eucharist and who reigns upon His heavenly throne . . . That practice in a special manner is to be highly praised according to which many exercises of piety, customary among the faithful, and with benediction of the Blessed Sacrament. For excellent and of great benefit is that custom which makes the priest raise aloft the Bread of Angels before congregations with heads bowed down in adoration, and forming with It the sign of the cross implores the heavenly Father to deign to look upon His Son who for love of us was nailed to the cross, and for His sake and through Him who willed to be our Redeemer and our brother, be pleased to shower down heavenly favours upon those whom the immaculate Blood of the Lamb has redeemed. (*Mediator Dei*, 129–35)

To this luminous doctrine of Pope Pius XII we can add the following admirable and precious words of Blessed John Paul II in his encyclical *Ecclesia de Eucharistia*:

Like the woman who anointed Jesus in Bethany, *the Church has feared no 'extravagance'*, devoting the best of her resources to expressing her wonder and adoration before the *unsurpassable gift of the Eucharist*.

Could there ever be an adequate means of expressing the acceptance of that self-gift which the divine Bridegroom continually makes to His Bride, the Church, by bringing the Sacrifice offered once and for all on the Cross to successive generations of believers and thus becoming nourishment for all the faithful? Though the idea of a 'banquet' naturally suggests familiarity, the Church has never yielded to the temptation to trivialize this 'intimacy' with her Spouse by forgetting that He is also her Lord and that the 'banquet' always remains a sacrificial banquet marked by the Blood shed on Golgotha. *The Eucharistic Banquet is truly a 'sacred' banquet*, in which the simplicity of the signs conceals the unfathomable holiness of God: *O sacrum convivium, in quo Christus sumitur!* The bread which is broken on our altars, offered to us as wayfarers along the paths of the world, is *panis angelorum*, the bread of angels, which cannot be approached except with the humility of the centurion in the Gospel: 'Lord, I am not worthy to have you come under my roof' (Mt. 8.8; Lk. 7.6). With this heightened sense of mystery, we understand how the faith of the Church in the mystery of the Eucharist has found historical expression not only in the demand for an interior disposition of devotion, but also *in outward forms* meant to evoke and emphasize the grandeur of the event being celebrated. (48–9)

The Blessed Pope affirms in the same encyclical: 'If, in the presence of this mystery, reason experiences its limits, the heart, enlightened by the grace of the Holy Spirit, clearly sees the response that is demanded, and bows low in adoration and unbounded love' (62).

The Concretization of Adoration in the Eucharistic Liturgy

The attitude of habituating oneself to Adoration, in a love without limits, must be present and expresses itself in concrete gestures above all in the Eucharistic celebration. The whole Eucharistic celebration must by its nature be impregnated and pervaded also in its details by the attitude of Adoration, expressed by the most appropriate words and gestures. The external gestures of Adoration are necessary so that by means of them man can unite himself to God in reverence. In fact St Thomas Aquinas says: '*totus exterior cultus Dei ad hoc praecipue ordinatur ut homines Deum in reverentia habeant*' (*S.Th.*, I–II, 102, 4, c). Beyond this, St Thomas affirmed that by means of external gestures the soul and the mind of man are moved to exercise the spiritual acts which unite him to God (cf. *S.Th.*, II–II, 81, 7, c).

The sacred humanity of Christ, by means of the hypostatic union with the Person of the Divine Word, must be adored with acts of Adoration reserved to God Himself. The Sacred Body and Blood of Christ, really present in the Eucharistic species, consequently must be adored with the act of worship reserved to God Himself (*cultus latriae*). This is the constant doctrine of the Church (cf. St Thomas Aquinas, *S.Th.*, III, 25, 2, c). The Real Presence of the immolated and living Lamb, hypostatically united to the Second Divine Person, requires of all those who participate in the Eucharistic celebration the attitude of loving and reverent Adoration.

An expression of this attitude is the prayer of the Sanctus or of the Trisagion which is recited before the Eucharistic consecration since the most ancient times in all Liturgies whether Eastern or Western. The prayer of the Sanctus reminds us of the presence of the angels, of the Church Triumphant at the Eucharistic sacrifice. The eschatological, transcendent, supernatural and, in consequence, Christocentric orientation are in evidence. St John Chrysostom puts in relief this aspect of the mystery, of the transcendent, to the drawing close to the moment of the Eucharistic consecration, saying, 'In the moment in which Christ immolates Himself, the Lamb of the Lord, when you see drawn the curtains of the doors of the altar, then think that it is heaven which is opened and the angels are descending' (*Hom in Eph.*, 3, 5). The holy Fathers of the Church taught us that the angels cover their face when Christ the Lamb is immolated on the Eucharistic altar (cf. St Ephrem, *Hymn of the Crucifixion*, 2, 6; St John Chrysostom, *De paenitentia*, Hom. 9).

The presence of the angels in the Sacred Liturgy breaks the closed circle, the anthropocentric dimension, which constitutes the tendency and the principle wound of man, heir to original sin. Liturgical anthropocentrism is a manifestation of sinful man's tendency to celebrate himself. This manifests itself in the Eucharistic sacrifice, that is, in the most sacred and transcendent moment, by means of a closed circle where the priest and the faithful look at each other reciprocally and continuously. This gesture, on a symbolic level, evidences anthropocentrism and favours, often unknown to the participants, a similar internal attitude. Instead, being turned to face in the same direction, at least in the moments par excellence of prayer and Adoration, underlines that they are precisely the most sacred and sublime moments, where man is focused on God's Saving activity, not himself.

As a result, Adoration of Christ Incarnate and immolated is most clearly manifested in this manner, as Christ the heavenly High Priest. The exclamation 'conversi ad Dominum' with which St Augustine usually finished his homilies, designated the common bodily posture of the liturgical assembly, that all were to turn to face the same direction, the East, symbol of the Lord in His Parousia. This expression, additionally, certainly also designated the interior conversion of heart and mind. St Thomas Aquinas synthesized in the following explanation all the biblical and patristic tradition on this theme:

> There is a certain fittingness in adoring towards the east. First, because the Divine majesty is indicated in the movement of the heavens which is from the east. Secondly, because Paradise was situated in the east according to the Septuagint version of Genesis 2:8, and so we signify our desire [by means of prayer] to return to Paradise. Thirdly, on account of Christ Who is 'the light of the world' and is called 'the Orient'. Who mounts above the heaven of heavens to the east, and is expected to come from the east, according to Matthew [24:27], 'As lightning cometh out of the east, and appears even into the west; so shall also the coming of the Son of Man be.' (*S.Th.*, II–II, 84, 3, ad 3)

The same orientation of the celebrant and the faithful during the Eucharistic canon should be without doubt an enrichment in the celebration of the Mass and would favour more clearly the attitude of Adoration. Liturgical orientation is not, however, a particularity of the Roman rite in its more ancient use (*usus antiquior*), but belongs also to the ordinary form of the Roman rite, as the Congregation for Divine Worship has declared (cf. Response of 25 September 2000).

In the Roman Rite in its more ancient use (*usus antiquior*), as it is designated in the Instruction *Universae Ecclesiae* (5 May 2011), concrete and expressive gestures of Adoration are added immediately after pronouncing the words of consecration over the bread and wine. Pronouncing these words, the celebrant, before proceeding with the rite, immediately genuflects and adores, respectively, the Body and Blood of the Christ, the Immolated Lamb. Then the celebrant elevates, respectively, the Body and Blood of Christ and then genuflects again in a new sign of Adoration. These simple and silent gestures of Adoration which surround the most sacred moment of the Eucharistic sacrifice can seem irrelevant and to some liturgists seem excessive so much that, in the recent liturgical reform, the number of genuflections were reduced from four to two. But looking with the eyes of faith at the immense sacredness, the immense act of Adoration and love that Christ fulfils when, in the double consecration, the sacrifice of the Cross comes to be represented, the believing soul of the celebrant, moved, cannot desire a reduction in the number of genuflections. The faithful prostrate instinctively on their knees for the duration of the prayer of the Eucharistic canon, adoring in profound silence in the same manner as the saints and angels who surround the altar. Could it not be these precious details of the *usus antiquior*, which could be the source of enrichment for the ordinary form of the Roman Rite?

Another concrete form of the attitude of Adoration is the silence maintained during the celebration and the rite of Holy Mass itself. The Second Vatican Council teaches us in the Constitution *Sacrosanctum concilium*, how even sacred silence can be a form of active participation of the faithful (cf. n. 30). In the *usus antiquior* of the Roman rite, silence as an attitude of Adoration and of active participation of the faithful manifests itself in the clearest and most solemn way in the fact that the canon, or the Eucharistic prayer, is pronounced 'sotto-voce' by the celebrant, in such a way as to furnish for those present an ample space for silence and the opportunity to be able to thus more easily participate in the most sacred moments of the Eucharistic sacrifice in an adoring attitude of silence. St John Chrysostom warned that the most sacred moments of the Eucharistic sacrifice should be surrounded by silence: 'In the hands of the priest is the Host, and all is prepared. The angels and archangels are present, and the Son of God is present. With what reverence everyone assists! All are in absolute silence. Do you think that all this is done uselessly? Far be it from you to think thus! All this is done with faith when the Lord is present and His death is celebrated, this tremendous sacrifice of His, these ineffable mysteries' (*In Act. Apost., Hom.* 21, 4).

Practical Proposals

At the beginning of his pontifcate, Blessed John Paul II in his Apostolic Letter *Dominicae cenae* exhorted the whole Church with these words: 'Our adoration never ceases' (3). We only arrive at true renewal of the Church when the worship of Adoration is given to the Divine majesty, in interior and, necessarily, exterior worship. The most Sacred Prayer of Adoration is the liturgy of the Eucharistic sacrifice because it is, in the first place, the worship which Christ the High Priest renders to the Father in the Holy Spirit, uniting to Himself all His Mystical Body (cf. Pius XII, Encyclical *Mediator Dei*, 20; Vatican II, *Sacrosanctum concilium*, 7). Therefore, the entire Eucharistic liturgy must be pervaded by the spirit of Adoration: the words, the gestures, the music, the silence. To encourage the spirit of Adoration one must begin to favour those elements in the Sacred Liturgy which unequivocally express Adoration and the millenary experience left to us by the Church, illumined by faith and sanctified by the example of generations of saints. Among these one can mention these in order of precedence: genuflection, silence, and the orientation of the

Eucharistic prayer. These are the elements which are most present in the usus antiquior of the Roman Rite. The recovery of such elements for use in the ordinary form would also be a concrete way of realizing that mutual enrichment desired by our Holy Father Benedict XVI. If one could advance the proposal to permit, as *ad libitum* choices in the ordinary form, the following elements of the usus antiquior: (1) The prayer and the rite of the Offertory. (2) The gestures during the recitation of the Roman canon (genuflections and signs of the Cross). (3) Silence, at least partial, during the Eucharistic prayer. There are two other elements which are not, however, particular to the *usus antiquior*. (4) Orientation during the Eucharistic prayer. (5) The distribution of Holy Communion received kneeling and on the tongue, introducing the use of kneelers, or of the altar rail.

Our Holy Father Benedict XVI proposes to us the latter two elements by his teaching, as can be read in the preface to the first volume of his *Opera Omnia* which concerns orientation during the Eucharistic prayer, and by the example which he has given before the eyes of the whole Church in distributing Holy Communion on the tongue to the kneeling faithful and with the use of kneelers. These two elements can be already introduced and, thanks be to God, some bishops have already put them into practice. God willing there will be an ever greater number of bishops with this spirit who will become advocates of this liturgical practice: it would be a convincing sign of effective collegiality with the Supreme Pastor of the Church, a thinking and acting 'cum Petro'.

All these elements express more clearly the sublimity and sanctity of God, present and operating in the liturgy. They are placed like an echo of Ps. 113: 'Non nobis, Domine, non nobis, sed Nomini Tuo da gloriam!' Based on an erroneous understanding of the principle of noble simplicity, formulated in *Sacrosanctum concilium* (34), during the process of liturgical reform after the Second Vatican Council, fewer signs, words and gestures of Adoration remained. Sometimes it happens that the empty spaces are filled by the celebrant with an excess of words – and often banal words – or by the exaltation of the human person. Often, in some celebrations, signs, gestures and words are invented which express the 'glory of man' rather than the glory of God. Assisting at such celebrations of the 'glory of man', justified by the celebrant with the principle of 'noble simplicity', one has the clear impression that instead of expressing the desire 'non nobis, Domine, non nobis, sed nomini Tuo da gloriam', such celebrations express the desire 'nobis, Domine, nobis, et nomini nostro da gloriam'.

The introduction of the elements mentioned, for example facing east in the Eucharistic prayer, and the rite of Communion received kneeling and on the tongue, can also be a convincing and efficacious help so that throughout the whole Eucharistic liturgy 'our adoration never ceases', to use the words of Blessed John Paul II. And this will accelerate the springtime of the Church, so ardently desired by Blessed John XXIII and by the Second Vatican Council, for which the constitution *Sacrosanctum concilium* establishes as the condition for true renewal of the Sacred Liturgy the principle by which words and gestures the holy and the sacred should be more clearly expressed (cf. 21).

The proposals mentioned for the enrichment of the ordinary form of the Roman Rite in view of an increase of the spirit of Adoration, would contribute to a renewal of the spiritual youth of the Church. Giving more glory to God would favour an increase of true spiritual joy in the Church. We hope that an ever greater number of churches and chapels in the Catholic world will resound with the words 'Introibo ad altare Dei, ad Deum qui laetificat iuventutem meam', expressing the joy and that spiritual youth which results from the true spirit of Adoration.

In the Encyclical Ecclesia de Eucharistia Blessed John Paul II has left us this pressing appeal so that the Sacrament of the Eucharist may be lived and celebrated with the maximum of faith and of Adoration:

> In the Eucharist we have Jesus, we have his redemptive sacrifice, we have his resurrection, we have the gift of the Holy Spirit, we have adoration, obedience and love of the Father. Were we to disregard the Eucharist, how could we overcome our own deficiency? The mystery of the Eucharist – sacrifice, presence, banquet – *does not allow for reduction or exploitation*; it must be experienced and lived in its integrity, both in its celebration and in the intimate converse with Jesus which takes place after receiving communion or in a prayerful moment of Eucharistic adoration apart from Mass. These are times when the Church is firmly built up and it becomes clear what she truly is: one, holy, catholic and apostolic. (60–1)

We conclude with the words of our Holy Father Pope Benedict XVI:

> Certainly, the beauty of our celebrations can never be sufficiently cultivated, fostered and refined, for nothing can be too beautiful for God, who is himself infinite beauty. Yet our earthly liturgies will never be more than a pale reflection of the liturgy celebrated in the Jerusalem on high, the goal of our pilgrimage on earth. May our own celebrations nonetheless resemble that liturgy as closely as possible and grant us a foretaste of it! (Homily, 12 September 2008)

Eight

Eucharistic Adoration and Sacred Scripture

Bishop D. José Ignacio Munilla Aguirre
Bishop of San Sebastián, Spain
Translated from Spanish by Mauricio Rafael Gonzalez Bustillos

Background and Introduction

It is known that our beloved Pope, Benedict XVI, led Adoration of the Blessed Sacrament as a part of the events during World Youth Day (WYD). It is difficult to forget that occasion at the Marienfeld Esplanade in Cologne when this great 'sign' was revealed before the eyes of the entire world! It was there that the word of God was fulfilled, as is expressed in the Letter of Paul to the Philippians: 'That at the name of Jesus every knee should bow, in heaven and on earth and under the earth, and every tongue confess that Jesus Christ is Lord, to the glory of God the Father' (Phil. 2.10–11).

Three years later, at Randwick Racecourse in Sydney, the same act of Adoration was repeated, and, God willing, in Madrid at the Cuatro Vientos airfield, young people from around the world will bow down again to Christ our Lord.

Who says young people are insensitive to liturgical language? Is the prayer of Adoration reserved exclusively for those with contemplative vocations? What happens to all those clichés that have reduced youth ministry to a series of 'group dynamics' devoid of any content and of dubious educational value?

It is not the time for fuzzy and inconsistent offers. As Pope Benedict XVI says: 'Young people do not seek a juvenile church but one that is young at heart, a church where Christ, the New Man, is made evident'. Right now a 'strong' style of youth ministry is springing forth, which was launched by Blessed John Paul II and consolidated by his successor on the Chair of Peter.

Is it true that you have to be young to reach the hearts of young people? On the one hand, it seems a true statement, but is contradicted by many concrete examples of older Holy Pastors. It ought to be recognized that certain senior people in the style of Blessed John Paul II and Benedict XVI have never been old, but simply have 'accumulated youth'.

Well, just before the start of WYD in Madrid, this First International Conference on Eucharistic Adoration is held, and I would like my conference on the biblical foundations of adoration also to serve as an aid to deepen Eucharistic Youth Ministry.

Eucharistic Adoration: Profession of the Divinity of Jesus Christ

According to the tradition of the Church the following theological axiom has been formulated: 'Lex orandi, lex credendi'. This expression comes from a collection of ten proposals on grace that came about because of the Pelagian controversy. Today it is often cited when dealing about the dogmatic value of the Liturgy, which helps us to understand more precisely the faith of the Church. The prayer with which the People of God have prayed in the Liturgy comes before its dogmatic formulation to the point that in the Liturgy we find an important element of discernment in order to define the contents of faith.

Without trying to univocally apply this axiom to the study of Adoration in the New Testament, it is possible to do so analogically. In the Gospels we find several passages in which Jesus is adored, which is then followed by a profession of faith in His divinity. If Jesus is adored, it is a sure sign that He is confessed as the true God. Not surprisingly, in the Old Testament, the people of Israel had been taught to worship only The LORD, 'You shall not bow down to their gods' (Exod. 23.24), 'for you shall worship no other god' (Exod. 34.14), 'You shall worship the Lord your God and him only shall you serve' (Mt. 4.10). Now, I want to show here some New Testament passages where Jesus is worshiped:

The birth of Jesus: 'Where is he who has been born king of the Jews? For we have seen his star in the East, and have come to worship him. (proskyneo)' (Mt. 2.2; 'and going into the house they saw the child with Mary his mother, and they fell down and worshipped him. Then, opening their treasures, they offered him gifts, gold and frankincense and myrrh' (Mt. 2.11).

The healing of the blind man: 'Jesus heard that they had cast him out, and having found him he said, 'Do you believe in the Son of man?' He answered, 'And who is he, sir, that I may believe in him?' Jesus said to him, 'You have seen him, and it is he who speaks to you'. He said, 'Lord, I believe'; and he worshipped him (proskyneo) (and knelt down before him)' (Jn 9.35–38).

Jesus walks on water: 'Jesus immediately reached out his hand and caught him, saying to him, 'O man of little faith, why did you doubt?' And when they got into the boat, the wind ceased. And those in the boat worshipped him (proskyneo) (knelt down before him), saying, 'Truly you are the Son of God' (Mt. 14.31–33).

The appearance of the Risen Jesus: 'And behold', Jesus met them and said, 'Hail!' And they came up and took hold of his feet and worshipped him (proskyneo) (knelt down before him) (Mt. 28.9).

The Ascension into Heaven: 'Then he led them out as far as Bethany, and lifting up his hands he blessed them. While he blessed them, he parted from them, and was carried up into heaven. And they worshipped him, (proskyneo) (knelt down before him) and returned to Jerusalem with great joy' (Lk. 24.50–52).

The mission of the disciples: 'Now the eleven disciples went to Galilee, to the mountain to which Jesus had directed them. And when they saw him they worshipped him (proskyneo) (knelt down before him); but some doubted. And Jesus came and said to them, 'All authority in heaven and on earth has been given to me. Go therefore and make disciples of all nations, baptizing them in the name of the Father and of the Son and of the Holy Spirit, teaching them to observe all that I have commanded you; and lo, I am with you always, to the close of the age' (Mt. 28.16–20).

Worship expressed in St Paul's letters: 'That at the name of Jesus every knee should bow, in heaven and on earth and under the earth, and every tongue confess that Jesus Christ is Lord, to the glory of God the Father' (Phil. 2.10–11).

The worship of Jesus in the New Testament comes with the rejection of the worship of the Apostles, the Roman emperors, and even the angels. Obviously, this gives an even greater authority, if possible, to the Gospel passages that we have shown, in which Jesus is worshiped. Here are some texts:

Rejection of the worship of the Apostles: 'When Peter was about to enter, Cornelius met him and fell down he wanted to pay tribute. But Peter lifted him up saying, "Arise, for I am a man like you" ' (Acts 10.25–26).

Rejection of the worship of Roman emperors (represented as the beast from the book of Revelation): 'If any one worships the beast and its image, and receives a mark on his forehead or on his hand, he also shall drink the wine of God's wrath, poured unmixed into the cup of his anger, and he shall be tormented with fire and sulphur in the presence of the holy angels and in the presence of the Lamb' (Rev. 14.9–10).

Rejection of the worship of the angels: 'Then I fell down at his feet to worship him, but he said to me, "You must not do that! I am a fellow servant with you and your brethren who hold the testimony of Jesus. Worship God". For the testimony of Jesus is the spirit of prophecy' (Rev. 19.10).

After examining these texts, where a prostration to Jesus Christ is fully equivalent to the worship given to The LORD, we can and must make an application to our situation today and the Church. Currently, in secular milieu there has been a diffusion of different representations of who Jesus is, where His divinity is plainly absent. The Arian tendency has been constant throughout the history of the Church, but it has now reached a special strength. Rather than specifically denying the divinity of Jesus Christ, the strategy seems to be in not explicitly stating it, by diluting the mystery of the incarnation into a theory of religious pluralism, and thus considering Him one among the prophets.

During the LXXXVI Plenary Assembly of the Spanish Episcopal Conference, the Pastoral Instruction 'Theology and Secularization in Spain', was published in which these Christological deviations are described in detail:

> This approach leads to consequences difficult to reconcile with the faith, namely: 1) by rendering the ontological foundation of the divine sonship of Jesus meaningless, 2) by denying that the Gospels affirm the pre-existence of the Son of God, and 3) by considering that Jesus did not live his passion and his death as a redemptive giving of himself, but as a failure. These errors are a source of serious confusion, leading many Christians to conclude mistakenly that the Church's teachings about Jesus are not based on Scripture or must be radically reinterpreted. (*Teología y secularización en España*, 30)

It is impossible that it is a coincidence that the obscuring of the affirmation of the divinity of Jesus Christ in these Spanish and Western theological circles has coincided with the questioning or the abandonment of Eucharistic Adoration. Building upon the above axiom, 'Lex orandi, lex credendi', I am confident that the expansion in Spain of Eucharistic Adoration, embodied especially in 'Perpetual Adoration', will be the germ from which will sprout a healthy Christology according to the tradition of the Church and Sacred Scripture.

Worshippers in Spirit and in Truth

The biblical text that is undoubtedly the most important for Adoration is the one given to us by the Gospel of St John as he presents us with the dialogue of the Samaritan woman. A detailed exegetical commentary on the key verses of this passage (Jn 4.19–26), will enable us to draw some lessons that can help in our vocation as worshippers.

Verse 19: 'The woman says, "Lord, I see you are a prophet"'.

The Samaritan woman opens her heart to Jesus when she realizes that He is a prophet. This man has the ability to know her life from inside, and that is a sign that He is a man of God. It is before men of God that one tends to open up ones heart by raising doubts and specific questions about our existence.

Verse 20: 'Our fathers worshiped on this mountain; and you say that in Jerusalem is the place where men ought to worship'.

The Samaritan points out to the 'prophet' the old controversy between Samaritans and Jews about the true place of worship. The question arises due to the fact that Jacob's well looks out to Mount Gerizim: Was is at Gerizim or in Jerusalem where worship was due to God?

Verse 21: 'Jesus said to her, "Woman, believe me, the hour is coming when neither on this mountain nor in Jerusalem will you worship the Father" '.

Jesus responds to the Samaritan woman with a word of prophecy: 'The hour is coming' when both sanctuaries will lose their meaning. This phrase from St John ('the hour is coming'), can be found in other passages of his Gospel (Jn 5.25, 28), and has an eschatological nuance: the light dawns on the person of Jesus in Him is announced the new form of worship, by which the place of worship becomes irrelevant.

When the time comes the Samaritans will also worship the Father. Here is a veiled promise that everyone – Jews, Samaritans, pagans – are called to the knowledge and worship of the true God. At the summit of revelation belonging to a specific people will not be the factor that distinguishes the true worshippers from false ones, but it shall be the personal disposition of accepting the light of revelation that is addressed to all peoples.

Verse 22: 'You worship what you do not know; we worship what we know, for salvation is from the Jews'.

Now, Jesus notes that salvation has had a historical path established by God through the Jewish people. The worship of the Samaritans had its origins in political ambition and confrontation. Therefore, the expected Messiah comes from the Jews.

Israel's role has been very important in the history of salvation, but has come to a final end (v. 17 'For the Law was given through Moses, but grace and truth came by Jesus Christ'.) Christ now having come, the Samaritans and all other peoples are on equal footing in order to embrace the fullness of revelation.

Verse 23: 'But the hour is coming, and now is, when the true worshipers will worship the Father in spirit and truth, for such the Father seeks to worship him'.

With an insurmountable conciseness and density, Jesus formulates the following verse: 'The true worshipers will worship the

Father in spirit and truth'. Some have interpreted this double worship either the wrong way or insufficiently:

'Worship in spirit' is to be understood as the interior moral attitude, in contrast to the mere outward ritualistic worship the Old Testament that was criticized by the prophets.

'Worship in truth' is understood by the reference to the newness of Christ, in contrast to the 'shadows' of the Old Testament. For example, animal sacrifices were shadows of Christ's sacrifice, circumcision was a shadow of Baptism (cf. Col. 2.11–12), and so on.

But these interpretations do not seem adequate. The word 'pneuma' (spirit) cannot be understood in a moral or anthropological sense but rather in the sense of 'divine spirit' as is normally used in the Gospel of St John. In addition, in this instance there is no doubt whatsoever, as is seen in the following verse (v. 24) when it is specified that 'God is pneuma'.

Therefore, in this case Jesus Christ was not merely opposing ritualistic worship to spiritual worship, but goes much further: 'spirit' and 'truth' refers to the 'Holy Spirit' and 'Word'. That is, the true worshippers will worship the Father in the Holy Spirit and Jesus Christ. The second and third person of the Trinity, introduce us to their school of worship . . . worship for them, with them and in them.

In Jesus' conversation with Nicodemus (Jn 3.3–8), it is clear that man must be born again, born of the Spirit to receive the gift of God. Man has no ground for access to God Himself instead that intimacy with God is a free gift. God enables man to relate to, him man's encounter with God is a gift of the latter, which raises him up freely to the status of 'son'. We are 'children' in the Son by the Holy Spirit. The worship in 'spirit' takes place in the only temple pleasing to the Father, the Body of the Risen Christ (Jn 2.19–22).

Verse 24: 'God is spirit, and those who worship him must worship in spirit and truth'.

Jesus gives the profound reason for this worship, the very being or nature of God: 'God is spirit', which brings to mind that God is inaccessible for those who are corporal and material beings; to meet God requires an elevation of man to the condition of 'spiritual man'. Therefore, what matters is not the place where worship is performed externally (in Jerusalem or Gerizim), but our access to the deification in Christ through the Holy Spirit.

This passage of the Samaritan women makes clear the gap between Christian and Gnostic soteriology (where the divine is accessible only to the wise or the pure: cf. the Nag Hammadi writings), the Gospel St John focuses on the God's merciful revelation to all nations manifested in the mediator between God and men, the Saviour of the world, Jesus Christ.

Verse 25: 'The woman said to him, "I know that Messiah is coming (he who is called Christ); when he comes, he will show us all things"'.

The Samaritan does not understand the words of Christ, and looks to the future hoping for the Messiah, who will announce everything. Jesus wants to make her understand that the future has arrived: it is today!

Verse 26: 'Jesus said to her, "I who speak to you am he"'. Jesus is made known to the woman as the expected Messiah by the formula of revelation 'Ego Eimi'. Here we hear, without doubt, the Johanine term that refers to Christ the 'I AM' (The LORD) of the Old Testament.

Here the dialogue's climax between Jesus and the Samaritan woman is reached: He is the giver of living water, as well as the 'place' of the new worship to God. The Samaritans are the image of each one of us that finally comes to faith in Jesus Christ, the Saviour of the world.

The conclusion of this Gospel passage of St John, where one finds the true summit of the pedagogy with which Sacred Scripture introduces us to the school of worship, is this: Worship is none other than the expression of baptismal spirituality, the logical consequence of having been introduced into the bosom of the Trinity. We are sons in the Son, and in Him, through the Holy Spirit, we are worshipers of the Father.

This is in the present life and will be for all eternity our vocation: to be worshippers of the Father, in the Son, through the Holy Spirit. At this point, why not bring up the words of my dear countryman and patron saint, Ignatius of Loyola: 'Man was created to give glory to God'. St Paul stresses this by a beautiful hymn in the Letter to the Ephesians: 'Blessed be the God and Father of our Lord Jesus Christ, who has blessed us in Christ with every spiritual blessing in the heavenly places, even as he chose us in him before the foundation of the world, that we should be holy and blameless before him. He destined us in love to be his sons through Jesus Christ, according to the purpose of his will, to the praise of his glorious grace which he freely bestowed on us in the Beloved' (Eph. 1.3–6).

Proskynesis and *Ad-oratio*
To return to the WYD in Cologne, we find there a rich vein of thought. During the closing Sunday Mass, Pope Benedict XVI took the opportunity to give a memorable catechesis on worship. (Here's

a prime example of that 'strong' youth ministry to which I referred to at the beginning of this talk!). Given the fact that the Eucharist is the actualization of the Sacrifice of Christ, the Pope says:

> This first fundamental transformation of violence into love, of death into life, brings other changes in its wake. Bread and wine become his Body and Blood. But it must not stop there; on the contrary, the process of transformation must now gather momentum. The Body and Blood of Christ are given to us so that we ourselves will be transformed in our turn. We are to become the Body of Christ, his own Flesh and Blood. We all eat the one bread, and this means that we ourselves become one. In this way, adoration, as we said earlier, becomes union. God no longer simply stands before us as the One who is totally Other. He is within us, and we are in him. His dynamic enters into us and then seeks to spread outwards to others until it fills the world, so that his love can truly become the dominant measure of the world. I like to illustrate this new step urged upon us by the Last Supper by drawing out the different nuances of the word 'adoration' in Greek and in Latin. The Greek word is *proskynesis*. It refers to the gesture of submission, the recognition of God as our true measure, supplying the norm that we choose to follow. It means that freedom is not simply about enjoying life in total autonomy, but rather about living by the measure of truth and goodness, so that we ourselves can become true and good. This gesture is necessary even if initially our yearning for freedom makes us inclined to resist it. We can only fully accept it when we take the second step that the Last Supper proposes to us. The Latin word for adoration is *ad-oratio* – mouth to mouth contact, a kiss, an embrace, and hence, ultimately love. Submission becomes union, because he to whom we submit is Love. In this way submission acquires a meaning, because it does not impose anything on us from the outside, but liberates us deep within.

Let us examine the etymological reflections that Pope Benedict XVI presents about the term Adoration according to its Greek and Latin meanings.

Proskynesis: In worship, the holiness and greatness of God are somewhat overwhelming for the creature, which sees itself immersed in its nothingness. Faced with the vastness and the holiness of God, we wonder and marvel in His presence, and we recognize our smallness and unworthiness.

Ad-oratio: But on the other hand, there also takes place a second and complementary experience, inseparable from that of above. We are moved by the fact that God Who is infinitely superior to us has looked upon our smallness, and loves us tenderly.

Adoration is the expression of man's reaction overwhelmed by the nearness of God, due to His beauty, goodness and truth.

We can see examples of the attitude towards worship, from the perspective of *proskynesis*, in biblical texts such as when the prophet Ezekiel is struck by the glory of The Lord (Ezek. 1.27–28), or when the Risen Christ appears to Saul. Let's read from the latter:

> Now as he journeyed he approached Damascus, and suddenly a light from heaven flashed about him. And he fell to the ground and heard a voice saying to him, 'Saul, Saul, why do you persecute me?' And he said, 'Who are you, Lord?' And he said, 'I am Jesus, whom you are persecuting; but rise and enter the city, and you will be told what you are to do.' The men who were travelling with him stood speechless, hearing the voice but seeing no one. Saul arose from the ground; and when his eyes were opened, he could see nothing; so they led him by the hand and brought him into Damascus. And for three days he was without sight, and neither ate nor drank. (Acts 9.3–9)

Moreover, an example of the attitude of Adoration under the second perspective, *ad-oratio*, is found in the biblical text of the Adoration of the Christ-child by the Magi: 'And going into the house they saw the child with Mary his mother, and they fell down and worshipped him . . .' (Mt. 2.11). The infinite transcendence of God is 'contained' and 'hidden' in the frail humanity of that child of Bethlehem. God the Father sends His 'kiss' of love for humanity in the tenderness of that child. The only appropriate response from our part is to return the kiss to God in the act of Adoration. The traditionally performed gesture at Christmas of kissing the image of the Christ-child, is one of the most significant expressions of the *ad-oratio* referred to by the Pope. Worship is not only submission, but also translates into the mystery of 'communion' and 'union'.

Commenting on the biblical passage of the 'Infancy Gospel' found in St Mathew, Pope Benedict XVI remarked during the Adoration at WYD in Cologne:

> Dear friends, this is not a distant story that took place long ago. It is with us now. Here in the Sacred Host he is present before us and in our midst. As at that time, so now he is mysteriously

veiled in a sacred silence; as at that time, it is here that the true
face of God is revealed. For us he became a grain of wheat that
falls on the ground and dies and bears fruit until the end of
the world (cf. Jn 12:24). He is present now as he was then in
Bethlehem. He invites us to that inner pilgrimage which is
called adoration. Let us set off on this pilgrimage of the spirit
and let us ask him to be our guide.

We must keep in mind that these two facets or perspectives of worship, *proskynesis* and *ad-oratio*, are not separate but are integrated
in the same act of worship. In other words, worship is something
simple and complex at the same time: the closer we get to God, the
simpler worship becomes to the point that *proskynesis* and *ad-oratio*
are confused and identified with each other. In worship the 'fear
of God' and 'love God' are fully integrated as one and the same
reality.

On the contrary, to the extent that our sin keeps us away from
God, these two aspects – *proskynesis* and *ad-oratio* – may be experienced in a discordant and even contradictory manner. Therefore, it is
important to return to the Sacred Scriptures, as a school of worship.
In them we learn that worship is an expression of man struck by the
nearness of God. Indeed, worship is the lively awareness of our sin,
of our silent confusion (Job 42.1–6), of our lively worship (Ps. 5.8), and
of our joyous tribute (Ps. 95.1–6).

Acts of Adoration

As worship is described in Sacred Scripture, it implies our whole
being. It is therefore logical that we express it through external
gestures, where the divine sovereignty and the response it stirs up
in us is manifested. Moreover, given that there is in us a tendency to
resist the will of God and to reduce our prayer to mere external rites,
it is important to stress that the sincere worship that pleases God is
that which springs from the heart.

The two key gestures in expressing worship are 'prostration' and
'the kiss' in which the creature's reverent awe and captivated attraction converge towards God:

Prostration, outside its religious connotation, expresses an attitude
imposed by force by a more powerful adversary. For example, what
Babylon imposed upon the captive Israelites (Isa. 51.23). In this sense,
it is often found in Assyrian bas-reliefs where vassals are kneeling
before their king with head bowed down to the ground. But in Sacred
Scripture we are invited to make the sign of prostration as a sign of
free, conscious, and joyful submission to the majesty of God. Thus,
we imitate Moses, prostrate in the Sinai at the moment of receiving
the Tablets of the Law (cf. Exod. 34.8), we learn from the prophet

Daniel who three times a day, with outstretched hands, knelt before the Lord (cf. Dan. 6.11); humbly we welcome the invitation of Psalm 95 – 'O come, let us worship and bow down, let us kneel before the Lord, our Maker' (cf. Ps. 95.6) – we recall the leper that on bent knees before Jesus begged to be cleaned (Mk 1.40), we follow the steps of that fisherman of Galilee, the first of the popes of the Church, who fell to his knees and prayed fervently, asking God the resurrection of Tabitha in Joppa (Acts 9.40).

A kiss adds to respect and submission the sign of the intimate and loving commitment. The pagans kissed their idols, but that gesture, for the faithful Israelite, is reserved for the The Lord: 'Yet I will leave seven thousand in Israel, all the knees that have not bowed to Baal, and every mouth that has not kissed him' (I Kings 19.18).

Only the Lord has the right to be worshiped. While the Old Testament acknowledges prostration before men (Gen. 23.7, 12; 2 Sam. 24.20; 2 Kings 2.15; 4.37), it strictly forbids any gesture of Adoration, whether it be to idols, or stars (Deut. 4.19) or other gods (Exod. 34.14; Num. 25.2), that can be interpreted as a rivalling of The Lord. There is no doubt that the eradication of every sign of idolatry was educating the people of Israel into an authentic worship. In this light the courage of Mordecai is understood:

> And all the king's servants who were at the king's gate bowed down and did obeisance to Haman; for the king had so commanded concerning him. But Mordecai did not bow down or do obeisance. And when Haman saw that Mordecai did not bow down or do obeisance to him, Haman was filled with fury. (Est. 3.2,5)

We see the same consistency in other passages, such as the three Jewish youths before the statue of Nebuchadnezzar, Shadrach, Meshach, and Abednego answered the king,

> O Nebuchadnezzar, we have no need to answer you in this matter. If it be so, our God whom we serve is able to deliver us from the burning fiery furnace; and he will deliver us out of your hand, O king. But if not, be it known to you, O king, that we will not serve your gods or worship the golden image which you have set up. (Dan. 3.16–18)

Within this biblical context, we understand Jesus' answer to the tempter when asked to kneel before him: 'You shall worship the Lord your God and him only shall you serve' (Mt. 4.10).

With regard to external gestures of worship (prostration and the kiss), I would draw attention to the process of secularization that is often found in many liturgical celebrations.

Some priests and lay people suppress or change the language by which the liturgy refers to God's transcendence. For example, instead of praying, 'God Almighty' they correct it by saying 'God who is nearby', and so on.

In many churches the gesture of kneeling at the time of the Consecration has largely been eliminated. The same is true with respect to genuflecting before the tabernacle.

The kiss that traditionally is used to worship the Christ-child at Christmas, or the cross of Christ on Good Friday, is also frequently deleted or substituted by mere inclinations, citing health reasons or brevity.

All this, in addition to a lack of obedience to our Mother the Church, accepts the assumptions of secularism uncritically.

Worship: The Combat of Purification

The true worship of God involves a full cleansing of both religious conceptions, and of our criteria, judgments and emotions. To clarify this point, we could use the gesture of purification that Jesus used in the Temple of Jerusalem, as is told by the Gospel of St John (Jn 2.13–25). Indeed, the expulsion of the merchants from the Temple is an image of the purification for each of us, as well as for ecclesial structures, so that in us may only dwell the glory of God. Seeing the prophetic gesture of the Master, the disciples recalled the words of the Old Testament: 'Zeal for thy house will consume me' (Jn 2.17), that is, where the love of God fills everything idolatry has no place.

But now, let us look at text of Genesis, which recounts the mysterious episode of Jacob wrestling with God (Gen. 32.23–33), for it is a paradigm. The catechesis on this text that the Holy Father preached, in his General Audience of 25 May 2011 has given this passage a special relevance.

> Therefore, as is also affirmed in the Catechism of the Catholic Church, 'from this account, the spiritual tradition of the Church has retained the symbol of prayer as a battle of faith and as the triumph of perseverance' (n. 2573). The biblical text speaks to us about a long night of seeking God, of the struggle to learn his name and see his face; it is the night of prayer that, with tenacity and perseverance, asks God for a blessing and a new name, a new reality that is the fruit of conversion and forgiveness.

> For the believer Jacob's night at the ford of the Jabbok thus becomes a reference point for understanding the relationship

with God that finds in prayer its greatest expression. Prayer requires trust, nearness, almost a hand-to-hand contact that is symbolic not of a God who is an enemy, an adversary, but a Lord of blessing who always remains mysterious, who seems beyond reach. Therefore the author of the Sacred Text uses the symbol of the struggle, which implies a strength of spirit, perseverance, tenacity in obtaining what is desired. And if the object of one's desire is a relationship with God, his blessing and love, then the struggle cannot fail but ends in that self-giving to God, in recognition of one's own weakness, which is overcome only by giving oneself over into God's merciful hands.

During prayer in general, and especially during the prayer of worship, a great battle is fought against my own ego. Worship is a radical change in the way we conceive our vital existence. This is a passage from an 'egocentric' worldview to another one that is 'Christ-centred'. Now, obviously, the task of focusing our life in Christ, is not reduced to a rational conviction, but rather it supposes the task of detachment from all that throws us off the true 'centre'.

The first battle that takes place with the prayer of Adoration is the firm decision to do it. Karl Rahner said that 'whoever prays only when he feels like it means that he has resigned himself to feel less likely to pray'. Adoration without perseverance is already to have the battle, because prayer is the first duty of a Christian, the first of his apostolates. The famous Spanish proverb: 'First is the obligation and then the devotion', forgets that prayer is our first obligation.

In an environment where pragmatism and the search for quick and easy success reigns, one falls frequently into the danger of seeing prayer as an activity to be postponed, or simply dispensable. We remember in reference to this, the words of Jesus: 'This kind cannot be driven out by anything but prayer' (Mk 9. 29). Without fidelity to prayer, by overcoming our appetites, our spiritual life will soon peak.

In the rich tradition of the Desert Fathers, prayer has more often been described in the terms of 'battle' and 'combat' which is a healthy counterpoint to the concept of prayer tied to the 'New Age' mentality that merges prayer with a relaxation technique and the search for inner wellbeing. It suffices to quote the following:

Some brothers asked the abbot Agathon: 'Father, what is the virtue that requires more effort in religious life?' He replied: 'Forgive me, but I think that nothing requires as much work as praying to God. If a man wants to pray to his God, demons,

his enemies, hasten to interrupt his prayer, knowing full well
that nothing will do them as much damage as prayer rising to
God. In any other work undertaken by the man in religious life,
for all the hard work and patience that such work requires he
will have and achieve some rest. Prayer requires a painful and
hard fight up to the last breath.'

Saint Teresa of Jesus, who is the pinnacle of Spanish mysticism,
bears witness to the inner struggle that occurs during the battle
of perseverance in prayer, and she does so with her usual wit and
charm: 'And very often, for some years, I was more occupied with the
wish to see the end of the time I had appointed for myself to spend
in prayer, and in watching the hour-glass, than with other thoughts
that were good. If a sharp penance had been laid upon me, I know of
none that I would not very often have willingly undertaken, rather
than prepare myself for prayer by self-recollection' (*The Life*, 8, 10).

Once having overcome the temptation against perseverance,
which we must always be attentive to, the second battle to be waged
in the prayer of Adoration is the purification of our fears, uncertain-
ties, emotions, ways of thinking and judging our existence, and so
on. As Jean Lafrance, well known author of several books on prayer,
said:

True prayer has more to do with rock climbing than with
mountaineering. Climbing to the top of the ladder of prayer is
primarily a descent into the depths of humility . . . If he makes
you experience the misery of your helplessness in order to pray,
at the same time he gives you the strength to bear it, and he
will show you the means to call upon him. The more you touch
the bottom of your poverty, the more you will rise to God in
supplication. The greater the force with which a ball is thrown
to the ground, the more it bounces up.

Let no one think that these reflections on the 'dark night' refer exclusively to the mystics who are on the highest levels of the spiritual
life. In fact, the purification of the soul begins the moment we take
seriously the prayer of Adoration. What takes place in the soul of
every worshiper is very similar to that described by St John of the
Cross in his example of the 'log thrown into the fire':

First of all the flames begins to dry it, by driving out its mois-
ture and causing it to shed the water which it contains within
itself. Then it begins to make it black, dark and unsightly, and
even to give forth a bad odour, and, as it dries it little by little, it

brings out and drives away all the dark and unsightly accidents which are contrary to the nature of fire. And, finally, it begins to kindle it externally and give it heat, and at last transforms it into itself and makes it as beautiful as fire. (cf. *The Dark Night of the Soul*, Book II, 10)

In short: Worship is purification, purification is sanctification, and sanctification is the glorification of God.

In the School of WYD: Towards a Spirituality of Worship
The various reflections that Pope Benedict XVI gave us about Eucharistic Adoration during the WYD in Cologne are a good reference to draw our conclusions and make applications to the spirituality of the worshiper.

Taking advantage of the motto of this WYD in Germany – 'We have come to adore him' – let's look at the Pope's words, uttered on the eve of his trip to Germany, after the Angelus on Sunday, 7 August 2005.

Thousands of young people are about to leave or have already set out for Cologne for the 20th World Youth Day, whose theme, as you know, is: We have come to worship him. (Mt. 2.2)

One might say that the whole Church has been spiritually mobilized to live this extraordinary event, looking to the Magi as unique models of people seeking Christ, before whom to kneel in adoration. But what does 'worship' mean? Might it be an expression of past times, meaningless to our contemporaries? No! A well-known prayer that many recite in the morning and the evening begins precisely with these words: I adore you, my God, and I love you with all my heart.

Every day, at sunrise and sunset, believers renew their 'adoration' or acknowledgement of the presence of God, Creator and Lord of the Universe. This recognition is full of gratitude that wells up from the depths of their heart and floods their entire being, for it is only by adoring and loving God above all things that human beings can totally fulfil themselves.

The Magi adored the Child of Bethlehem, recognizing him as the promised Messiah, the Only-begotten Son of the Father in whom, as St Paul says, 'the fullness of the deity resides in bodily form' (Col. 2:9). The disciples Peter, James and John, to whom Jesus revealed his divine glory – as the feast of the Transfiguration celebrated yesterday reminds us – predicting his definitive victory over death, experienced something similar on Mount Tabor. Subsequently, with Easter, the crucified and Risen Christ was fully to manifest his divinity and offer to all men and women the gift of his redeeming love. Saints are those who accepted this gift and became true worshippers of the living God, loving him without reserve at every moment of their lives. With the forthcoming meeting in Cologne, the Church wants once again to present this holiness, the peak of love, to all the young people of the Third Millennium.

Who can accompany us better on this demanding journey of holiness than Mary? Who can teach us to adore Christ better than she? May she help especially the new generations to recognize the true face of God in Christ and to worship, love and serve him with total dedication.

Certainly this shows a heart in love with God, the heart of Benedict XVI, who will be remembered for his persistent invitation to Adoration. The Pope speaks of the saints as true worshippers of the living God, among them are the Magi, who left everything, in order to meet the God-man. Above all, he proposes the model of Mary, who having begotten her Son in the flesh, adored Him in 'spirit and truth'.

If holiness is the vocation to which all Christians are called, and if, as Benedict XVI had underlined, holiness is the necessary condition for us to be true worshippers of God, then, the conclusion to be drawn is blunt: 'Adoration is not a luxury but a priority' (Angelus, 28 August 2005).

In other words, Benedict XVI included Eucharistic Adoration in WYD, in order to crown the invitation that his predecessor, Blessed John Paul II, gave us, 'Do not be afraid to be saints'. Holiness and Adoration are closely linked concepts. Sanctity enables true worship; while worship is the source of holiness.

The Attitude Towards Worship as a Christian Lifestyle

It is sometimes wrongly emphasized that Eucharistic Adoration underlines a unilaterally vertical dimension of Catholic spirituality at the expense of the horizontal dimension, social or charitable. Nothing could be further from the truth! It would suffice to quote many healing experiences of the 'poor of The Lord' which are taking place around the chapels of Perpetual Adoration.

The acknowledgment that God becomes one of us, putting Himself in our hands, giving Himself as food for the life of the world, underpins the Christian model of solidarity and charity. On the night of the Eucharist's institution, Jesus girded Himself with a towel around His waist and knelt before us, while washing our feet. Eucharistic Adoration feeds in us the same feelings of the Heart of Christ, 'who, though he was in the form of God, did not count equality with God a thing to be grasped, but emptied himself, taking the form of a servant, being born in the likeness of men' (Phil. 2.6–7).

So that my neighbour, and especially the poor, occupy the central place that they should occupy in our lives, it is essential that our 'self' be dethroned. And in order to dethrone my 'ego' it is essential that Adoration put Christ at the centre of our existence. When Christ takes the place due to Him, the other concerns and occupations (especially our relationship with others) are ordered as a result.

Imagine a jacket lying on the ground. If someone picks up the garment holding it from the end of one of its sleeves, or from one of its pockets, the result would be a considerable mess. You have to take the jacket from the shoulders to hang it properly.

Something similar happens with worship: to adore is to take life by the shoulders and not by the sleeve. Anyone who puts God at the top of the values of their existence, notes that 'everything else' happens to occupy the place it should. By worshiping God one learns to relativize all things which, although important, should not be at the centre, that do not relate to it. Education in worship is absolutely necessary for the overcoming of the temptation to idolatry in all its versions and facets: 'You shall worship the Lord your God and him only shall you serve' (Mt. 4.10).

In the school of Jesus, the true worshiper of the Father, we learn that Adoration is not confined to a point in time done in the chapel, but it is an essential dimension of the believer's life. It is a way of life, the way of worship, as St Paul puts it: 'I appeal to you therefore, brethren, by the mercies of God, to present your bodies as a living sacrifice, holy and acceptable to God, which is your spiritual worship' ('latreia' from the verb to worship) (Rom. 12.1).

In short, Sacred Scripture not only invites us to 'do' prayer of Adoration, but to 'be' worshippers in spirit and in truth, living our life as a providential opportunity to witness the glory of God. Here is a good definition of the worshiper, 'the witness of the glory of God'.

In the Bull of the Jubilee for the year 2000, Blessed John Paul II spoke these beautiful words: 'For two thousand years the Church is the cradle where Mary places Jesus and entrusts him to the Adoration and contemplation of all peoples'. Let us conclude by invoking the Blessed Virgin Mary, she who gave us and gives us still the Body and Blood of her Son in order to worship him.

From the hand of Mary, may we worship Jesus Christ!

Nine

The Eucharist, Adoration and Healing

Father Nicholas Buttet
Moderator of the Eucharistein Community, St Maurice, Switzerland
Translated from French by Gary Holmes & Sean Davidson

I would like to make five preliminary remarks.

First: There exists today some confusion between health and salvation. In many languages, there is a correspondence between these two words. We realize that in a world that has lost the sense of God, health becomes an obsession. What used to concern the human heart before: salvation, redemption, eternal life, to the point of risking everything for that treasure, has been substituted today for health. We see a practically religious quest for health with its own rites, rituals and even magic. Benedict XVI told the young prisoners in the prison of Casal del Marmo in Rome on 18 March 2007:

> We have recalled that God loves us: this is the source of true joy. One can having everything one wants and still be some-times unhappy. On the contrary, one could be deprived of everything, even freedom or health and still be in peace and joy, if God is in our heart. So therein lies the secret: that God is always in the first place in our life.

Before him, St Augustine said, 'Sometimes the doctor makes a mistake in promising the patient health of the body. God gives you a sure and free healing, that is salvation'. This is the first point: this confusion between health and salvation. Make no mistake, let us look for salvation and many things will follow.

Second: What does it mean to be healed or to be sick in the Bible? Or even to be alive or dead? We see Jesus who speaks to the dead: 'Lazarus, come forth from the tomb'. We are used to it because we often hear of it. But talking to a dead person is not something we do too often! We also notice that Jesus remained silent although some people addressed Him because they were dead in some sense.

The Bible contains stories of salvation which are completely paradoxical. In the tales and the stories of the world, we learn that the heroes were young, beautiful, strong and that they set off on an adventure. In the Bible, they were old, sterile and powerless and God chose them (e.g., Abraham and his wife Sarah). For us it always starts on the wrong foot! What is important in the Bible is not so much to be healthy or ill, but to be with God. One is healthy and holy when one is with God Who comes to meet us in our weakness. The place of our wound, our vulnerability, is the place where God meets us.

A friend of mine, Philippe, died of AIDS. Six months before he died he wrote me a letter saying, 'I want to die alive'. And this letter struck me: to die, but already living from the true life which awaits me. Because one usually dies dead! In this case he wanted to die living because there was another more important life that had penetrated his vulnerability.

After she had her third heart attack Blessed Teresa of Calcutta was on life support. She was visited by a priest and a Hindu doctor, who said to the priest, 'Father, get the small box, quickly'. The priest replied, 'The medicine box? What box?' 'No, the small box. You know that when it's there, Mother Teresa is completely calm'. The priest realized that it was the tabernacle. The Indian doctor said: 'When this little box is in her room, she just looks, looks, and looks again at that box'. You see, to be sick or healed is not quite what one imagines!

Third: Christ tells us: 'Come to me all ye who labour and are burdened and I will give you rest'. I believe that Eucharistic Adoration becomes the place of the incarnation of these words of Christ: 'Come to me'.

'For you who fear his name', said the prophet Malachi, 'the sun of justice will shine, bringing in its rays your healing'. This is one of the last words of the first covenant, the Old Testament. The prophet, Malachi concludes the history of the preparation of the coming of the Messiah with this prophetic and deeply moving announcement: 'The sun of justice will shine, bringing in its rays your healing'. The sun of justice is the Host exposed on our altars. And in saying that I will emphasize another point. We often hear of people putting Adoration and mental prayer in opposition to each other. For those who have understood the meaning of contemplative prayer, 'that dialogue of love with the God who we know loves us and wants our love in return', there is no opposition possible between these two. There is a modality that can be a bit different for entering into intimacy with God, but in both cases, the same attitude of a man, a human being who casts himself into the arms of a Father to experience the love that unites us to Him by the grace of Christ and the Holy Spirit.

Fourth: I would like to recall the difference between healing and treating. Treating is an art, says St Thomas Aquinas, and it is the medical art that can do a certain number of things for a sick person. A doctor can treat, he can never heal. St Thomas Aquinas says the power of healing is an inner principle. It is necessary to make this distinction. Sometimes we seek in our spiritual life to be treated for, seeing Jesus as the substitute physician and not the physician Who deeply heals the heart of wounded man. It is the inner principle of my life and of the abundant life promised to me, and that is the true life. The book of Sirach (38.11): 'My son, when you are sick, do not get annoyed (It's normal everyone does, but he says it just to remind us), pray to the Lord to heal you, renounce your faults, keep your hands clean of all sin, purify your heart, offer incense and a memorial of fine flour (the Eucharist), and have recourse to the doctor, because the Lord has created him too, do not exclude him because you need him'. We need to distinguish between the healing that comes from God and the treatment that comes from the doctor. If we are not clear on this, we will be greatly confused when it comes to praying to the Lord, when we come to meet God in Adoration.

Fifth: I would like to speak to you mainly of the Eucharist; not of the whole mystery of the Eucharist, as the sacrificial mystery which we saw yesterday in the Liturgy and what it means, but this particular dogma of the real presence which is highlighted by Eucharistic Adoration. In Eucharistic Adoration we profess that Christ is really, corporally, substantially present in the Most Blessed Sacrament. It is this real presence of a person whom we meet. There is no reason to go to Adoration if Christ is not present in the Most Blessed Sacrament. We would be crazy, sick – we would need to be treated by a physician. But if Christ is there, we're right! Blessed Dina Bélanger, an extraordinary Canadian, said: 'If one only understood the presence of Christ it would be necessary for bodyguards to be in front of churches since they would be taken by storm by people trying to see the King of kings'.

I shall now discuss the Eucharist and healing under four perspectives: a theological aspect, an anthropological aspect, a historical aspect and an eschatological aspect.

Theologically, Adoration completely reverses the order of the world, or rather puts the world back in order. St Thomas defines sin as 'turning away from God and towards the creature'. Adoration instils in the soul the exact opposite movement: turning away from creatures to turn towards the Creator. Adoration is at the heart of the world's redemption – by the Eucharistic Sacrifice, for sure, but I want to emphasize the specificity of Eucharistic Adoration which has not yet been fully developed in the Church. A complete reversal of movement, an ecstasy of man, not an ecstasy in the mystical sense of the term in particular phenomena: a coming out of oneself. Philosophers distinguish two kinds of mystics: inward mysticism which focuses on ourselves, particularly with Buddhism, and that of ecstasy, which turns us towards God. One can live Adoration in a Buddhist way, being a practicing Catholic before the Most Blessed Sacrament and closed in on oneself. It is necessary to come out of oneself, to be in ecstasy in an exodus of self, leaving the land of bondage to go into the Promised Land. This passes way through the desert, by asceticism, by murmuring (not too long because one loses a lot of time when one murmurs!). Sometimes this passes by a deepening of this mystery.

Eucharistic Adoration is the providential response to the first moral duty of man which is attached to the virtue of justice and especially to the virtue of religion. The first moral, philosophical duty of the human being in the virtue of religion is to adore God, to recognize God as the creator of all things. Then, I think there is something new for us to reflect upon more deeply. We have attached, which is absolutely true theologically, Eucharistic Adoration to the celebration of the mystery as a prolongation of thanksgiving after Communion and as a preparation for the next Communion. Benedict XVI recalled in 2005, this order of perfection in some way if I may say so, the primacy of Adoration over all things. Before the Eucharistic sacrifice itself, there was the Adoration of God. And this Adoration finds, thanks to the gift of the Eucharist, a sublime, extraordinary and unique form of expression. You see, in a world that has forgotten God, to proclaim the moral duty of man to adore God with a no longer interior but exterior gesture, which is manifest in prostrating oneself before the Host, becomes a kind of prophetic revolution. It is necessary to really deepen this mystery of Adoration as an expression of the first duty of the human heart to God the Creator. We can live it in a theological way, but first from a moral point of view. It is important to render to God this cult of Adoration. And this act of Adoration, first and foremost, before the origin of origins, even before the Word became flesh, will find its expression now in Eucharistic Adoration. Benedict XVI himself said this in Christmas 2005: 'Precisely in a world where the guiding criteria are progressively lacking and where the threat exists that everyone makes for himself his own criterion, it is essential to emphasise adoration.' Quoting St Augustine: 'Let no one eat this flesh without first having adored it. We would sin, if we did not adore it'. It seems essential to me to underline this approach to Adoration in the theology of Eucharistic Adoration.

The catastrophe of the original sin caused us to lose the dignity of the children of God: sanctifying grace. That which gives us Christ is this dignity of being a child of God, is this ability to be like Jesus, of being modelled on Christ and to be able to say by the power of the Holy Spirit to God, 'Abba, Father'. So, there is in Eucharistic Adoration this mystery which must be lived. Both Blessed John Paul II and Benedict XVI have stressed that Pentecost was not an historical event but is an ongoing event and that this Pentecost is realized in the Eucharist. There are two Pentecosts in Sacred Scripture: the Pentecost of John, the Johannine Pentecost, that of the open Heart of Christ, the last breath of Jesus which became the first breath of the believer – that of Jesus who breathes on the Apostles on the evening of His Resurrection. The gift of the Holy Spirit in St John is a gift that makes us children of God. God was so eager to give back to humanity, and through humanity the entire cosmos (cf. Romans) that filial return, that He breathed. This open heart is the gift of the Holy Spirit. Where does this heart beat today so that we may live this Johannine Pentecost? Well, it is the Heart of Christ beating in the Most Blessed Sacrament of the Altar. All the theology of the Heart of Christ leads to the Eucharistic Heart of Christ with Pius IX and then Pius XI who took this up after him. So we're truly in the apotheosis of the mystery of the Heart of Christ revealed to St Gertrude of Helfta in the Middle Ages, passing by St Margaret Mary Alacoque in the revelation of Paray-le-Monial, to arrive at the Eucharistic Heart. But why is this heart so important? Because from there is given the Holy Spirit for us to live as children of God. And when Cardinal Ratzinger commented on the third secret of Fatima, he said, 'But how could one imagine the triumph of the Immaculate Heart of Mary? Not in extraordinary signs and wonders, but in the filial return to God. Because the first quality of the Heart of Mary was 'Fiat' – yes – to the Father's will. In Eucharistic Adoration, we live a *kairos*. The tragedy of today's world is its distance from the Heart of God. The filial spirit is the 'Our Father' prayer. It is the language of hope. We live in a world that has lost hope and so which has fallen into both serious sins that are the caricatures or the opposite of hope: presumption and despair. Humanity hovers between presumption – wanting to save itself, by succeeding in its science, its technology, in this ideology of perpetual progress, where salvation would be the end of this progress; we lost the radiant future, with globalization remaining with us. It is believed that through this man will succeed in creating a world of happiness and perfection: a tragic mistake – and conversely, despair: a depressive society plagued by non-sense. Standing between them is the crest of hope: Abba, Father, Our Father Who art in heaven.

In Eucharistic Adoration, by the outpouring of the Holy Spirit that flows from the Eucharistic Heart of Christ, we are called to enter into the mystery of our dignity as children of God – in childlike confidence, in the language of a child, not in words but in the filial attitude towards the Father. We must become what we are due to our Baptism. Therefore we must struggle prophetically against the presumption and despair that plague our society today.

Humanity, thanks to Eucharistic Adoration, can prostrate before God present in the Most Blessed Sacrament. I quote here the deeply moving homily of Benedict XVI on the feast of *Corpus Christi* in 2008:

> Kneeling in adoration before the Lord. Adoring the God of Jesus Christ, who out of love made himself bread broken, is the most effective and radical remedy against the idolatry of the past and of the present. Kneeling before the Eucharist is a profession of freedom: those who bow to Jesus cannot and must not prostrate themselves before any earthly authority, however powerful. We Christians kneel only before God or before the Most Blessed Sacrament because we know and believe that the one true God is present in it, the God who created the world and so loved it that he gave his Only Begotten Son (cf. Jn 3.16). We prostrate ourselves before a God who first bent over man like the Good Samaritan to assist him and restore his life, and who knelt before us to wash our dirty feet. Adoring the Body of Christ, means believing that there, in that piece of Bread, Christ is really there, and gives true sense to life, to the immense universe as to the smallest creature, to the whole of human history as to the most brief existence.

That's where I think we find the source of the true revolution against idolatry. The world which is not in Adoration of God is necessarily idolatrous. Man can not help but adore! The Adoration of false gods: ego, money, power, sex, all the idolatries of our modern world, can only be changed by the prophetic Adoration of the true God.

We welcome young people to our community who have been through drugs, alcohol, depression, violence. And the true healing, the authentic healing comes from kneeling before the Most Blessed Sacrament. I remember a young man who came to me one night and said, 'I can't go on anymore, I must take heroin, I can't go on'. I said to him, 'I cannot put you in handcuffs, I can not bind you, I can only do one thing, and that is to pray with you before the Most Blessed Sacrament'. We both went to the chapel for the whole night, 11 p.m. to 6 a.m. He was clinging to the altar, just below the Monstrance, and if he could have dug his nails into the altar, he would have done so. He held the altar like that, gazing at Jesus. After that, he has never had any temptation to take heroin. He was there before Jesus, you see, Who was present.

Another girl, who was on drugs, who had made five suicide
attempts, had been on drugs for three years and who had fought
with batons against the police, said one day: 'I don't believe in this
life any more at all'. She spent one hour before the Blessed Sacrament
(an hour with her stopwatch in hand), after she had already spent
hours shouting and screaming. 'Jesus, if you do not show me that it's
you, I will go, it's over, I'll kill myself, my life has no meaning'. As she
got up to leave, saying it's over, she said to me: 'I do not know what
happened'. I saw her at the door of the chapel. She held her heart and
said to me: 'Have my heart'. I said to her: 'Let's go immediately to
the hospital'. 'No, it's love'. She said: 'As I said to Jesus, I am going,
I do not know what happened but my heart was pierced by the tenderness of God. So I knew he was there, that he loved me and that
my life had meaning'. Today she has completed her Masters degree
in political science, after having been heavily involved with drugs.
Jesus is there, you see. And before the idolatries of the world, there
is only Adoration the true God. You must go on your knees before
God in order to put man back on his feet. The glory of God is man
on his feet, man fully alive. Only the prostration before God can put
man back on his feet.

Anthropologically, the first illness of the heart of man, a tragic
and horrible illness, 'the source of all illnesses', said St Augustine 'is
pride'. The reversal of pride is the self-abasement of God. He is naked
in the manger, he is naked on the cross, he is naked in the Host, to the
point that Blessed John Paul II could say in *Fides et ratio*: 'From this
vantage-point, the prime commitment of theology is seen to be the
understanding of God's kenosis, a grand and mysterious truth for the
human mind, which finds it inconceivable that suffering and death
can express a love which gives itself and seeks nothing in return'
(93). The Greek word *kenosis* means emptying of self: a God Who
humbled Himself. This is presented in the hymn to the Philippians:
'Who being in the form of God, did not count equality with God
something to be grasped. But he emptied himself, taking the form
of a slave . . . obedient unto death, death on a cross'. The whole task
of theology consists in deepening the mystery of the kenosis of God.
Benedict XVI made a deeply moving observation at Christmas 2005:
'His way of being God challenges our way of being human'. His way
of being God is a child in a manger among an ox and a donkey, one
crucified between two thieves, an apparently inert piece of bread on
an altar. His way of being God challenges our way of being human.
The healing of pride is in the contemplation of the Eucharistic Christ.
If the Prophet Isaiah can tell us that in the Passion, Christ no longer
has a human face, no longer has the features, nor the appearance of
a son of Adam, we must understand that this word is improperly

applied to the Passion, but that it applies fully to the Eucharist. There He no longer has a human face, He no longer has the features of the son of Adam: He has the appearance, the look of a piece of bread! And it is God Who is there! In these hours of Adoration that we spend, who are we then to demand something else? How can our pride still resist before Christ present in the poverty of the Eucharist. Everything else falls away! What have you that you did not receive? If you received it, why do you boast as if you had not received it? Who could humble oneself to the point of rendering oneself present under the appearance of an inert material? Who could humble themselves that far? Our God has gone that far! Pride shatters, it destructs before this way of being God, which consists in presenting Himself to us in the radical poverty of the Eucharist.

Blessed John Paul II said in Poland after the fall of the Berlin Wall: 'We need a Eucharistic school of freedom'. A school that speaks to us the language of giving. The great tragedy of our world is selfishness, the withdrawal into oneself. Man wants to keep himself for himself. The antidote is the Gift.

When we come before the Most Blessed Sacrament, the Eucharist speaks to us this language of Gift. He has given Himself up in total vulnerability. One can take Him. We can move Him. He lets it happen. Not only is He given, but given up, that is to say thrown to the wolves. And for those who want to nourish themselves on Him, He becomes the food of eternal life. But for those who want to profane Him, an act of sacrilege is possible. He permits Himself to be thrown to the wolves. The Eucharist teaches us the logic of the Gift.

I have a friend who lived nine and a half years in the Gulags: Alexander Ogorodnikov was tortured, beaten, abused. I asked him: 'but how did you resist so many horrors, so much suffering?' While being very discreet about what he experienced, he told me about some of the torture to which he was subjected to. According to him, without the grace of God it was impossible to bear them. He said, 'You know when you have given everything to God, down to the last cell of our body, they can no longer take anything from you, even when they tear your flesh, it is already given'. Here, you see, we kneel. We'll have to move from servitude of myself to the freedom of self-donation. The Eucharist, the Most Blessed Sacrament teaches us that freedom.

There are psychological considerations also. Our society has a lot of problems of self-esteem, illnesses of the refusal to live, because the looks we get are non-loving, and because of the fear of being rejected. So many people have received the look which establishes what the psychiatrist Eric Ericsson described as the foundation of the first essential trust, that look which is the look of love laid on us in the first years of our lives, by the father, by the mother and by the grandparents. It is a tragedy not to have received that first trust! But this is not the dead end it seems. God has set His eyes on me in the Eucharist.

A drug addict, Malika, had disappeared. It was thought that she had run away. Finally, she was found that evening in a small oratory of a big religious house where a few people had gathered. She was asked what she was doing there. 'I spent my day here, before the Most Blessed Sacrament'. Before Jesus exposed, she said, 'he gazed at me all day!' She explained to us that she had wanted to run away, but the gaze of Christ had kept her. Jean-Paul Sartre, who went on to reject God, experienced this. He had done something wrong and said:

> I was among those who could have been made saints. But one day I burned the carpet in the house and suddenly God was watching me. I was trying to escape his gaze. I ran into the bathroom to hide under the sink but He was still looking at me! And I started to swear like my grandfather: 'By the Holy Name of God, in the name of God, do not look at me anymore!'

There are two wounds in humanity today. The first is that of not having been looked upon and the second is to refuse to be looked at. The Eucharist can heal both. The first is existential, the second is philosophical and is linked to freedom. It is necessary to let oneself be looked at by God. The Eucharist is the place where God looks at me and gives me my dignity. It's not a look that stares at me. I can rediscover my self-esteem, because I can look at myself like God looks at me, not as the world looks at me in terms of having, of power, of doing, of knowing, but in being. The Eucharist heals me, 'He who looks at him will shine without shadow nor troubled face. A poor man cries out and the Lord hears him. He saves him from all his troubles. Taste and see that the Lord is good! Happy is he who finds refuge in him' (Ps. 34). St Ambrose of Milan said about the encounter of Jesus and Mary Magdalene: 'Who are you looking for?' asks Christ, 'But look at me, Mary. As long as you do not look at me, I shall call you woman and as soon as you look at me, I shall call you Mary'.

I lived five years in a hermitage. A 15-year-old girl who had made five suicide attempts arrived there. What I did not know was that she had a gun in her bag. There, on a ridge 150 meteres above steep rocks, she came and wanted to shoot herself at the edge of a gap so as not to fail. She said to me: 'I do not believe in God'. I replied: 'There is only one thing that can save you, to let yourself be looked at by

Jesus'. 'But I do not believe in Jesus'. 'But He believes in you'. 'What does being looked at by Jesus mean?' 'I spend nights of Adoration in the chapel. If you want, come and spend a night of Adoration from 10 p.m. to 6 a.m. before Jesus present in the Host'. Then she ran away, but she came back and said to me, 'Okay, but I want to spend nine nights'. I later learned that her grandmother made novenas and now she also wanted to make a novena. She came on the first night from 9 p.m. to 6 a.m. and was still, practically frozen before Jesus present in the Host. She later wrote to me:

> At the end of the school year I wanted to scream to my com-
> rades about the distress that was wearing me down, the disgust
> of life that pushed me to do anything. So I decided to spend
> nine nights in adoration. The Lord will surely hear me, this
> time I will go before Him, I'll beg Him. So I did nine whole
> nights of adoration. For nine nights, I let myself be looked at by
> Jesus. I presented my wounds to the Most Blessed Sacrament
> and Jesus healed them. For nine nights, I let out all the pains of
> my soul and the Virgin Mary cradled me in her arms to soothe
> me. After these nine nights, I emerged transformed.

She was confirmed six months later. She had a baccalaureate, and now she has completed her degree in medicine. Nine nights to save a soul. Jesus looked at her. She thought she was ugly, and even – par-don the expression – a bitch. She said: 'I realized that I was beautiful, I had a price in his eyes, that he loved me and that what is important is not what I thought of me or what my father thought of me (he had told her: 'You can die; I have no concern with you'), or what my friends thought of me; only what Jesus thought of me.

Paradoxically, the rationalism of the eighteenth century has caused humanity to lose its reason. Rationalism has released an emo-tional romanticism that has taken different forms over the centuries, but which is a kind of emotionalism, ending in an emotionalization of the conscience (cf. Karol Wojtyla, *The Acting Person*). This is a kind of personal life lived simply at an emotional level, and a social life in which ethics itself is defined in terms of felt emotion. Thus we lose the sense of reason.

It is true that to believe in the existence of God is first an act of reason before it is an act of faith as to who this God is. It is also true that today, it takes a lot of effort to reach God by reason alone. Here is a categorical imperative: it is Jesus Christ who gives to reason its nobility. Adoration delivers us from emotionalism and enables us to live the theological life of faith, hope and charity. If you spend 3 hours honestly before the Sacred Host, where Jesus is present, looking at Him without doing anything else – I do not say in silence, but before Him – then you will necessarily need to perform acts of faith, hope and charity. Otherwise, you will be dreaming or imagining. Eucharistic Adoration obliges us to live in a theological way which is the only way to reach God; that is to say through faith, hope and charity. Adoration is summed up with the most disarming simplicity as posing acts of faith, hope and charity.

Recently we were with children before the Most Blessed Sacrament. I said to them: 'you can say some prayers'. There was a little boy there and he did not budge. Everyone prayed for an intention. So I said to this little boy, who was about three: 'Would you like to pray for someone?' 'Jesus I love you', he made an act of charity. He had touched God by this act of charity. 'Jesus, you are there', he touched God by an act of faith. 'Jesus one day I'll see you face to face'. He was a small child, who one day before the Most Blessed Sacrament, said: 'Jesus, You do not let me see you but I know it's you who are there!' (His faith almost exceeded that of God, I was going to say!) The Eucharist will restore to us our original dignity: to that of rational beings: not rationalists but rational ones, perfected by the grace of faith, hope and charity. This is a healing from a deviant emotionalism that is wrought by an authentic theological life, which puts the emotions and feelings in their rightful place. Otherwise, one is faced with two temptations: either lose oneself in emotion, or reject it categorically, which in both cases is a tragedy for the humanity of the person. Only an authentically theological life restores to human affectivity its legitimate and rightful place, including in our devotional lives.

The healing of the worst spiritual illnesses, *acedia*, spiritual sadness, is crucial. This kind of carelessness, this torpor, when one is no longer hungry, no longer thirsty, when one is weary, no longer desiring Jesus, everything becomes a burden. Prayer becomes a burden. Praying the Divine Office becomes a burden. This is a very common illness which Eucharistic Adoration can cure. Before the Most Blessed Sacrament, I can make acts of desire: 'My soul thirsts for the living God, as a deer longs for running streams so my soul thirsts for You, Lord'. We must hunger and thirst for Him.

I used to go mountain climbing. One day we were at the creeks near Marseille. We had nothing much left to eat. In the evening, we had a little bread which we had finished and had only four oranges left. There were four of us and we said: 'We'll climb the mountain path early tomorrow morning. At the top we will eat the oranges'. But the path we took was too difficult. One friend had no more strength and became stuck half way. Instead of arriving at the summit at 8 a.m. as we had expected, we arrived at 2 p.m. We had to pull him up from above. We had saved his orange for him.

When he saw the orange, his eyes lit up. He crawled to the orange and ate it together with the peel. That's how we must go before the Most Blessed Sacrament, not physically, but with desire. I am going to eat you Lord and Eucharistic Adoration is always a communion of desire. It is You Lord, my soul thirsts for You. Saint Peter Julian Eymard said, 'Our adorations bear little fruit because we always start with ourselves and so not with God'. We're not going to Him with this desire and thus, tragically, one can fall into *acedia* while adoring. And it's not simply because my eyes are tired, but because my heart does not look any more. If I sleep but my heart watches, that's good. But if I sleep and my heart no longer watches, that is a catastrophe! There is a theology of sleep to be developed which is that of having the heart awake. *Acedia* is a true tragedy and therefore we have to heal it through hunger and thirst, through the desire for God, the desire to see God, the desire for Christ. Joy comes from this hunger and this thirst. My heart is hungry and thirsty for the living God, and my joy, nourished from this source of life that flows from the Heart of Christ, will glorify this God. I will discover authentic joy.

Our world now lives from a drive for exterior perfection, of the need to be a superman. It does not seek the perfection of holiness. Holiness is firstly the acceptance of poverty, into which the merciful grace of God can dive. Before the Eucharist, I do not have any masks, I do not have to play a sociological role. I can be poor before the Most Blessed Sacrament. We have Perpetual Adoration of the Most Blessed Sacrament in Freiburg and sometimes I spend the night in Adoration. These are mind-blowing encounters. One day, at 4 a.m., I saw a politician before the Most Blessed Sacrament. I saw him on his knees like me; no difference. When St Alphonsus Liguori, who was, it was said, the best dressed in all of Rome and St Benedict Joseph Labre, who put fleas inside his shirt so that they would not get cold in winter, adored the Most Blessed Sacrament together side by side for 40 hours, we had man in his most sublime dignity in the presence of God, it was not about appearances, it was not the dignity of a well-known lawyer or a poor beggar that was their difference: they were unique, children of God. The Most Blessed Sacrament will teach me to accept my vulnerability, my poverty, my misery, my sin, my nothingness. I can only be there in the truth, down to the last detail.

I have a friend who had come to Adoration that we had organized in order to accompany his wife. When we had finished the procession of the Most Blessed Sacrament, he said,

I wanted to scream: don't get on your knees, you're crazy! It's nonsense: you do not believe these charlatans of priests who make you believe that God is there. But I did not dare to say anything, so as not to shame my wife.

He himself had had a serious car accident and could no longer bend his knees. He suddenly felt himself being put on his knees before the Most Blessed Sacrament. As he went down to the ground he realized he no longer had any pain in his knees. As a result, he had to convert and every morning at 5 a.m. before going to work, he made an hour of Adoration.

One day before the Most Blessed Sacrament, Jesus said to a businessman, 'About your taxes: where are you with them?' He replied, 'Lord, I am here to adore, not to talk about taxes!' The Lord said, 'I am very interested in your taxes and your tax return!' And he said: 'No, no, Lord, I am considering more elevated things!' Well he had to go and see his tax agent to correct his tax return, and the Lord did not give up until he had been honest about his tax declaration before the Blessed Sacrament. The Lord requires us to go to the end of our misery, our poverty, our sin when we are before the Most Blessed Sacrament. Being poor, this is our title of nobility.

We live in an emotional world and therefore with deep emotional dependences and deficiencies which often manifest themselves in sexual deviancies. I believe that Adoration is the place to acquire the virtue of chastity. First Jesus says, 'Your eye is the window of your soul. Keep your eyes pure so that your heart is pure'. Laying my eyes on the Eucharistic Body of Christ, I am called little by little to no longer gaze elsewhere, but to look at things, people, with a look purified by Eucharistic Adoration. This Body of Christ, this flesh of Christ compels me to look at the flesh of others and my own flesh differently. The way I look at and to touch the flesh of the Son of man, this Sacred Body of Jesus, will compel me to rethink my way of touching my body, of living my body, of looking at the body of another, of touching the body of another. There is a way of living the body through Eucharistic Adoration. There is a way to rediscover my radical dependence with respect to God. The human being is a being of a necessarily dependent relationship. If I do not depend dramatically on Christ in this intimacy lived in Adoration, I will be emotionally dependent on human beings. Thus Eucharistic Adoration is the place to acquire the virtue of chastity, of vulnerability experienced, of poverty lived, of the beggar who cries and of the one that will gradually be transfigured by gazing at is flesh, in this relationship with the Body of Christ, with the bodies of others. In the hospice of Blessed Teresa of Calcutta it is very nice to see in the bathroom where they wash the people who have been brought in from the street, written in large letters: 'the Body of Christ'.

We are told that people are no longer capable of being attentive. It's like channel-hopping on the TV! Moving from one thing to another prevents us from being attentive. But the ancients said that attention was the mother of prayer. What is providential about the Eucharist, is that the sense which at once makes us the most ecstatic and which also gives us the most attention, is vision. The Eucharist is first a gaze at the Host. If we began to expose the Most Blessed Sacrament from the twelfth to the thirteenth centuries, it was to correct the heresy of Beranger of Tours who denied the Real Presence of Christ in the Most Blessed Sacrament. The People of God responded first by saying 'We want to see him! Show us Jesus and we will demonstrate our faith by looking at the Host'. Adoration is a mystery of vision, a gazing upon me by Christ who heals me. My gaze is fixed on Him in return. I look at the Host; otherwise there is no need to expose the Most Blessed Sacrament, go before the tabernacle – He is there. Even the largest armoured door will never prevent the radiation of the Real Presence, because Eucharistic Adoration is a mystery of love. I want to see, because love is in the gaze. Have you ever seen two people in love? They look at each other all the time. They seek each other. They are constantly trying to see each other. Love wants to see the beloved. You can hear the beloved on the phone. But when I at look at the beloved, it changes everything. There is one person who was healed of blindness from birth before the Most Blessed Sacrament in a place of Marian pilgrimage. She said:

> I saw my daughter for the first time. And God has been kind; it took three months to heal. I would never have been able to bear to see face to face at once. Here I had three months to fully regain my sight. God has been good.

This is Adoration: I do not see God face to face, and thankfully so, because otherwise I would die. The look is so important, that St Pius X gave a partial indulgence, at the time 300 days, for anyone who looked at Jesus in the Most Blessed Sacrament, at the elevation during the Mass and said 'My Lord and my God'. At the time, people were bowing their heads at the elevation and, historically speaking, it's not the original purpose of the Eucharist. Jesus said to St Gertrude of Helfta: 'As many times as man looks with love at the Host that contains the Body and Blood of Christ, as many times he increases his future merits'. There will be delight in heaven for those who have laid their eyes of flesh on His Eucharistic Body.

There are two types of solitude: the original solitude, that of our first parents: 'it is not good for Adam to be alone', not man and woman, not masculine and feminine, but it is not good that a human being should be alone. And there is the emotional solitude that we live in the world today.

What is original solitude? It was Blessed John Paul II, who stated that: 'It does not belong to the prehistory of man, but to the theological prehistory of each of us'. Each of us has to discover his place in the world. God alone suffices, and no creature can fill my heart. This is the essence of this solitude which is the *sine qua non* condition of all relationships with other human beings and with the world. We will have to conquer this original solitude. God alone suffices, and no creature will fill my life. So, in Eucharistic Adoration, I learn to live this original solitude. At the same time, I am healed according to my relationships with others. Not only my emotional solitude is filled by that of Christ, but I am also capable of living with others in an authentic relation of human being to human being, person to person, and not from emotional thirst to emotional thirst.

The historical aspect of the Eucharist is important. Jesus said to St Faustina: 'Tell the whole world, that the world will not find peace on earth until it comes back to my Heart, to my mercy'. Yet, Jesus said, 'The throne of My mercy is the Holy Sacrament'. This is to say: 'Tell the whole world that peace is impossible in the heart, in families and in the world if one does not adore the Eucharistic Jesus'. I believe that visiting the Eucharistic Christ in Adoration is a revolution. It is the only revolution beside which Lenin, Che Guevara and Mao are mere children. Their revolutions were for the death of man but the revolution for the life of man is the solemn proclamation, by Eucharistic Adoration, of the Sovereignty of God. I put this prophecy of Jesus to St Faustina at the same level as the prophecy of Mary at Fatima: 'If you do not convert, there will be a more serious war (than WWI)'. And war broke out. If there is no return to the Eucharist, a global catastrophe could happen. The response to this catastrophe which we see emerging everywhere, to this economic crisis which is just beginning, will be Eucharistic Adoration, reparative Adoration and healing.

Two more things on the Eucharist: first, eschatologically, it is the drug of immortality. I taste already eternal life, the divine life for which I was made. Second, in adoring the Eucharist I implore the coming of Christ in glory, the *parousia*. We await His coming in glory, but He that comes in glory is already present in the Most Blessed Sacrament. It is the same and I am already inserted into the *parousia*, into the presence and the coming, through Adoration. Heaven is already there and it is not so much heaven that descends, but the earth that rises to heaven in this great ascending movement. The whole creation is waiting in the pains of childbirth for the revelation of the sons of God. Creation aspires that we conduct ourselves as children of God, so that the entire cosmos will find in Christ its completion and fulfilment. The answer to the ecological crisis of the world today is also found in Adoration. Already in it, the radiation of Christ will be able to emerge, through the energy issued from this Eucharistic nuclear fission – to use the image of Benedict XVI – rediscovering an order of the cosmos ordered by the Creator, an order of humanity, ordered by the Redeemer, and to proclaim the Lordship of God over all flesh and over all the cosmos, so that the peace of God can penetrate hearts and the world.

Ten

Homily: Eucharistic Adoration, Self-Offering and Martyrdom

Francis Cardinal Arinze
Prefect Emeritus of the Congregation for Divine Worship and the Discipline of the Sacraments, Vatican City

In the Collect for the Mass of St John Fisher and St Thomas More, the Church prays today to God Who in martyrdom has brought true faith to its highest expression. We admire the workings of God's grace in these two great witnesses of Christ. We listen to the Lord Who in the readings at this Mass invites us to a radical following of Him. This leads us to reflect on how Eucharistic Adoration increases our union with Christ. We shall close with a meditation on the close relationship between the Holy Eucharist and martyrdom.

Two Giant Witnesses of Jesus Christ
Our Holy Mother, the Church, celebrates today two giant witnesses of our Lord and Saviour, Jesus Christ: St John Fisher and St Thomas More.

St John Fisher (1469–1535) did his theological studies in Cambridge and eventually became bishop of Rochester, in England. He led an austere life, was a zealous pastor who regularly visited his flock, and composed works against the errors of his time.

St Thomas More (1477–1535) studied at Oxford, married and had one son and three daughters, was Chancellor in the King's Court in London, and wrote works on government and in defence of the faith.

After many vexations, both were beheaded in 1535 by order of King Henry VIII because they did not go against God's law and against their conscience to support the king's divorce. In his letter from prison to his daughter, Margaret, St Thomas More beautifully exposes his state of soul. It is one of total abandonment to God and reliance on divine grace for the trial ahead:

> I cannot but trust in his (that is, God's) merciful goodness. His grace has strengthened me until now and made me content to

lose goods, land and life as well, rather than to swear against
my conscience . . . By the merits of his bitter passion joined to
mine and far surpassing in merit for me all that I can suffer
myself, his bounteous goodness shall release me from the pains
of purgatory and shall increase my reward in heaven besides
. . . Nothing can come but what God wills. And I am very sure
that whatever that be, however bad it may seem, it shall indeed
be the best.[1]

Here is faith at its highest manifestation. Here is love of God pure
and splendid. As we sing in the psalm, the martyrs give us moving
example of love and faith: 'Those who are sowing in tears will sing
when they reap. They go out, they go out, full of tears, carrying seed
for the sowing, they come back, they come back, full of song, carrying their sheaves' (Ps. 125.5–6).
  The Church, therefore, rightly prays in the Collect:

O God, who in martyrdom have brought true faith to its highest expression, grant graciously that, strengthened through
the intercession of Sts John Fisher and Thomas More, we may
confirm by the witness of our life the faith we profess with our
lips. (*Roman Missal*, revised English translation)

Jesus Invites us to Follow Him, Carrying our Cross

The celebration of the Eucharistic sacrifice and the contemplation of
the Eucharistic mystery in the Adoration of this ineffable Sacrament
are powerful in introducing and encouraging us to a radical following of Christ. Jesus consummates His sacrifice of love for His Spouse,
the Church, in His passion, death and resurrection. He puts into the
hands of His Church the sacramental re-presentation of the Sacrifice
of Calvary in the Eucharistic Celebration. He wants our participation
in the sacrifice. He loves us so much that in the Real Presence He has
devised a wonderful way to remain with us after Mass. He invites us
to visit Him in the Most Blessed Sacrament, to express our love for
Him, to adore Him, and to learn from Him how to carry our cross
daily and follow Him.
  The *Catechism of the Catholic Church* puts it beautifully:

It is highly fitting that Christ should have wanted to remain
present in his Church in this unique way. Since Christ was

---

[1]   *The English Works of Sir Thomas More*, London 1557, p. 1454.

about to take his departure from his own in his visible form, he wanted to give us his sacramental presence; since he was about to offer himself on the cross to save us, he wanted us to have the memorial of the love with which he loved us 'to the end', even to the giving of his life. In his Eucharistic presence he remains mysteriously in our midst as the one who loved us and gave himself up for us, and he remains under signs that express and communicate this love. (1380)

In the Gospel of this Mass, Jesus invites us to follow Him. The call is unequivocal, clear, even radical:

He who loves father or mother more than me is not worthy of me; and he who loves son or daughter more than me is not worthy of me; and he who does not take up his cross and follow me is not worthy of me. (Mt. 10.37–38)

Jesus goes so far as to ask of His followers' readiness to make the supreme sacrifice of their lives for His sake: 'He who finds his life will lose it, and he who loses his life for my sake will find it' (Mt. 10.39). Jesus carried His cross. He invites us to do the same. He gave witness to the truth right up to laying down His life in its defence. He invites us to do that same:

If any man would come after me, let him deny himself and take up his cross and follow me . . . Whoever is ashamed of me and of my words in this adulterous and sinful generation, of him will the Son of man also be ashamed, when he comes in the glory of the Father with the holy angels. (Mk 8.34, 38; cf also Lk. 9.23–26)

St Peter in the First Reading of this Mass teaches us not to be surprised if as followers of Christ we meet suffering; rather we should be ready to offer it with Christ and through Christ:

Rejoice in so far as you share Christ's sufferings, that you may also rejoice and be glad when his glory is revealed. If you are reproached for the name of Christ, you are blessed, because the spirit of glory and of God rests upon you . . . Therefore let those who suffer according to God's will do right and entrust their souls to a faithful Creator. (1 Pet. 4.13, 14, 19)

Active participation in the Eucharistic Celebration and intensive Adoration of our Eucharistic Lord outside Mass are very conducive to this readiness to offer oneself with Christ, through Christ and in Christ.

The Second Vatican Council says that Christ's faithful, instructed by God's word and refreshed at the table of the Lord's Body,

> should give thanks to God by offering the Immaculate Victim, not only through the hands of the priest, but also with him, they should learn to offer themselves too. Through Christ the Mediator, they should be drawn day by day into ever closer union with God and with each other, so that finally God may be all in all. (*Sacrosanctum concilium*, 48)

Eucharistic Adoration Increases Union with Christ

There is no doubt that Eucharistic Adoration increases our union with Christ. As Pope Benedict XVI teaches,

> Eucharistic adoration is simply the natural consequence of the Eucharistic celebration which is itself the Church's supreme act of adoration . . . The act of adoration outside Mass prolongs and intensifies all that takes place during the liturgical celebration itself. (*Sacramentum caritatis*, 66)

Blessed John Paul II already wrote in his last Encyclical Letter: 'The Eucharist is a priceless treasure: by not only celebrating it but also by praying before it outside of Mass we are enabled to make contact with the very wellspring of grace' (*Ecclesia de Eucharistia*, 25).

The testimony of St Alphonsus de Liguori is powerful: 'Of all devotions, that of adoring Jesus in the Blessed Sacrament is the greatest after the sacraments, the one dearest to God and the one most helpful to us'.[2]

By kneeling or sitting in the presence of our Eucharistic Lord habit-ually, we gradually begin to absorb His spirit, to have in us something of that mind which was in Christ Jesus (cf. Phil. 2.5). 'The Eucharist', says Pope Benedict XVI, 'draws us into Jesus' act of self-oblation. More than just statically receiving the incarnate *Logos*, we enter into the very dynamic of his self-giving' (*Deus caritas est*, 13). Jesus in the Holy Eucharist, both as received and as adored, is the inspiration and strength of martyrs, confessors and virgins. 'The gaze of the Church is constantly turned to her Lord, present in the Sacrament of the Altar, in which she discovers the full manifestation of his boundless love' (*Ecclesia de Eucharistia*, 1). In the adoring presence of Jesus in the tabernacle or exposed in the monstrance, the follower of Christ

---

2   *Visite al SS. Sacramento e a Maria Santissima,* Introd. *Opere Ascetiche*, Avellino, 2000, p. 295.

grows in love of Christ and the Church, in sentiments of repentance, in readiness to offer self together with Christ, and in preparedness to spread the Gospel and extend Christian solidarity to the suffering and the needy. To the diligent and loving Christian, Adoration of the Most Blessed Sacrament 'becomes an inexhaustible source of holiness' (*Ecclesia de Eucharistia*, 10).

Eucharistic Adoration and Martyrdom

The martyr follows our Eucharistic Lord. In the Holy Eucharist we adore Jesus who laid down His life for us. 'Greater love has no man than this, that a man lay down his life for his friends' (Jn 15.13). Jesus did precisely that. 'For this reason the Father loves me, because I lay down my life, that I may take it again. No one takes it from me, but I lay it down of my own accord' (Jn 10.18). At Mass, we celebrate the saving mystery of the suffering, death and resurrection of our Saviour. After Mass, Jesus remains with us in this ineffable Sacrament in the tabernacle or in the monstrance. There we adore Him for His great love for us, we thank Him, and we show Him our love by professing our readiness to be sacrificed with Him, offering with generosity, love and patience our sufferings, setbacks, disappointments and humiliations through Him, with Him and in Him.

The Summit of Such Loving and Unifying Self-Offering is Martyrdom

Martyrdom is the highest demonstration of love of Jesus of which we are capable. It is a rare grace given only to a few. None of us dare presume to have the strength to make this sacrifice. But we can rely on God to give us the grace if He so calls us to this supreme demonstration of love. During the persecution of Diocletian the 40 martyrs of Abitina in Proconsular Africa gave this supreme witness by laying down their lives to defend their fidelity to Sunday Mass. They declared in front of their persecutors: 'Without fear of any kind we have celebrated the Lord's Supper, because it cannot be missed; that is our law. We cannot live without the Lord's Supper'.[3]

Dear brothers and sisters in Christ, let us adore and thank our Eucharistic Jesus for the magnificent witness given by St John Fisher and St Thomas More. Let us pray to our Blessed Mother Mary, woman of the Eucharist and Queen of Martyrs, to obtain for each of us growing Eucharistic faith and devotion and readiness with St Paul to see our sufferings as carrying out in our flesh 'what is lacking in Christ's afflictions for the sake of his Body, that is, the Church' (Col. 1.24).

---

[3]   *Acta SS. Saturnini, Dativi et aliorum plurimorum Martyrum in Africa*, 7, 9, 10: PL 8, 707, 709–10; quoted by Blessed John Paul II in *Dies Domini*, 46.

Eleven

Adoration in the Formation and Life of Priests

Raymond Leo Cardinal Burke

Prefect of the Supreme Tribunal of the Apostolic Signatura, Vatican City

Introduction

My presentation is inspired both by the theological reflection upon the Mystery of Faith, the Eucharistic Mystery, and its essential relationship to the ordained priesthood, and by my personal experience as a priest who, on this coming 29 June 2011, will have completed 36 years of priestly life and ministry. To the degree that I have been a good and faithful priest, the truth of what the Church teaches concerning the relationship of the Holy Eucharist and the Holy Priesthood has been at the heart of my priestly life and ministry, that is, it has kept me focused on my priestly identity, and it has been the source from which I have drawn the wisdom and strength to respond to my priestly vocation with an undivided heart.

Blessed John Paul II, in *Gift and Mystery*, written on the occasion of the fiftieth anniversary of his priestly ordination, commenting on the words of the priest, 'The Mystery of Faith', after the consecration of the bread and wine, changing them into the Body and Blood of Christ, wrote:

> *Is this not the deepest reason behind the priestly vocation?* Certainly it is already fully present at the time of ordination, but it needs to be interiorized and deepened for the rest of the priest's life. Only in this way can a priest discover in depth the great treasure which has been entrusted to him. Fifty years after my ordination, I can say that in the words *Mysterium fidei* we find ever more each day the meaning of our own priesthood.[1]

---

[1] Blessed John Paul II, *Gift and Mystery: On the Fiftieth Anniversary of My Priestly Ordination*, New York: Doubleday, 1996, p. 79.

In the end, a priest is conscious that his entire priestly life is at the service of the Mystery of Faith, the Mystery of the Redemptive Incarnation, which is experienced directly in the Sacrament of the Holy Eucharist.

The first intimations of the vocation to the priesthood in my life came by way of wonder at the Eucharistic Mystery. In the growing awareness of God's call to the priesthood in my life, which led to my entrance into the seminary, it was, most of all, participation in the Eucharistic Sacrifice and in Eucharistic Adoration which continued to draw me to the priesthood and helped me to understand, more and more, the meaning of the priestly vocation.

Having grown up during a time of strong Eucharistic devotion, my last years in the seminary and my first years of priestly life coincided with a period of crisis in Eucharistic faith and an abandonment of Eucharistic devotion by many. During the crisis, it was my earlier strong formation in Eucharistic faith and devotion, at home and in the minor seminary, which sustained me. The suffering of the crisis taught me even more the essential importance of Eucharistic faith and devotion both for the response to the vocation to the priesthood and for the fulfilment of the mission entrusted to the ordained priest.

The reflection on the objective reality of the essential relationship of the ordained priesthood to the Holy Eucharist, in fact, naturally leads to a deep conviction about the essential place of Eucharistic faith and devotion in the life of the seminarian or priest. I now offer some reflections on the Holy Eucharist and the Holy Priesthood with the specific purpose of underlining various aspects of Eucharistic devotion in the response to the priestly vocation and mission.

The Priesthood and the Pastoral Charity of Our Lord Jesus Christ

The ordained priest, by the grace of the Sacrament of Orders, acts in the person of Christ, Head and Shepherd of the flock, in every time and place, by his teaching, his sacramental ministration and his governance. Blessed John Paul II, in his Post-Synodal Apostolic Exhortation *Pastores dabo vobis*, making reference to *Presbyterorum ordinis*, 'On the Life and Ministry of Priests', of the Second Vatican Council, declared: 'By sacramental consecration the priest is configured to Jesus Christ as Head and Shepherd of the Church, and he is endowed with a 'spiritual power' which is a share in the authority with which Jesus Christ guides the Church through his Spirit' (21). He goes on to explain that, by the grace of priestly consecration, 'the spiritual life of the priest is marked, moulded and characterized by the way of thinking and acting proper to Jesus Christ, Head and Shepherd of the Church, and which are summed up in his pastoral charity' (21).

It is clear that the offering of the Holy Mass is the fullest expression of the pastoral charity of Our Lord Jesus Christ. Through the grace of ordination to the Sacred Priesthood, the priest is conformed to the person of Christ in His pastoral charity. His soul is indelibly marked for the exercise of the pastoral charity of Christ on behalf of all men. Offering the Holy Sacrifice of the Mass for the salvation of the world, the priest most fully and perfectly carries out the high-priestly ministry of Christ to which he has been called and for which he has been configured to the person of Christ.

In *Pastores dabo vobis*, Blessed John Paul II made specific reference to the highest expression of the priestly office, recalling the words of the ordaining bishop, when he places the offerings for the Holy Mass in the hands of the newly-ordained priest, 'Understand what you do, imitate what you celebrate, and conform your life to the mystery of the Lord's cross'.[2] Regarding what has been called the *traditio instrumentorum*, the handing-over of the paten with the bread and the chalice with the wine for the celebration of the Holy Mass, and the accompanying words, Blessed John Paul II declared:

> This is the invitation and admonition which the Church addresses to the priest in the Rite of Ordination, when the offerings of the holy people for the Eucharistic Sacrifice are placed in his hands. The 'mystery' of which the priest is a 'steward' (cf. 1 Cor. 4.1) is definitively Jesus Christ himself, who in the Spirit is the source of holiness and the call to sanctification. This 'mystery' seeks expression in the priestly life. For this to be so, there is need for great vigilance and lively awareness. (*Pastores dabo vobis*, 24)

At every moment of the priest's life and ministry, he is returning to the Eucharistic Sacrifice, as the highest and most perfect expression of his priestly identity, in order to understand his priestly mission of pastoral charity and to have the strength to carry out his divinely-given mission.

Discernment of the Priestly Vocation and Eucharistic Devotion

Clearly, then the discernment of the call to the priesthood must come by way of growing knowledge and love of the Holy Eucharist. So often, during my life as a priest and bishop, I have encountered young

---

2   *Rites of Ordination of a Bishop, of Priests, and of Deacons*, 'Ordination of Priests', United States Conference of Catholic Bishops, Washington, DC, 2003, p. 91.

men who are struggling to know whether Our Lord may be calling them to the priesthood. Surely, the struggle is made increasingly more difficult by the secularization of the society in which we live.

My first counsel to a young man who is struggling to discern the priestly vocation is to spend time daily in the presence of the Most Blessed Sacrament, that is, to participate in daily Mass, if possible, and to spend an extended time, a holy hour, if possible, in prayer before the Blessed Sacrament reposed in the tabernacle or exposed in the monstrance for Eucharistic Adoration. Unfailingly, prayer in the presence of our Eucharistic Lord opens the mind of a young man to know God's will for him and gives him the courage to respond with an undivided heart.

Even if some doubt remains, I encourage the young man to enter the seminary, as the Church's chosen place for the discernment of the priestly vocation and of preparation to receive, God willing, the call to the priesthood from the Diocesan Bishop or religious superior. In the seminary, he will find that the Holy Eucharist is at the heart of the formation which is offered to him, in accord with the discipline of the universal Church. Can. 246 §1, reads: 'The Eucharistic celebration is to be the centre of the entire life of a seminary in such a way that, sharing in the very love of Christ, the students daily draw strength of spirit for apostolic work and for their spiritual life from this richest of sources'.

In *Pastores dabo vobis*, Blessed John Paul II is emphatic about the essential place of Eucharistic faith and devotion in the life of the priest and, therefore, in the formation of seminarians, of candidates for priestly ordination. Commenting on the essential importance of participation in the sacramental life of the Church 'for the gift and task of that "pastoral charity" which is the soul of priestly ministry', he noted, above all, the importance of participation in the Holy Eucharist, '[f]or priests, as ministers of sacred things, are first and foremost ministers of the Sacrifice of the Mass: the role is utterly irreplaceable, because without the priest there can be no Eucharistic offering' (48).

Regarding the place of the Holy Eucharist in the life of the seminarian or priest, Blessed John Paul II, quoting at length from his *Angelus* Address of 1 July 1990, declared:

> This explains the essential importance of the Eucharist for the priest's life and ministry and, as a result, in the spiritual formation of candidates for the priesthood. To be utterly frank and clear, I would like to say once again: 'It is fitting that seminarians take part *every day* in the Eucharistic celebration, in such a way that afterwards they will take up as a rule of their priestly life this daily celebration. They should moreover be trained to

consider the Eucharistic celebration as the *essential moment of their day*, in which they will take an active part and at which they will never be satisfied with a merely habitual attendance. Finally, candidates to the priesthood will be trained to share in the *intimate* dispositions which the Eucharist fosters: *gratitude* for heavenly benefits received, because the Eucharist is thanksgiving; *an attitude of self-offering* which will impel them to unite the offering of themselves to the Eucharistic offering of Christ; *charity* nourished by a sacrament which is a sign of unity and sharing; *the yearning to contemplate and bow in adoration* before Christ who is really present under the Eucharistic species.' (*Pastores dabo vobis*, 48)

To daily participation in the Holy Mass, the seminarian or priest will naturally unite Eucharistic devotion, above all, visits to the Blessed Sacrament and extended prayer before the tabernacle or before the Eucharistic Host exposed in the monstrance. Only through Eucharistic devotion will the seminarian or priest be able to extend and deepen the communion in the Body, Blood, Soul and Divinity of Christ, which is Christ's supreme gift to him in the Eucharistic Sacrifice. It is through Eucharistic devotion that the '*intimate* dispositions' to which Blessed John Paul II refers are safeguarded and cultivated.

In my experience as a bishop, I have remained singularly impressed, during my regular visits to the seminary, to find always, when I made my visit to the Blessed Sacrament, a good number of seminarians in prayer. Also, it was common for the seminarians to ask for some extended period of Eucharistic Adoration, even every day, so that their communion with the Lord in the Holy Mass could be extended and deepened by keeping company with Him through His Real Presence in the Most Blessed Sacrament.

Eucharistic devotion in no way detracts from the central importance of the seminarian's participation in the Holy Mass. It rather prepares him to be more fully engaged in the Eucharistic Sacrifice. At the same time, the reality of the Holy Eucharist, containing the entire good of our salvation, is so great that it connaturally inspires the desire to manifest, in a concrete way, love and devotion to our Eucharistic Lord.

Eucharistic devotion, especially the Holy Hour, does not take away from the other aspects of seminary formation, for instance, the intellectual or the pastoral formation. Rather, it grounds all aspects of formation in the objective reality of the priestly vocation. Regarding intellectual formation, one thinks, for example, of St Thomas Aquinas, whose love of our Eucharistic Lord, expressed in hours spent in prayer before the Blessed Sacrament and in wonderful texts and hymns which he composed for the Holy Mass and Eucharistic devotion, was openly acknowledged by him to be the font of his theological reflection. On his deathbed, when he had made his last confession and received Viaticum, the Angelic Doctor declared: 'I am receiving thee, Price of my soul's redemption: all my studies, my vigils and my labours have been for love of thee'.[3] Regarding pastoral formation, one thinks, for instance, of St John Mary Vianney, who addressed the extreme spiritual poverty of the parish at Ars, to which he was assigned as parish priest, by making the celebration of the Holy Mass the heart of his service of the faithful, and by spending long hours before the Blessed Sacrament in prayer for his own conversion and the conversion of the souls entrusted to his priestly care.

St John Mary Vianney, Model of Priestly Eucharistic Devotion

It will be helpful to extend the reflection on the place of Eucharistic devotion in the life of St John Mary Vianney. In his letter (16 June 2009) proclaiming a Year for Priests on the occasion of the 150th anniversary of the Death of St John Mary Vianney, the Curé of Ars, Pope Benedict XVI underlined, in a particular way, the centrality of Eucharistic faith and devotion in the life of the patron saint of parish priests. The Holy Father recalled how St John Mary Vianney, arriving as the parish priest of Ars, a village known for a coldness or tepidity in the practice of the faith, chose 'to "*live*"', physically, in his parish church'.

The Curé of Ars, by seeking constantly the company of our Eucharistic Lord, drew the faithful to Christ in His Real Presence in the Most Blessed Sacrament. Seeking out the parish priest, they found him in the parish church, keeping company with the Lord. St John Mary Vianney's exemplary Eucharistic faith rekindled the Eucharistic faith and practice of the parishioners.

In time, the evident identification of the Curé of Ars with Christ in His Eucharistic Sacrifice also attracted the faithful to the Sacrament of Penance. In his letter, the Holy Father observed: 'This deep personal identification with the Sacrifice of the Cross led him – by a sole inward movement – from the altar to the confessional'. Pope

---

[3]   Herbert Thurston, S.J., and Donald Attwater, eds, *Butler's Lives of the Saints*, Complete Edition, New York: P.J. Kenedy & Sons, 1956, Vol. 1, p. 511. See: Jean-Pierre Torrell, O.P., *Saint Thomas Aquinas, Vol. 1: The Person and His Work*, Revised Edition, trans. Robert Royal Washington, DC: The Catholic University of America Press, 2005, p. 136.

Benedict XVI underlined the essential relationship between the Sacraments of the Holy Eucharist and Penance, as it is exemplified in the priestly ministry of St John Mary Vianney. He observed:

> [The Curé of Ars] sought in every way, by his preaching and his powers of persuasion, to help his parishioners to rediscover the meaning and beauty of the sacrament of Penance, presenting it as an inherent demand of the Eucharistic presence. He thus created a *'virtuous' circle*. By spending long hours in church before the tabernacle, he inspired the faithful to imitate him by coming to visit Jesus with the knowledge that their parish priest would be there, ready to listen and to offer forgiveness. (Letter, 16 June 2009)

The faithful did not fail to identify their parish priest with Christ who is all merciful toward us, pouring out His life for the salvation of men, without boundary, in the Sacrament of the Holy Eucharist, and hearing the confession of their sins and absolving them from their sins in the Sacrament of Penance. Here, it must be noted that the Eucharistic devotion of a seminarian or priest will always be closely connected with the daily examination of conscience and act of contrition, and the regular encounter with Christ in the Sacrament of Penance for the confession of sins and the reception of absolution.

The faithful, observing the fervent Eucharistic devotion of St John Mary Vianney, were given the grace of a conversion of heart, which expressed itself in Eucharistic devotion. Pope Benedict XVI, commenting on the profound effect of the example of the priest on the Eucharistic devotion of the faithful, declared: 'St John Mary Vianney taught his parishioners primarily by the witness of his life. It was from his example that they learned to pray, halting frequently before the tabernacle for a visit to Jesus in the Blessed Sacrament' (Letter, 16 June 2009).

St John Mary Vianney urged the faithful, notwithstanding their unworthiness, to draw close to Our Lord in the Most Blessed Sacrament. At the same time, his manner of offering the Holy Mass taught the people the truth of the Real Presence and of the thirst of Christ for their souls. They learned from the example of the Curé the great mystery of God's all-merciful love of us, which is expressed most fully and compellingly in Christ's making present for us anew, in the Eucharistic Sacrifice, the outpouring of His life for our salvation.

St John Mary Vianney, from his Eucharistic devotion, understood that he, like Christ, was both Priest and Victim. His Eucharistic devotion developed in him an ever greater disposition to pour out his life in pure and selfless love of the faithful, as Christ did through His death on the Cross. Quoting the Curé, Pope Benedict XVI observed: 'He was accustomed, when celebrating, also to offer his own life in sacrifice: "What a good thing it is for a priest each morning to offer himself to God in sacrifice" ' (Letter, 16 June 2009).

In the same way, the Curé was convinced that any laxity of a priest in carrying out his sacred ministry flowed necessarily from a lack of fervour in offering the Holy Mass. Once again quoting St John Mary Vianney, Pope Benedict XVI commented on the saint's conviction 'that the fervour of a priest's life depended entirely upon the Mass' (Letter, 16 June 2009). The Curé of Ars declared: 'The reason why a priest is lax is that he does not pay attention to the Mass! My God, how we ought to pity a priest who celebrates as if he were engaged in something routine' (Letter, 16 June 2009). The saintly Curé manifested the total sincerity of his words in his own priestly life centred in the Holy Eucharist.

In fidelity to the Magisterium, St John Mary Vianney taught the essential bond of the Holy Priesthood with the Most Blessed Sacrament. Regarding the priestly vocation, the saint declared: 'O, how great is the priest! . . . If he realized what he is, he would die . . . God obeys him: he utters a few words and the Lord descends from heaven at his voice, to be contained within a small host' (Letter, 16 June 2009).

On many occasions, the Curé of Ars led the faithful to a deeper faith in and devotion to the Sacrament of the Holy Priesthood by reminding them that the Holy Priesthood exists primarily for the celebration of the Holy Eucharist and that the celebration of the Holy Eucharist cannot take place without the Holy Priesthood.

Eucharistic Wonder and the Priestly Vocation

Blessed John Paul II strikingly described the wonder which should fill the mind and the heart of every priest when he is offering the Holy Mass. Christ's action, through the priest's ministry, truly unites Heaven and Earth, for it makes present the glorious Body, Blood, Soul and Divinity of Christ for the salvation of the world. Blessed John Paul II wrote these words about the 'profound amazement and gratitude' before the reality of the Eucharistic Sacrifice, which should fill the minds and hearts of all the faithful and, especially, of priests:

> This amazement should always fill the Church assembled for the celebration of the Eucharist. But in a special way it should fill the minister of the Eucharist. For it is he who, by the authority

given him in the Sacrament of priestly ordination, effects the consecration. It is he who says with the power coming to him from Christ in the Upper Room: 'This is my Body which will be given up for you. This is the cup of my Blood poured out for you. . . .' The priest says these words, or rather *he puts his voice at the disposal of the One Who spoke these words in the Upper Room* and who desires that they should be repeated in every generation by all those who in the Church ministerially share in His priesthood. (*Ecclesia de Eucharistia*, 5)

In the Eucharistic Sacrifice, all of the faithful witness the mystery of the immense love of Our Lord Jesus Christ for all men, without boundary. It is the mystery which Our Lord expressed with His words, as He was dying upon the Cross for the salvation of the world: 'I thirst' (Jn 19.28). The ordained priest is called to share in the thirst of Christ for souls, which is immeasurable and without cease. Through the Eucharistic devotion of the priest, the priest comes to a deeper appreciation of his call to pastoral charity, and the faithful understand the true meaning of the priest's care of their souls.

In *Ecclesia de Eucharistia*, Blessed John Paul II described Eucharistic faith in a striking manner. He reminded us that the life of the Church has its 'foundation and well-spring' in the Sacred Triduum, which is fully contained in the Eucharistic Mystery. As he wrote, the Paschal Triduum 'is as it were gathered up, foreshadowed and "concentrated" for ever in the gift of the Holy Eucharist' (5). He continued: 'The thought of this leads us to profound amazement and gratitude. In the paschal event and the Eucharist which makes it present throughout the centuries, there is truly enormous "capacity" which embraces all of history as the recipient of the grace of the redemption'. How much the attitudes, words and actions of the priest who is devoted in his love of the Most Blessed Sacrament will give witness to the truth of the Mystery of Faith, the Holy Eucharist, which, at its every celebration, embraces the entire world. Christ suffered, died and rose from the dead for the salvation of all men, without boundary.

Eucharistic devotion in the seminarian or priest keeps ever before his mind the apostolic origin of the priestly ministry, that is, its unbroken succession from the ordination of the Apostles, the first priests, by Christ at the Last Supper, to the ordination of the newest priest in the world today. Blessed John Paul II declared:

The ministry of priests who have received the sacrament of Holy Orders, in the economy of salvation chosen by Christ, makes clear that the Eucharist which they celebrate is *a gift which radically transcends the power of the assembly* and is in any event essential for validly linking the Eucharistic consecration to the sacrifice of the Cross and to the Last Supper. (*Ecclesia de Eucharistia*, 29)

Through Eucharistic faith and devotion, both the priest and the faithful will be always deeply conscious that the priesthood is a gift given by Christ to His Church, so that He might be present, in every time and place, as Head and Shepherd of the flock, giving His life for the flock, above all through the offering of the Holy Sacrifice of the Mass.

Quoting his Apostolic Letter *Dominicæ cenæ*, written to all of the bishops of the Church on Holy Thursday of the second year of his pontificate, Blessed John Paul II underlined again the essential and central place of Eucharistic Adoration in the life of the priest. He declared:

> If the Eucharist is the centre and summit of the Church's life, it is likewise the centre and summit of priestly ministry. For this reason, with a heart filled with gratitude to our Lord Jesus Christ, I repeat that the Eucharist 'is the principal and central *raison d'être* of the sacrament of priesthood, which effectively came into being at the moment of the institution of the Eucharist'. (*Ecclesia de Eucharistia*, 31)

Commenting on the number and variety of the responsibilities of the priest, Blessed John Paul II observed that Eucharistic devotion alone will permit the priest to remain focused in his priestly life, so that every act of his ministry may express the pastoral charity which has its source in the Eucharistic mystery.

In his last letter to priests on the occasion of Holy Thursday 2004, referring to his last Encyclical Letter *Ecclesia de Eucharistia* and to his book written on the occasion of his fiftieth anniversary of priesthood ordination, Blessed John Paul II wrote:

> We were born from the Eucharist. If we can truly say that the whole Church lives from the Eucharist (*'Ecclesia de Eucharistia vivit'*), as I reaffirmed in my recent Encyclical, we can say the same thing about the ministerial priesthood: it is born, lives, works and bears fruit *'de Eucharistia.'* There can be no Eucharist without the priesthood, just as there can be no priesthood without the Eucharist. (2)

Contemplating the mystery of the ordained priesthood, Blessed John Paul II declared to his brother priests in the same letter:

Before this extraordinary reality we find ourselves amazed and overwhelmed, so deep is the humility by which God 'stoops' in order to unite himself with man! If we feel moved before the Christmas crib, when we contemplate the Incarnation of the Word, what must we feel before the altar where, by the poor hands of the priest, Christ makes his Sacrifice present in time? We can only fall to our knees and silently adore this supreme mystery of faith. (2)

Both the seminarian who is deepening his knowledge of the call to the priesthood and the priest who is deepening his knowledge of the gift of his priestly vocation will seek daily the occasion to fall to their knees and adore the great Mystery of Faith.

The Hermeneutic of Discontinuity and the Crisis of Eucharistic Devotion

In the Postsynodal Apostolic Exhortation *Sacramentum caritatis*, Pope Benedict XVI exhorted all of the faithful to cultivate Eucharistic devotion. Emphasizing 'the orderly development of the ritual forms in which we commemorate the event of our salvation' (3), he addressed a mistaken notion regarding Eucharistic Adoration, which had developed after the Second Vatican Ecumenical Council. He wrote:

> During the early phases of the reform [following the liturgical renewal desired by the Second Vatican Council], the inherent relationship between Mass and adoration of the Blessed Sacrament was not always perceived with sufficient clarity. For example, an objection that was widespread at the time argued that the eucharistic bread was given to us not to be looked at, but to be eaten. In the light of the Church's experience of prayer, however, this was seen to be a false dichotomy. As St Augustine put it: *'nemo autem illam carnem manducat, nisi prius adoraverit; peccemus non adorando* – no one eats that flesh without first adoring it; we should sin were we not to adore it.' In the Eucharist, the Son of God comes to meet us and desires to become one with us; eucharistic adoration is simply the natural consequence of the eucharistic celebration, which is itself the Church's supreme act of adoration. (66)

Pope Benedict XVI, in accord with the teaching which he had set forth, in magisterial form, in his Christmas discourse to the Roman Curia in 2005, described the connatural relationship between participation in the Eucharistic Sacrifice and Eucharistic Adoration: 'The act of adoration outside Mass prolongs and intensifies all that takes place during the liturgical celebration' (66).

In this 2005 Christmas Address to the Roman Curia, the Holy Father explained how the development of Eucharistic Adoration in the Church, especially as it took shape in the Middle Ages, is a fruit of the Eucharistic mystery itself and the Church's Eucharistic faith. Referring to the post-Conciliar hermeneutic of discontinuity, which effectively suppressed all forms of Eucharistic devotion and Adoration in some parts of the Church, he wrote:

> Receiving the Eucharist means adoring the One whom we receive. Precisely in this way and only in this way do we become one with him. Therefore, the development of Eucharistic adoration, as it took shape during the Middle Ages, was the most consistent consequence of the Eucharistic mystery itself: only in adoration can profound and true acceptance develop. And it is precisely this personal act of encounter with the Lord that develops the social mission which is contained in the Eucharist and desires to break down barriers, not only the barriers between the Lord and us but also and above all those that separate us from one another. (Discourse, 22 December 2005)

Eucharistic Adoration is essential for seminarians and priests, if they are to grow, in the words of Pope Benedict XVI, in 'profound and true acceptance' of the priestly vocation and of the pastoral charity of Christ, which is its essence.

In *Sacramentum caritatis*, Pope Benedict XVI comments at some length on the relationship between Eucharistic spirituality and the daily life of Christian charity. Noting how the growing secularization of society leads to the relegation of Christian faith 'to the margins of life as if it were irrelevant to everyday affairs', Pope Benedict XVI articulated 'the need to rediscover that Jesus Christ is not just a private conviction or an abstract idea, but a real person, whose becoming part of human history is capable of renewing the life of every man and woman' (77).

The temptation, for a seminarian or priest, to reduce Christ to an abstract idea is most destructive of the spiritual life. It leads to the loss of his own identity and prevents him from accomplishing his first and most important mission of leading the faithful in his care to a knowledge, love and service of Christ as He is alive for us in the Church. Devotion to the Most Blessed Sacrament draws the priest into an ever deeper personal encounter with Christ Who, in turn, inspires in him a life defined by pastoral charity. At the same time, it prepares the priest to encounter Christ personally in his life, above all in the Eucharistic Sacrifice and through Eucharistic devotion, and to bring Him to others with pure and selfless love.

Blessed John Paul II, in his book, *Gift and Mystery*, underlined the essential relationship of the priest's Eucharistic devotion to the effective fulfilment of his mission. He wrote:

> If we take a close look at what contemporary men and women expect from priests, we will see that, in the end, they have but one great expectation: *they are thirsting for Christ*. Everything else – their economic, social, and political needs – can be met by any number of other people. From the priest they ask for Christ! And from him they have the right to receive Christ, above all through the proclamation of the word. As the Council teaches, priests 'have as their primary duty the proclamation of the Gospel of God to all' (*Presbyterorum ordinis*, 4). But this proclamation seeks to have man encounter Jesus, especially in the mystery of the Eucharist, the living heart of the Church and of priestly life. The priest has a mysterious, awesome power over the Eucharistic Body of Christ. By reason of this power he becomes the steward of the greatest treasure of the Redemption, for he gives people the Redeemer in person. Celebrating the Eucharist is the most sublime and most sacred function of every priest. As for me, from the very first years of my priesthood, the celebration of the Eucharist has been not only my most sacred duty, but above all my soul's deepest need.[4]

Through Eucharistic devotion, the priest safeguards the heart of his priestly ministry and cultivates the gift of divine love in the Most Blessed Sacrament for the sake of the sanctification of the faithful.

In his last Encyclical Letter *Ecclesia de Eucharistia*, Blessed John Paul II commented, with deep sorrow, on shadows which had entered into the Church's Eucharistic faith and love. The first of the shadows he noted was that '[i]n some places the practice of Eucharistic adoration has been almost completely abandoned'. The other shadows which he noted and which are connected with the abandonment of Eucharistic Adoration, are liturgical abuses, the 'reductive understanding of the Eucharistic mystery' which strips it 'of its sacrificial meaning', the obscuring or the loss of the understanding that 'the ministerial priesthood, grounded in apostolic succession', is necessary for the celebration of the Holy Eucharist, and false ecumenical initiatives involving the celebration of the Holy Eucharist. Regarding these shadows, he strikingly concluded: 'How can we not express profound grief at all this? The Eucharist is too great a gift to tolerate ambiguity and depreciation' (10).

---

[4]   Blessed John Paul II, *Gift and Mystery*, pp. 85–6.

Setting forth anew the faith of the Church regarding the Holy Eucharist, he announced the purpose of the Encyclical Letter: 'I wish once more to recall this truth and to join you, my dear brothers and sisters, in adoration before this mystery: a great mystery, a mystery of mercy. What more could Jesus have done for us? Truly, in the Eucharist, he shows us a love which goes 'to the end' (cf. *Jn* 13:1), a love which knows no measure' (11).

Blessed John Paul II had a twofold desire at the end of his service as Successor of St Peter: to set forth the truth regarding the Holy Eucharist and to bow down in Adoration before the great Mystery of Faith.

Eucharistic Devotion and Devotion to the Most Sacred Heart of Jesus

Devotion to the Sacred Heart of Jesus both flows from Eucharistic devotion and, at the same time, increases its fervour. Entering the minor seminary in 1962, I was introduced to the practice of renewing each year the Consecration to the Sacred Heart of Jesus, which was made by St Margaret Mary.[5] With the maturing of my priestly vocation, over the years of seminary formation and the years of my ministry as a priest and bishop, the Sacred Heart of Jesus has never ceased to attract me and to draw me into a deeper appreciation of the Sacraments, especially the Sacraments of the Holy Eucharist and Penance, and to a fuller identification of myself with the reality of the priestly vocation which St John Mary Vianney, the Curé of Ars, so simply and powerfully described with these words: 'The priesthood, it is the love of the Heart of Jesus'.[6] The devotion to the Sacred Heart of Jesus has kept before my eyes the great wonder of being called to the priesthood, especially when I have faced temptations to doubt the reality of the priestly vocation or to treat the reality carelessly.

To put it simply, the devotion to the Sacred Heart of Jesus has helped me to recognize my priestly vocation, to embrace the vocation to the priesthood, and to grow more solidly in my priestly identity. While other devotions, such as Eucharistic devotion and devotion to the Blessed Virgin Mary, are an essential part of the spiritual life of seminarians and priests, the devotion to the Sacred Heart of Jesus, in a certain way, draws the whole devotional and prayer life of

---

[5]   Cf. John Croiset, S.J., *Devotion to the Sacred Heart of Our Lord Jesus Christ*, 2nd edn, Patrick O'Connell (trans.), St. Paul, Minnesota: The Radio Replies Press Society, 1959, pp. 242–3.

[6]   'Le sacerdoce, c'est l'amour du Cœur de Jésus', A. Monnin, *Esprit du Curé d'Ars, Saint J.-B.-M. Vianney dans ses Catéchismes, ses Homélies et sa Conversation*, Paris: Téqui, 2007, p. 90.

seminarians and priests together in the cultivation of a union of heart with the Heart of Jesus, Head and Shepherd of the flock in every time and place through His ordained priests. The words of Pope Pius XI, regarding the devotion to the Most Sacred Heart of Jesus, have been verified in my life as both seminarian and priest:

> For is not the sum of all religion and therefore the pattern of more perfect life, contained in that most auspicious sign and in the form of piety that follows from it inasmuch as it more readily leads the minds of men to an intimate knowledge of Christ Our Lord, and more efficaciously moves their hearts to love Him more vehemently and to imitate Him more closely? (*Miserentissimus Redemptor*, 8 May 1928, 3)

The Sacred Heart of Jesus is the pre-eminent symbol of Christ's love of us in the Church, which has its highest and most perfect expression in the Most Blessed Sacrament.

Having loved us 'to the end' by dying for us on the Cross, Christ permitted His heart to be pierced, giving us an unmistakable sign of His unfailing love poured out upon us in the Church from His glorious pierced Heart (Jn 13.1; cf. Jn 19.34). The Holy Eucharist, it is clear, is the greatest gift given to us from the Heart of Jesus. Holy Mass and, above all, Holy Communion are the most privileged and most perfect meeting with Christ, mysteriously and really present for us in the Church. We experience directly the love from the Heart of Jesus in priests, especially when they are offering the Holy Mass.

The devotion to the Sacred Heart of Jesus helps the seminarian or priest to keep focusing on the essence of his life in the Church, namely knowing and loving Christ, and giving himself to Him totally. For that reason, the devotion to the Sacred Heart assists very much the discernment of the call of Christ to follow Him as a true shepherd of the flock. It keeps the seminarian focused on the essential place of the Sacraments of the Holy Eucharist and Penance in his daily life, so that Christ can really speak to his heart and draw him to the Holy Priesthood. Devotion to the Sacred Heart of Jesus leads a young man to the most powerful helps in knowing the vocation to the priesthood and in finding the courage to embrace the vocation, namely, participation in the Holy Mass and prayer before the Most Blessed Sacrament, and frequent access to the Sacrament of Penance.

Devotion to the Sacred Heart of Jesus helps a seminarian or priest, in a particular way, to avoid the temptation to envision the priestly life as a job, a function or a profession in the Church, and instead to see the priesthood as his identity, the identity of Christ the Shepherd, of a man transformed by the mystery of Holy Orders to be truly the love of the Sacred Heart of Jesus for all His brothers and sisters, especially those in most need. In the Sacred Heart of Jesus, the seminarian or priest comes to understand that priestly ordination changes his life completely, that priestly ordination consecrates every fibre of his being to Christ the High Priest for the sake of His pastoral charity, of His boundless and ceaseless care of the Father's flock.

Devotion to the Sacred Heart of Jesus helps him never to lose sight of the pre-eminent place which prayer and the Sacraments must have in his life as a priest. Entering into the mystery of the Heart of Jesus, first of all, uncovers the greatest gifts which flow unceasingly from His glorious pierced Heart, above all the gift of His Body, Blood, Soul and Divinity in the Holy Eucharist. The Sacred Heart of Jesus points to the unfathomable mystery of the personal encounter with Him in the Sacraments and, above all, in the Sacraments of Penance and of the Holy Eucharist. Devotion to the Sacred Heart of Jesus keeps liturgical piety correctly focused on the mystery of the meeting of Heaven and earth which takes place at every celebration of the Sacred Liturgy. The devotion to the Sacred Heart also confirms the importance of the daily Holy Hour, the treasured time spent simply before the Eucharistic presence of Christ, during which the seminarian or priest gives his heart again and completely to the Heart of Jesus.

Conclusion

It is my hope that these few reflections on the essential relationship of the Mystery of Faith, the Eucharistic Mystery, to the ordained priesthood, as I have experienced the relationship in my own priestly life, are helpful to understanding the fundamental and critical importance of Adoration of the Most Blessed Sacrament in the formation and life of seminarians and priests. In a particular way, I hope that the heroic teaching and example of St Thomas Aquinas, St John Mary Vianney and Blessed John Paul II, and the magisterium of our Holy Father, Pope Benedict XVI, have opened up the beauty and power of the relationship of the priestly vocation to its fundamental reason for existence, namely, the daily celebration of the Eucharistic Sacrifice for the salvation of the world.

As we strive to deepen our understanding of the great gift of Eucharistic Adoration for our life in Christ and, in particular, for the life of those called to follow Christ in the ordained priesthood, let us call upon the intercession of the Blessed Virgin Mary, the first and best of the disciples of Our Lord and our model of Eucharistic faith and practice. The Blessed Virgin Mary, in her maternal love, draws us to her Immaculate Heart, so that she might lead us to the Heart of her Son, as she led the wine stewards at the Wedding Feast of Cana to Jesus with the clear and firm instruction: 'Do whatever he tells you'

(Jn 2.5). In a particular way, she draws those called to the priesthood to join her, with St John the Apostle, at the foot of the Cross, and to lift up their hearts, with her Immaculate Heart, to the pierced Heart of Jesus, ever open to receive us, to heal us and strengthen us, through His Eucharistic Sacrifice.

I close with the exhortation of St John Eudes to priests, regarding the place of Eucharistic devotion among their many duties:

> Have a most profound devotion to the Blessed Sacrament, for it is the unspeakable treasure of the priest, who should have in his own heart a burning zeal towards so holy a possession. It should be his one and constant desire to honour the Blessed Sacrament and to make it honoured by others and to see that the abiding place of the Lord is clean, honourable and edifying. The priest should be unfailing in his efforts to teach the faithful to act reverently in the presence of Christ in the Tabernacle; he should spare no pains to encourage them to assist frequently and devoutly at Holy Mass.[7]

---

7   St John Eudes, *The Priest: His Dignity and Obligations*, W. Leo Murphy (trans.), New York: P.J. Kenedy & Sons, 1947, p. 23.

Twelve

Addressing Objections to Adoration

Malcolm Cardinal Ranjith
Archbishop of Colombo, Sri Lanka

> *When we are before the Blessed Sacrament, instead of looking about, let us shut our eyes and our mouth; let us open our heart; our Good God will open His; we shall go to Him. He will come to us, the one to ask, the other to receive; it will be like a breath from one to the other.*[1]

These were the words with which the Curé of Ars, St John Mary Vianney wished to explain what Adoration was all about. Adoration is someone's presence before the Almighty God in an attitude of silent, yet powerful expression of faith: 'Speak Lord, Thy servant is listening' (1 Sam. 3.10). It is truly unexplainable in human terms. Pope Benedict XVI explained the meaning of the expression Adoration as a *Proskynesis* – a 'gesture of submission, the acknowledgement of God as our true measure, the norm which we accept to follow', and as *'ad-oratio'* 'the mouth to mouth contact, the kiss, an embrace which is implicit in the idea of Love' (Homily, 21 August 2005). It is this process of presence before God which transforms us. St Paul speaking of those who turn to the Lord in the way Moses did states 'when we shall turn to the Lord the veil shall be taken away . . . we all with open face beholding as in a glass the glory of God are transfigured (*meta morfoumetha*) into the same image from glory to glory' (2 Cor. 3.16, 18). It is interesting to note that the verb used here is the same which explains the transfiguration of Christ on Mount Thabor (*metemorfothè*).

The presence before God of the adorer transforms him. This is beautifully mentioned in the book of Exodus which states:

---

[1] St John Mary Vianney, *The Little Catechism of the Curé of Ars*, Rockford, IL: Tan, 1951, p. 42.

when Moses came down from Mount Sinai, with the two slabs of the statement in his hands he was not aware that the skin on his face was radiant after speaking with The Lord. Aaron and all the sons of Israel saw that Moses' face was radiant and they were afraid to go near him. (Exod. 34.29–30)

It is like the case of someone who gazes at a sunset; after a while his face too takes on a golden glow. Explaining this experience the Servant of God Fulton Sheen remarks that when we look at the Eucharist in an attitude of Adoration, of profound reverence and love: something happens to us similar to that which happened to the disciples at Emmaus. On Easter Sunday afternoon when the Lord met them, He asked why they were so gloomy. After spending some time in His presence and hearing again the secret of spirituality – 'the Son of Man must suffer to enter into His glory' – their time with Him ended and their 'hearts were on fire'.[2]

Eucharistic Adoration, then, is a profoundly personal and to that extent also communitarian encounter with the Lord. Its inborn attitude of reverence is not motivated by any sense of submissiveness but by an attitude of profound faith and the yearning for a dialogue or rather attitude of presence and listening between the 'I' and the great 'Thou' – this search for communion.

It is like Moses looking at the burning bush. The bush itself continues to burn but is not destroyed. Our presence before the Eucharistic Lord does not diminish His glory but speaks to us and we dialogue with Him. In fact we are transformed in the process. He does not change but we do. Yet, along the history of the Church, this great belief in the Presence of Jesus in person in the Most Holy Eucharist, has not been without its detractors, especially those that objected to the ecclesial practice of Eucharistic Adoration.

Objections to Adoration

The earliest objections to Eucharistic Adoration arose in the context of a contestation that Christ was really and physically not present in the consecrated species of the bread and wine. It was Berengarius (999–1088), the Archdeacon of Angers in France, who surprisingly advocated this position in the Middle Ages. Ipso facto, Eucharistic Adoration would have been rendered redundant by such a position. Yet, Pope St Gregory VII, the then reigning head of the Church, ordered Berengarius to sign a retraction on the basis of the constant

---

[2]   Fulton Sheen, *A Treasure in Clay: Autobiography of Fulton J. Sheen*, San Francisco: Ignatius Press, 1993, p. 189.

faith of the Church, which document became the first definitive pronouncement of the Eucharistic faith of the Church. It stated:

> I believe in my heart and openly profess that the bread and wine that are placed on the altar are, through the mystery of the sacred prayer and the words of the Redeemer, substantially changed into the true and proper and life-giving Flesh and Blood of Jesus Christ, our Lord, and that after the consecration they are the true Body of Christ which was born of the Virgin and which hung on the Cross as an offering for the salvation of the world – and the true Blood of Christ – which flowed from His side – and not just as a sign and by reason of the power of the Sacrament but in the very truth and reality of their substance and in what is proper to their nature.[3]

Along with this conviction of faith the Church gave weight to a true intensification of Eucharistic worship in the form of Eucharistic processions, of acts of Adoration, visits to Christ in the Pyx, etc. These traditions became expressions of that faith. Later on other significant moves such as the institution of the feast of Corpus Christi by Pope Urban IV were made. Eucharistic miracles gave further impetus to that. All of this was based on that ever intensifying faith of the Church that the consecrated species of Bread and Wine are really and integrally the Body and Blood of Christ, faith held firmly by the Apostles and confessed all along as a core doctrine by the Church. Indeed it is what the Lord Himself had stated and had wanted the Church to follow. 'This is my Body, this is my Blood' (cf. Lk. 22.19–20) and 'do this in memory of me' (Lk. 22.19) were those determining words of the Lord which Paul too speaks about when discussing the Eucharist (1 Cor. 4.23–27).

This Eucharistic faith of the Church became definitively defined and affirmed by the Council of Trent in the background of the Lutheran revolution. It affirmed that 'In the Blessed Sacrament of the Holy Eucharist, after the consecration of the bread and wine, our Lord Jesus Christ, true God and true man, is truly, really and substantially contained under the perceptible species of bread and wine' (canon 719), and again

> Because Christ our Redeemer said that it was truly His Body that He was offering under the species of bread (Mt. 26.26ff; Mk 14:22ff; Lk. 29.19ff and 1 Cor. 12.24ff) it has always been

---

3   Giovan Domenico Mansi. *Sacrorum conciliorum nova, et amplissima collectio.* Florence, 1759, XX 524D.

the conviction of the Church, and this holy council now again declares that, by the consecration of the bread and wine a change takes place in which the whole substance of the bread is changed into the substance of the Body of Christ our Lord and the whole substance of the wine into the substance of His Blood. This change the holy Catholic Church fittingly and properly names transubstantiation. (canon 722)

Besides, it refuted the error being propagated especially by the protestant reform which declared that transubstantiation was untrue. Zwingli preferred to interpret the words consecration in the sense of a transignification: Not 'this is my Body' but 'this is like my Body'. He argues that it cannot be 'is' for if it is so we should be literally eating flesh and the Lord would be torn apart by our teeth. And since this actually does not happen, transubstantiation cannot be true.[4] The Council thus decreed that:

> If anyone denies that the Body and Blood, together with the soul and divinity of our Lord Jesus Christ and therefore the whole Christ is truly, really and substantially contained in the sacrament of the most Holy Eucharist, but says that Christ is present in the Sacrament only as a sign or figure or by His power: let him be anathema. (canon 728)

The Church thus steadfastly held to the truth that the consecrated bread and wine is in its very substance truly and integrally the Body and Blood of Christ. This faith was re-affirmed over and over again by the Councils that followed and by the Supreme Pontiffs. In *Mediator Dei*, Venerable Pius XII reaffirmed this faith when he stated that 'By transubstantiation of bread into the Body of Christ and of the wine into His Blood, His Body and Blood are really present' in the Church (70). The same has been re-affirmed by Pope Paul VI (*Mysterium fidei*, 46); Blessed John Paul II (*Ecclesia de Eucharistia*, 15) and Pope Benedict XVI (*Sacramentum caritatis*, 10, 11, 66).

In fact the Servant of God Paul VI was gravely concerned about a certain trend in the Church in the aftermath of the Council to dilute the substance of its Eucharistic faith especially on transubstantiation and the permanent presence. The Pope stated . . . 'We can see that some . . . are disseminating opinions on Masses celebrated in private or on the dogma of transubstantiation that are disturbing the minds of the faithful and causing them no small measure of confusion'

---

[4]   Cf. Huldreich Zwingli, *On the Lords' Supper* (1526) in: *Corpus Reformatorum*, *Huldreich Zwingli Sämtliche Werke*, vol. 91, Leipzig: Heinsius, 1927, 796–800.

(*Mysterium fidei*, 10). The Pope proceeds 'we cannot approve the opinions that they set forth, and we have an obligation to warn you about the grave danger that their opinions involve for true faith' (14). The Pope, during whose lifetime the Second Vatican Council deliberated for the longest period, affirmed:

> For the constant teachings that the Catholic Church has passed on to her catechumens, the understanding of the Christian people, the doctrine defined by the Council of Trent, the very words that Christ used when He instituted the Most Holy Eucharist, all require us to profess that 'the Eucharist is the flesh of our Saviour Jesus Christ which suffered for our sins and which the Father in His loving kindness raised again' (St Ignatius of Antioch, *Epistle to the Smyrnians*, 7.1; PG 5, 714). To these words of St Ignatius, we may well add those of Theodore of Mopsuestia, who as a true witness to the faith of the Church on this matter addressed the people saying: 'The Lord did not say: This is a symbol of my Body and this a symbol of my Blood, rather: This is my Body and my Blood. He teaches us not to look to the nature of what lies before us and is perceived by the senses, because the giving thanks and the words spoken over it have changed it into flesh and blood'. (*Mysterium fidei*, 44)

Indeed Pope Paul VI's entire encyclical is a solid defence of the true faith of the Church on the Most Holy Eucharist. In his solemn profession of faith dated 30 June 1968, Paul VI held that:

> Every theological explanation which seeks some understanding of this mystery, in order to be in accord with the Catholic faith, must firmly maintain that in objective reality, independently of our mind, the bread and wine have ceased to exist after the consecration, so that the adorable Body and Blood of the Lord Jesus from that moment on are really before us under the sacramental species of bread and wine. (25)

The Pope thus urged the bishops 'To preserve [this faith] in its purity and integrity among the people . . . with all false and pernicious opinions being completely rejected' and 'to foster devotion to the Eucharist, which should be the focal point and goal of all other forms of devotion' (*Mysterium fidei*, 64).

It is then clear that the objections to Eucharistic Adoration based on a contestation or misinterpretation of the ecclesial faith and doctrine on the Eucharist stands disapproved and firmly rejected.

In *Sacramentum caritatis* Pope Benedict XVI mentions an opinion spreading during 'the early phases' of the Conciliar liturgical reform which did not perceive with sufficient clarity 'the inherent relationship between the Mass and Adoration of the Blessed Sacrament'. The Pope states that 'for example, an objection that was widespread at the time argued that the Eucharistic bread was given to us not to be looked at, but to be eaten' (66). This situation possibly arose due to some influence of protestant theology, since vestiges of this error reflect what happened during the protestant reformation. Most of the reformers disputed the Tridentine doctrine of the continuous and transubstantiated presence of Christ in the consecrated bread and wine reducing it to a mere symbolic one and they also argued that the Eucharist was just a community meal and not a sacrifice renewed and hence was not for Adoration. Though Luther, Zwingli, Melanchthon and John Calvin had their own specific outlooks, sometimes even contradictory, by and large they interpreted the Eucharist in opposition to the Catholic theology of the time. Luther's view was that the real presence was limited to the reception of Holy Communion (*in usu, non extra*). In fact the Lutherans believe in the real presence only between the consecration and the Holy Communion. This position however was firmly condemned by the Council of Trent which decreed that 'If anyone says that after the consecration, the Body and Blood of our Lord Jesus Christ are not present in the marvellous Sacrament of the Eucharist, but are present only in the use of the Sacrament while it is being received and not before or after, and that the true Body of the Lord does not remain in the consecrated hosts or particles that are kept or are leftovers after communion: let him be anathema' (canon 731). For the Catholic Church then the presence of Christ in the consecrated species of the Eucharist is not limited to the moment of reception only but continues. In other words it is not there only for the 'eating' but also for Adoration.

Pope Benedict XVI stresses this fact when he states 'Receiving the Eucharist means adoring Him Whom we receive' (*Sacramentum caritatis,* 66). As a matter of fact the Eucharist is not just merely the joyful anticipation of the heavenly banquet at the *parousia,* but is also the Sacrifice on Calvary and its memorial. It is not just a feast for our hunger but for our eyes too, for, we gaze in wonder at this self-offering of love for our salvation. Luther does not look at it that way. For him there is no ontological link between what happened on Calvary and what happens on the altar and hence Lutheran Theology does not give adequate weight to the sacrificial aspect of the Holy Mass. It places greater accent on the communion meal aspect. Perhaps that was the reason why he did not give much importance to the Theology of the priesthood especially its sacrificial dimension as explained in the letter to the Hebrews. But for Catholic theology, each time the Eucharist is celebrated the sacrifice of Christ on Calvary is renewed and as Venerable Pius XII stated:

> The august sacrifice of the altar, then, is no mere empty commemoration of the passion and death of Jesus Christ, but a true and proper act of sacrifice, whereby the High Priest by an unbloody immolation, offers Himself a most acceptable victim to the eternal Father, as He did upon the Cross (*Mediator Dei*, 68).

At the Eucharist, our eyes are raised in deep faith, humble honour and Adoration before the august person of Jesus on the Cross. In fact St John's Gospel (19.37) presents the crucifixion as the fulfilment of the prophecy of Zachariah: 'They shall look upon him whom they have pierced' (Zech. 12.10). It is this sacrifice at which the centurion gazed and experienced faith when he recognized the Saviour in Jesus 'truly this man was the Son of God' (Mk 15.39).

The Eucharist by the strength of what it re-enacts – that powerful and most radical expression of God's love in the self-offering of Jesus, the Son of God, calls upon us to direct our gaze upon Him and to proclaim our faith in Him. This is the basis for the faith of St Augustine who so clearly announces that we would sin if we do not adore Him before we receive Him. This wondrous sacrifice of Christ;this breaking of self becoming our heavenly food need to be seen with wondrous awe and deep faith. Indeed Jesus predicted the need for us to look up to Him recognizing His divinity on the Cross, at the moment of His salvific death: 'When you have lifted up the Son of man, then you will know that I am He' (Jn 8.28). It is the same verb that is being used by the Lord to explain 'lifting up' here and the 'lifting up' of the bronze serpent by Moses in the wilderness to save the people of Israel referred to in Jn 3:14. And interestingly on both occasions Jesus refers to recognition of His person in faith ('that whosoever believeth in Him' Jn 3.15) and ('that you may know, I am He' Jn 8.28). It is looking at Christ's sacrifice that one's faith in Him is confirmed and one is saved. At each Eucharist where Christ's unique sacrifice on Calvary is re-enacted, faith is born and we adore Him as the Son of God. There lies a foretaste of our salvation – a foretaste of paradise. Hence, Eucharist without that adoring gaze on Christ would be poorer. It is this that constitutes true Adoration. If that is not assured, whereby our hearts are lifted up to the wonder of salvation on the Cross, the Eucharist itself would turn out to be yet another formality, a noisy brawl and an empty faithless and tasteless experience. This tendency therefore to make it modern and colourful is, to say the least, of poor taste. Unless we adore Him Whom we receive we would not even know who it is that comes to us and makes us His own. That kind of reception of the Eucharist will become meaningless. The Pope stresses this when he says: 'Only in Adoration can a profound and genuine reception mature' (*Sacramentum caritatis*, 66).

In this sense ensuring the devout and contemplated celebration of the Eucharist would become no more a matter of choice but of necessity. It is here that I would personally prefer the prayerful and devout atmosphere visible in the older (Tridentine) form of the Mass where participation of the assembly is more subdued, sedate and recollected. It is respectful of the great mystery that happens on the altar. Perhaps it is time to think of classifying what active participation truly means. Pope Benedict XVI dedicated an entire chapter to this in *Sacramentum caritatis*:

> It should be made clear that the word 'participation' does not refer to mere external activity during the celebration. In fact, the active participation called for by the Council must be understood in more substantial terms, on the basis of a greater awareness of the mystery being celebrated and its relationship to daily life. (52)

That is Adoration. And so considering all these factors one could state that the Eucharist is not just merely for eating but also for Adoration.

Another objection that was heard quite extensively in certain quarters was that Adoration was not congruous with the spirit of the celebration of the Eucharist or that it was just a pietistic activity with no link to the most Holy Eucharist. This position which the Church condemned earlier, at Trent, seemed to re-emerge rather forcefully in the aftermath of the Vatican II liturgical reforms, especially in the background of a reduction of the Eucharistic celebration to a mere banquet meal of fellowship, and at the cost of its sacrificial dimension. Indeed there was a time when such practices as Benediction of the Blessed Sacrament, Holy Hours and Perpetual Adoration were looked down upon as being contrary to the spirit of the Council. The Council of Trent denounced those who reject the centuries-long tradition of Eucharistic worship or devotion:

> If anyone says that Christ, the only begotten Son of God, is not to be adored in the Holy Sacrament of the Eucharist with the worship of latria, including the external worship and that the Sacrament, therefore, is not to be honoured with extraordinary festive celebrations nor solemnly carried from place to place in procession according to the praiseworthy universal rite and custom of the holy Church, or that the Sacrament is not to be

publicly exposed for the peoples' Adoration, and that those
who adore it are idolaters: let him be anathema. (canon 734)

This canon is congruous with the relative teaching of that same
Council that:

> The custom of reserving the Holy Eucharist in a sacred place is
> so ancient that it was recognized already in the Century of the
> Council of Nicea. That the Holy Eucharist should be taken to the
> sick and that it should be carefully kept in the Churches for this
> purpose is right and very reasonable. Moreover, many Councils
> prescribe this and it is a long standing custom in the Catholic
> Church. Consequently, this holy Council decrees that this most
> salutary and necessary custom be retained. (canon 724)

In this regard, it must be asserted that the practice of reserving the
Blessed Sacrament in order to take it to the sick or to the hermits
is truly an ancient one. It was a natural corollary of the Church's
ancient belief in the continuous and personal presence of Christ
in the consecrated species of the Eucharist. It is this belief that led
the Church to gradually introduce formal worship of the Eucharist
outside the Mass and led to such devotional practices as processions, acts of Adoration, visits to Christ in the pyx, windows from
the cells of monks by which they could view and adore Christ in the
tabernacle and then eventually to the festive celebration of *Corpus
Domini*, the Holy Hour, Perpetual Adoration, visits to the Blessed
Sacrament, Benediction of the Blessed Sacrament, confraternities
of adorers and Eucharistic Congresses. It has been a process of
continuous development. The important consideration was that
since Christ is present in the Eucharistic species not only during
the celebration of the Holy Mass but also afterwards, He needs to
be adored and glorified. The Eucharistic species once consecrated
remained divine and hence adorable – the visible presence of Christ
among us. This practice, of course, was ridiculed by the reformers and called idolatry. John Calvin, for example, who did not
consider the consecrated bread and wine to be the very Body and
Blood of Christ but only its sign or symbol, considered Eucharistic
Adoration as practiced in the Catholic Church as idolatry. Their use
of the sacred species was thus restricted to the rite of communion
only and the remainder was discarded. The same position more or
less was upheld by Luther, Zwingli and Melanchthon. The Catholic
Church is clear on this, for its Eucharistic devotions are but a natural consequence of our faith in the continuous and unchangeable
presence of Christ in the Eucharistic species.

It is in this light that the bi-millennial tradition and faith of the Church has to be understood – The Eucharist is there for Adoration as much as for communion. Pope Paul VI said so:

> The Catholic Church has always and still displays this latria that ought to be paid to the Sacrament of the Eucharist, both during Mass and outside of it, by taking the greatest possible care of the consecrated hosts, by exposing them for the solemn veneration of the faithful and by carrying them about in procession to the joy of great numbers of the people. (*Mysterium fidei*, 56)

There are some who unfortunately claim that the Second Vatican Council did not give such importance to Eucharistic devotions and so it need not receive so much of attention. Indeed this may be a correct analysis as the Constitution on the Sacred Liturgy, *Sacrosanctum concilium,* which in its general presentation as well as in its treatment of the most Holy Eucharist (ch. 2) and of the other sacraments and sacramentals did not make any mention of devotions to the Most Blessed Sacrament. It does mention popular devotions in a brief passage (13), but no is made mention of Eucharistic devotions. This is in stark contrast with the treatment on this subject in the decrees of the Council of Trent and the encyclical letter *Mediator Dei* of Venerable Pius XII. Whether that was a deliberate omission or an accidental one is a question that has to be answered. Most likely, those devotions were taken for granted as a given fact and not treated explicitly. Yet, at least some mention should have been made, given the importance of the Council's pronouncements for the future and the importance which had been given to these devotions all along the centuries before that event. This omission probably was also a reason for the above mentioned claim that the Eucharist is not for adoring but for eating and that the Council did not give much importance to that aspect of liturgical worship. This, too, may have prompted Pope Paul the VI's lament in *Mysterium fidei* that:

> There are . . . a number of reasons for serious pastoral concern and anxiety in this very matter that we are now discussing and because of our consciousness of our Apostolic office, we cannot remain silent about them. For we can see that some of those who are dealing with this Most Holy Mystery in speech and writing are disseminating opinions on Masses celebrated in private or on the dogma of transubstantiation that are distorting the minds of the faithful and causing them no small measure of confusion about such matters of faith. (9–10)

The Pope then goes on to explain what he means by 'opinions' and among them outlines a notion being spread around that 'Christ our Lord is no longer present in the consecrated Hosts that remain after the celebration of the Sacrifice of the Mass had been completed' (11). This last error mentioned shows a whittling down of the role of the Eucharistic faith of the Church and of its practice of Adoration. The Pope goes on to affirm the value of the Eucharistic Adoration at length in this encyclical. 'The Catholic Church' states the Pope 'has always displayed and still displays this latria that ought to be paid to the Sacrament of the Eucharist, both during Mass and outside of it. By taking the greatest possible care of consecrated Hosts, by exposing them to solemn veneration of the faithful and by carrying them about in procession to the joy of a great number of the people' (56). He then explains in great detail and with evidence from the Fathers various elements of Eucharistic devotion (56–65), and the need to preserve them. He exhorts the bishops to:

> take this faith which means nothing less than maintaining complete fidelity to the words of Christ and the Apostles, and preserve it in its purity and integrity among the people entrusted to your care and vigilance, with all false and pernicious opinions being completely rejected; and we beseech you to foster devotion to the Eucharist, which should be the focal point and goal of all other forms of devotion. (64)

And so, in the light of a quasi total absence of a mention of Eucharistic Adoration and devotion in the Conciliar Constitution on the Sacred Liturgy *Sacrosanctum concilium,* and a tendency which sought to down play or reject such faith raising its head in some quarters, this encyclical letter of Pope Paul VI published even before the formal conclusion of the council (8 December 1965), can be considered a suitable reply to these protestantizing elements within the Church and a due correction of course for which we should be grateful to Pope Paul VI.

With regards to the opinion that there is no continuity between the celebration of the Holy Eucharist and the relative devotions the answer is proved by *Mysterium fidei* itself which states: 'The Catholic Church has always displayed and still displays this latria that ought to be paid to the Sacrament of the Eucharist both during the Mass and outside of it' (56). Indeed Blessed John Paul II explained the ontological nexus between the celebration–reception and Adoration moments of the Eucharist by stating that the Eucharist 'is at one and the same time a sacrifice-sacrament, a communion-sacrament and a presence-sacrament' (*Redemptor hominis,* 20). They are all linked

together. It is not possible to separate them. Indeed one cannot celebrate the Eucharist without being aware of the grandiosity of what
happens at the altar and assuming an attitude of awe and veneration
towards the Lord Who gives Himself up daily for our salvation on
our altars. What really takes place at the celebration of the Eucharist
is that the priest celebrant, totally identified with the Supreme High
Priest, Christ, whose celebration of the paschal feast in the heavenly
Jerusalem, surrounded by the Choirs of angels continues without an
end, becomes the *altar Christus* and makes that feast of our redemption happen on our altars too. The invisible heavenly sacrifice of love,
of the 'lamb that was slain', comes down, in visible form, on to our
altars – the heavenly becomes earthly. Pope Benedict XVI explains
this as *veritatis splendor*:

> Jesus Christ shows us how the truth of love can transform
> even the dark mystery of death into the radiant light of the
> Resurrection. Hence the splendour of God's glory surpasses
> all worldly beauty. The truest beauty is the love of God who
> definitively revealed Himself to us in the paschal mystery.
> (*Sacramentum caritatis*, 35)

This cannot but fill us with awe and a spirit of adoring veneration.

The reception of communion too requires faith in the grandiosity
of what is about to happen – the Lord comes to me or rather coming
to me, He embraces me and wishes to transform me into His very
being. It is not just a mechanical act of reception of a piece of bread –
something done in an instant. It is this invitation to be in communion
with the Lord: invitation to love. The Pope explains Adoration in
these very same terms:

> The Greek word [for Adoration] is *proskynesis*. It refers to the ges-
> ture of submission, the recognition of God as our true measure,
> supplying the norm we choose to follow . . . The Latin word for
> Adoration is *ad-oratio* – mouth to mouth contact, a kiss, an embrace
> and hence ultimately love. In this way submission acquires a
> meaning, because it does not impose anything on us from outside
> but liberates us deep within. (Sermon, 21 August 2005)

Adoration then is submission for love and intimacy with the Lord.
Hence, the act of receiving the Lord, where we experience His love at
its highest point – inviting us to be with Him, cannot but take place
in an atmosphere of Adoration. So too the very self immolation of
Christ at the consecration of the bread and wine which is the high
point of His sacrifice out of love for us, cannot but be a moment that

calls for Adoration. Thus we can say that neither in its celebration nor in its reception can the Eucharist be detached from the call to Adoration. Cardinal Ratzinger wrote:

> Communion and Adoration do not stand side by side or even in opposition but are indivisibly on . . . Love or friendship always carries within it an impulse of reverence, of Adoration. Communicating with Christ therefore demands that we gaze on Him, allow Him to gaze on us, listen to Him, get to know Him.[5]

It is in this light that we ought to also understand the famous dictum of St Augustine: '*Nemo autem illam Carmen manducat, nisi prius adoraverit, peccemus non adorando*' – or: 'No one eats that flesh without first adoring it; we should sin were we not to adore it'.[6] Indeed only Adoration opens our hearts towards a true sense of participation in the Eucharist, for, it enlarges them to experience the profound love of God manifested in the Eucharist and towards a true and deeply personal union with Christ at the reception of communion. ('Behold, I stand at the door and knock; if any man hears my voice and opens the door, I will come into him and will dine with Him and he with Me'. Rev. 3.20.)

In this sense the words of the Pope are clear; 'receiving the Eucharist means adoring Him Whom we receive. Only in this way do we become one with Him and are given, as it were, a foretaste of the beauty of the heavenly liturgy' (*Sacramentum caritatis*, 66). Thus it is Adoration which would render the celebration of the Holy Eucharist and the reception of the Most Holy Body and Blood of Christ meaningful and profoundly transforming. Otherwise it would end in a purely mechanical exercise or a social cacophony; an event of man and not of God, for, Adoration renders the Eucharist an experience of salvific divine grace and of eternity. Besides, Adoration then would find a natural outflow into all the other Eucharistic devotions and give meaning and depth to them. The Eucharist is the supreme moment of Adoration, and its outflow, all the devotions connected to it. The one would give meaning and depth to the other. It is sad to note how in some places the Churches and sanctuaries have been turned into market places or theatres and concert houses. I once walked into a Cathedral Church in a prominent city in Europe and found some people waiting to celebrate a wedding Mass and it was like a big

---

[5] Joseph Cardinal Ratzinger, *God is Near Us*, San Francisco: Ignatius Press, 2003, p. 97.
[6] St Augustine, *Enarrationes in Psalmos*, 98:9, CCL XXXIX, 1385.

market place – everybody was engaged in animated conversation. There certainly was no spirit of recollection or any sense of adoring reverence in preparation for the Eucharist. Then there was this Eucharist in a parish church in Germany, at which I was told, they enacted a theatre drama with a lot of assembly participation by way of prayers and sketches with the parish priest as the compere. When I asked my friend who told me about this how he felt about it, he replied with the words 'much ado about nothing'. We ought to ask ourselves whether we are serious about the Catholic faith on transubstantiation and the continuous presence of Christ in the Eucharist and whether all of that faith has not been whittled away in the name of meaningless theories and pedantic theologizing which all the time seeks compromises with secularism and atheism. In conclusion, I must stress that the Eucharist which is not adored is a contradiction *in se* and Adoration without the Eucharist is a non-starter, because Eucharist and Adoration are like the two faces of the same reality.

Some complain that Eucharistic Adoration is too private, too personal and even too quiet. This seems to be based on erroneous contentions: that Adoration is only private in nature and that the worship of God has to always be a communitarian exercise. Both these positions are untenable. Adoration has a communitarian dimension too. For, when we adore the Lord, which means we enter into communion with Him or let Him absorb us unto His own being, we become united to others in Him. Pope Benedict XVI says: 'Union with Christ is also union with all those to Whom He gives Himself. I cannot possess Christ just for myself; I can belong to Him only in union with all those who have become or who will become, His own' (*Deus caritas est*, 14). Thus even when I adore the Lord in private I am being constantly placed in relationship with others and they too adore Him in me. Communion is thereby created. Private prayer does not necessarily take one away from the community. It builds community. Besides, each time the Church engages in public worship and in acts of Adoration it is the entire body of believers who pray and that includes the Church in its individual members too. Jesus too adored the Father in private as well as in public prayer, like those in the temple and those in the synagogue. Thus every act of Adoration, private or communitarian, has a salubrious effect on the community as well as the individual.

Besides, worship need not necessarily be communitarian only. It can very well be personal. As we mentioned above, Jesus too spent a lot of time by Himself in prayer. But that did not prevent Him from coming closer to the others. Indeed He was the one who gave up His life for the redemption of others; altruism at the highest level. Thus Adoration does not and need not take us away from communitarian prayer or from our communitarian obligations. It binds us even closer with one another in the Lord.

There are still others who object to Eucharistic Adoration saying that there is far too much of a 'Jesus and I' mentality behind it. One reason this is erroneous, as mentioned above, is that Adoration by bringing us closer to Jesus makes us more sensitive towards the others. And this comes out best in the lives of some of the greatest saints or saintly figures. I need only to mention the example of Blessed Teresa of Calcutta who insisted on several hours of prayer and Adoration before the Blessed Sacrament for her sisters each day before their visits to the streets to look for the sick and the dying. It was this feeling of the Lord's presence in their midst that energized them in their daily work. Facing criticism about the Sisters spending several hours of their valuable time in prayer and Adoration, Blessed Teresa once remarked 'If my Sisters did not spend so much time in prayer, they could not serve the sick and the poor at all'. Indeed as Pope Benedict XVI tells us, Adoration 'seeks to break down not only the walls that separate the Lord and ourselves but also and especially the walls that separate us from one another' (*Sacramentum caritatis*, 66). In *Deus caritas est* he states:

> Piety does not undermine the struggle against the poverty of our neighbours, however extreme. In the example of Blessed Teresa of Calcutta, we have a clear illustration of the fact that time devoted to God in prayer not only does not detract from effective and loving service to our neighbour but is in fact the inexhaustible source of that service. (36)

Personal prayer is not against community prayer. One is not exclusive of the other either. They really feed one another. Liturgical prayer creates and enhances the relationship not only between God and the community but also between God and me, and makes me sensitive to that need to be in constant touch with the divine in my life. Maybe a misunderstanding of this has led some to believe that individual devotions are not needed any more because of the post-Vatican II accent on liturgical and communitarian worship. That is not correct. *Sacrosantum concilium* says: 'The spiritual life, however, is not limited solely to participation in the Liturgy. The Christian is indeed called to pray with his brethren, but he must also enter into his chamber to pray to the Father in secret' (12). Thus liturgical prayer is strengthened and enriched through personal prayer. Adoration of the Most Blessed Sacrament as a personal devotion is then important and helps create an inner atmosphere in us which feeds into liturgical prayer and inner participation.

Let me conclude with the following beautiful words of the Curé of Ars, St John Mary Vianney, a true Apostle of Adoration:

> Ah! If we had the eyes of angels with which to see our Lord Jesus Christ, who is here present on this altar, and who is looking at us, how we should love Him! We should never more wish to part from Him. We should wish to remain always at His feet; it would be a foretaste of heaven: all else would become insipid to us.[7]

---

[7]   St John Marie-Baptist Vianney, *The Little Catechism of the Curé of Ars*, Rockford, IL: Tan, 2009, p. 41.

Thirteen

Adoration as the Foundation of Social Justice

Peter Cardinal Turkson
President, Pontifical Council for Justice and Peace, Vatican City

Introduction
In the mid-eighties, I served Catholic students and lecturers at the University of Cape Coast, Ghana, as their Chaplain. One afternoon, a Catholic student came to see me, very upset about an evangelical flier he had in his hand. In the anti-catholic tract, an American evangelical pastor denounced Catholics and their Church for worshipping a 'wafer-god' which was the Eucharist or Blessed Sacrament.[1] It is obvious where the flier was coming from, namely a recall of Eucharistic theology of the Protestant Reformation which, opposing Catholic teaching on transubstantiation, claimed that the elements of the Eucharist remain bread and wine which communicates the presence of the Lord because of the recipient's faith or which at best, according to Luther, mediate the Lord's presence through a 'consubstantiation'.

Catholic Doctrine of the Real Presence
The great Council of Trent drew upon the rich heritage of the Church to affirm, in its doctrine of transubstantiation, that during the Eucharist at the consecration, the elements of bread and wine are transformed into the Body and Blood of Christ. At the consecration the bread and wine become the Body and Blood of Christ and thereafter Christ is really and permanently present in the elements of the Eucharist.

---

[1] This is actually not the only denial of the Eucharist and the Real Presence of Jesus therein. Some have called it idolatrous, quoting Lev 26.1–2; others have rejected the Real Presence in the Eucharist as a reduction of an irreducible risen Jesus; and Mt. 28.6 is cited to claim that the risen Jesus was not seen to be present in the blood-stained cloths in the tomb.

At the thirteenth session of its 1551 sitting presided over by Pope Julius III, the Council of Trent enunciated decrees about the Eucharist that dealt with: transubstantiation as the conversion of the substances of bread and wine of the Eucharist into the Body and Blood of Christ; the worship or *latria* and veneration of the consecrated species as worship of the Godhead; the custody of the consecrated species and its carrying to the sick to be carried out with the dignity befitting God; the worthy preparation that must precede the reception of the Eucharist; the use of the Sacrament of the Eucharist.[2]

The observed relationship between the doctrine of transubstantiation and the decree on the veneration of the Eucharist is very significant, for it underlines the rootedness of Eucharistic Adoration in the sacramental celebration of the Sacrifice of the Mass. The veneration of the Eucharist is indeed rooted in the sacramental celebration in two inseparable ways: through the transformation of the bread and wine into the Body and Blood of Christ at the consecration, the Son of God in His crucified, risen and exalted state is present to receive the homage of redeemed humanity, wherever He is exposed or introduced; and, as such, during the sacramental celebration of the Eucharist itself, especially after the consecration, the reality of the presence of the Lord attracts gestures of reverence (e.g., elevation of the species; its Adoration through ejaculatory phrases, genuflection, acclamations) and gestures of special veneration (e.g., bells, candles, incense).

Although the Mass may never be celebrated together with the Blessed Sacrament exposed,[3] the *devotional worship* of the real presence of Jesus in the Eucharist derives from the character and conduct of the sacramental celebration of the same Eucharistic sacrifice of Jesus and is inspired by them. Pope Paul VI accordingly affirmed a unity that exists between Eucharistic Adoration and sacramental Communion; while Blessed John Paul II taught that Eucharistic Adoration prolongs and multiplies the fruits of the Holy Mass and makes it personal.[4]

The inherent relationship between the sacramental celebration of the Eucharist and its Adoration as Blessed Sacrament outside Mass has not always been clearly perceived, as Pope Benedict XVI observed:

An objection that was widespread [during the early post-Vatican-II reform] argued that the Eucharistic bread was given

---

[2]   *Decrees of the Ecumenical Councils,* Vol. II, ed. Norman Tanner SJ, London: Sheed and Ward, 1970, pp. 693–7.

[3]   Cf. CIC 941, in line with *Sacrosanctum concilium.*

[4]   Cf. Paul VI, *Mysterium fidei,* and Blessed John Paul II, *Ecclesia de Eucharistia,* 25.

to us not to be looked at, but to be eaten. In the light of the Church's experience of prayer, however, this was seen to be a false dichotomy. As St Augustine put it: *No one eats that flesh without first adoring it* [and Saints Bernard and Gertrude added that looking at the Sacred Host is a meritorious act]. Eucharistic adoration is simply the natural consequence of the Eucharistic celebration, which is itself the Church's supreme act of adoration . . . The act of adoration outside Mass prolongs and intensifies all that takes place during the liturgical celebration itself. Indeed, 'only in adoration can a profound and genuine reception mature. And it is precisely this personal encounter with the Lord that then strengthens the social mission contained in the Eucharist[5]

The Real Presence of the Lord in the Eucharist

The basic affirmation of the Church's doctrine of transubstantiation is the *reality* of the *presence* of the Lord under the species of bread and wine after the consecration.[6] The Holy Eucharist is a *presence* and a *reality*, which Pope Paul VI referred to as the cardinal mystery of Catholic Christianity.[7] The Holy Eucharist is Jesus Christ crucified and glorified, who is in the Blessed Sacrament both as a *reality* and as a *presence*. Following Fr John Hardon S.J., Christ is in the Eucharist as a *reality* because the Eucharist is Jesus Christ. He is in the Eucharist as a *presence* because, through the Eucharist, He affects us and we are in contact with Him, according to our faith and devotion. If reality means actuality and if actuality means objectivity, then the Catholic faith believes that the Christ who is in the Eucharist is the Christ of

---

5   *Sacramentum caritatis*, 66, quoting the Holy Father's Address to the Roman Curia 22 December 2005.

6   Christ 'is present in the Sacrifice of the Mass not only in the person of his minister, 'the same now offering, through the ministry of priests, who formerly offered himself on the cross', but especially in the Eucharistic species', *The Catechism of the Catholic Church*, 1088; cf. the profession of faith of Berengarius under Pope Gregory VII: 'I believe in my heart and openly profess that the bread and wine placed upon the altar are, by the mystery of the sacred prayer and the words of the Redeemer, substantially changed into the true and life-giving flesh and Blood of Jesus Christ our Lord, and that after the consecration there is present the true Body of Christ which was born of the Virgin and offered up for the salvation of the world, hung on the cross and now sits at the right hand of the Father, and that there is present the true Blood of Christ which flowed from His side. They are present not only by means of a sign and of the efficacy of the sacrament, but also in the very reality and truth of their nature and substance'.

7   Cf. Paul VI, *Mysterium fidei*.

history, the one who was conceived at Nazareth, born at Bethlehem, died and rose from the dead at Jerusalem, and is now seated at the right hand of God, the Father Almighty.

Now, this *reality* is a *presence* in the sense that it is a personal relationship between rational subjects. I am present to someone and he to me when I am aware of him and he of me; when I have him on my mind and in my heart, as he thinks of me and senses kinship with and affection for me. As such *presence* transcends space and time. Someone can be present to me mentally and volitionally. As soon as I think of someone with love, he is present to me. In sum, another person, another subject, can be *spiritually* present to me.

Presence therefore does not deny physical reality, because two people can be both near to each other in body and intimately united in spirit. But neither does *presence* require physical proximity. It rather stresses intimacy of mind and heart. Thus, *Eucharistic Adoration* involves my awareness of Christ in the Eucharist and my raising sentiments of love towards Him. But this does not mean that Christ's *presence* to me is purely psychological or subjective, as if a figment of my mind, without reference to the objective reality of Christ present in the Eucharist.

We might then say that the Eucharistic Presence of Christ is at once *a reality* and *a relationship*. It is a *reality* because Christ really is in the Eucharist; and it is a *relationship* because it is about having Christ in mind and in heart. It is ultimately a relationship that grows and matures by *faith* through prayer.

The Need for the Eyes and the Mind of Faith

It has been observed that the liturgical form of the Eucharist, where the actual sacramental actions with bread and wine were separated from the repast and combined with the Liturgy of the Word, expresses the conviction that the sacrament should only be celebrated in the *fullness of faith*, which is nourished by the Word of God.[8] The Liturgy of the Word furnishes the faithful with, as it were, *eyes and mind of faith* with which to behold the Lord present in the Eucharist;[9] and this is also true of the real presence of Jesus in the adored species. Some, indeed, have referred to this presence of Jesus

---

[8]   Karl Rahner et al., eds, *Sacramentum Mundi*, vol. 2, London: Burns & Oates, 1968, p. 261.

[9]   Indeed, when Blessed John Paul II exhorted us to enter the new millennium with our gaze firmly set on the face of the Lord, he went on to add that the contemplation of Christ's face is first done with and through Scriptures, which provide us with the *vision of faith*. It is only faith which fully enters the mystery of the face of Jesus (cf. *Novo millennio inuente*, 16, 19).

to *the eyes and mind of faith* as *the grace of a double real presence*, which the following story well illustrates.

Our story comes from a L'Arche household (*foyer*) for the profoundly disabled called La Forestière. Autistic from birth, Loïc has the ageing body of a young child. He is small, weak and unable to walk, wash or dress himself. Practically blind, he occasionally lets out a groan, babbles childishly, or cries with joy or anger. Lacking practically every human capacity or talent, from the world's point of view he would be considered worse than useless. Yet thanks to the great faith of his parents and of the L'Arche community, Loïc made his First Communion, attends the Eucharist, receives Holy Communion and obviously likes community prayers and Adoration. And he in turn has become a master teacher, especially of Adoration.

Now, knowing Loïc a bit, let me tell you a particular story. About 25 years ago, a Jesuit friend of mine was at L'Arche; he was with Loïc, by then in his thirties, in the L'Arche chapel. As Loïc cannot sit on his own (actually he can, but prefers not to), he was on my friend's lap. It was the weekly time of Adoration before the Blessed Sacrament. Given how they were seated, my friend could see both Loïc and the Blessed Sacrament at the same time, and after a while he noticed himself wondering: *Who is revealing whose Real Presence?*

For he had begun to notice some striking similarities: neither Loïc nor Our Lord speaks, in the normal sense; neither Loïc nor Our Lord 'does' anything, in the normal sense; to be with Loïc in community is to draw near, see beyond appearances, be present in silence, open one's heart, enter into communion more by listening than by speaking; to be with Our Lord in Adoration is to draw near, see with eyes of faith, be present in silence, open one's heart and enter into communion more by listening than by speaking.

The grace of the moment, the Jesuit told me, was how the several striking similarities or parallelisms mutually revealed each other, and he came to call it the grace of a 'double Real Presence'. On the one hand, from Loïc he learned about presence and, being present within Him in the chapel, both could be present to our Lord in His Real Presence. At the same time, my friend discovered that the Eucharistic Adoration he had been doing since six years of age was much more relevant to his relationship with Loïc than he had heretofore realized.

The Jesuit would be hard-pressed to say which was more revelatory, which was prior or posterior, which was primary and which secondary. Did he not need the Lord to discover who and how Loïc really is, hidden behind his human brokenness, indeed uselessness? Did he not need Loïc to reveal how Christ is gently, invitingly, quietly but really present while hidden within that implausible, virtually quality-less, wafer?

So coming to know Loïc is like learning to open one's own heart in Adoration; Loïc somehow teaches the meaning of real or radical presence. To see humanity in a broken person – to see divinity in a scrap of bread broken for the life of the world.

Eucharistic Adoration as the Foundation of Social Justice

Eucharistic Adoration as our act of worship and like any act of worship is first and foremost our *justice* towards God. Worship of God is an act of justice towards Him which disposes us, indeed sets us free, to be just towards one another, because it is the living out of *our filial relationship* towards God; and it is the living out of *our common filiation or sonship* in Christ. Worship is therefore in a very real way the basis of any human action, especially towards one another. Pope Benedict XVI echoed similar sentiments:

> Before any activity, before the world can change there must be worship. Worship alone sets us truly free; worship alone gives us the criteria for our action. Precisely in a world in which guiding criteria are absent and the threat exists that each person will be a law unto himself, it is fundamentally necessary to stress worship.[10]

The reality of the presence of Jesus in the Eucharist makes every Eucharistic Adoration, the Adoration and contemplation of Jesus present in the species of the bread and wine of the Eucharist; and the One present in the adored species is Jesus of Nazareth, once crucified, now risen and glorified. The contemplation of Jesus in the Eucharist is essentially the contemplation of the incarnate mystery of salvation.

In Jesus and His ministry, one sees the justifying grace of God at work, overlooking the just demands of the covenant law and, out of mercy,[11] and love, re-instating man in covenant relationship of communion with God. For 'by grace you have been saved through faith, and this is not your doing; it is the gift of God' (Eph. 2.8). God reconciles man to himself in Jesus and re-introduces man into a life of communion with God.

The bestowal of the Spirit of Jesus on the Church and her members, enables them to respond to God's justice or righteousness in faith and become the *justice of God in* Christ (2 Cor. 5.21), *justifying*, in their turn, one another out of mercy and love,[12] namely overlooking

---

[10]   Benedict XVI Address to the Roman Curia (22 December 2005).
[11]   Blessed John Paul II defines *mercy* as 'a special power of love, which prevails over sin and infidelity of the chosen people' (*Dives in misericordia*, 4.3).
[12]   Thus, Blessed John Paul II teaches that in relationships between individuals and social groups, etc., '*Justice is not enough*'. There is need for that '*deeper power, which is love*' (cf. *Dives in misericordia*, 12).

sins and injuries to their rights, socio-political relationships etc; and thereby restoring the *family of God* and the *family of society* in communion.

This sense of *justice* and *righteousness* suggests that our call to serve the cause of justice, to be *servants of justice,* is rooted in God's *justice* towards us. It is first and foremost a call to spiritual experience: the experience of God's *justification* in faith and, by witnessing to it in Church and society, *justifying* others. Our *social justice,* rooted in our justice towards God, is our response to His justice towards us. Our Eucharistic Adoration is to nourish our experience of God's justice in our encounter with Jesus, whose mission was to reveal the justice of God. 'In your light we see light'.

The 1976 Eucharistic Congress in Philadelphia, USA, had as its theme the essential link between the Eucharist and the *hungers of the human family,* the first time in history that the Church focused an entire international event on such a link.

The congress captured the hunger for simple bread expressed in the very bodies of delegates from Africa and Asia. It captured the hunger for the bread of justice and freedom expressed in popular Spanish hymns by delegates from Latin America who brought their *Mass of Protest.* And it captured the hunger for nourishment and unity between rich and poor nations expressed in speeches by Blessed Teresa of Calcutta and Fr Pedro Arrupe, Superior General of the Society of Jesus.[13]

Fr Arrupe explained the surprising connection of the Eucharist with a variety of social concerns in the following way:

> This rediscovery of what might be called the *social dimension* of the Eucharist is of tremendous significance today. In the Eucharist . . . we receive not only Christ, the Head of the Body, but its members as well . . . Wherever there is suffering in the Body, wherever members of it are in want or oppressed, we, because we have received the same Body and are part of it, must be directly involved. We cannot properly receive the Bread of Life without sharing bread for life with those in want.[14]

---

[13] Cf. David Leigh, S.J., 'Toward a Sacrament of the World', in: *Spirituality Today*, vol. 37, Spring 1985, pp. 33–46.

[14] Pedro Arrupe, S.J., 'The Eucharist and Hunger', *Justice with Faith Today,* St. Louis: Jesuit Resources, 1980), pp. 176–7, as quoted by Leigh, op. cit. See also: the theme of the 1964 Eucharistic congress in Bombay: *The Eucharist and the New Man*, where Cardinal Gracias said, 'To wish to unite all men in the partaking of spiritual bread, without at the same time providing material bread is only a dream' (Leigh, op. cit.).

In the subsequent 1981 Eucharistic Congress in Lourdes, France, the theme *Jesus Christ: bread broken for the world* explicitly affirmed the relationship between Adoration and social justice.[15] Addressing some 3,000 English-speaking pilgrims there, the late Cardinal John Krol, Archbishop of Philadelphia, said that, just as Jesus allowed Himself to be broken on the cross for the salvation of the world, 'so we who break the bread of the Eucharist must commit ourselves to the same task'. The Cardinal went on to articulate the link between the Eucharist and several important social issues, including hunger for which he used the word *starving*: 'Jesus is bread broken for the world not only that he might heal our wounded nature through Eucharistic nourishment but that we might see him in the broken bodies of those who are starving . . . of those who are refugees . . . of those who are victims of violence'.[16]

---

[15]   The first 24 International Eucharistic Congresses dealt mainly with activities relating to the Eucharist, *Oeuvres eucharistiques* – the cult of adoration, processions, Holy Communion (particularly of children), the Sacrifice of the Mass, Eucharistic associations and movements. Then, beginning with the 25th which was held in Lourdes, France, in 1914, every Congress has had a specific theme of its own and been 'a providential opportunity to solemnly show to humanity *The Eucharist [as] a gift of God for the life of the world*', itself the theme of the most recent Congress held in Québec City, Canada, in 2008 (Pope Benedict XVI, 'Address' to the Participants in the Plenary Assembly of the Pontifical Committee for International Eucharistic Congresses, Vatican City, 9 November 2006). It is instructive, when reviewing the list, to notice how many of the themes are explicitly social or public (i.e., not exclusively intra-ecclesial) and how few, by contrast, are explicitly about Adoration, contemplative prayer, holiness or spirituality: The Eucharist and the Social Reign of Jesus Christ (1914), The Peaceful Reign of Our Lord Jesus Christ in the Eucharist (1922), The Eucharist and Holland (1924), The Peace of Christ in the Reign of Christ (1926), The Madonna and the Eucharist (1928), The Eucharist in Africa's Testimony (1930), The Eucharist and Ireland (1932), The Social Reign of Our Lord Jesus Christ and the Eucharist (1934), The Eucharistic Apostolate in the Missions (1937), The Eucharist Bond of Charity (1938), The Eucharist and Peace (1952), The Eucharistic Reign of Christ the Redeemer (1955), *Pro Mundi Vita* (1960), The Eucharist and the New Man (1964), *Vinculum Caritatis* (1968), 'Love One Another as I Have Loved You' (1973), The Eucharist and the Aspirations of the Human Family (1976), Jesus Christ Bread Broken for a New World (1981), The Eucharist and the Christian Family (1985), *Christus Pax Nostra* (1989), The Eucharist and Evangelisation (1993), The Eucharist and Freedom (1997), Jesus Christ Only Saviour of the World, Bread for New Life (2000), The Eucharist, Light and Life of the New Millennium (2004), The Eucharist: God's Gift for the Life of the World (2008) and the theme of the next one: The Eucharist: Communion with Christ and with One Another, to be held in Dublin, Ireland (2012).

[16]   Cardinal John Krol in: *The Voice*, Miami, Florida, 31 July 1981, p. 15.

Christ in the Eucharist is both drawing us to Himself and driving us to make Him present to our brothers and sisters in every nation. Perhaps more clearly than other sacraments, the Eucharist not only nourishes our personal and parish lives but also suggests to us the importance of its connection with a variety of social concerns.[17]

These words of Jesuit Fr David Leigh hint, moreover, that the relationship goes both ways. It goes from Adoration to social justice, and also from social justice to Adoration. What Vatican II's *Lumen gentium* says about the Eucharist, namely that it is *the source and summit of the whole Christian life* (11), applies equally to Eucharistic Adoration. *It is through prayer that the Church engages in the battle for peace*, for prayer not only opens the heart to a meeting with the Most High but also disposes us to an encounter with our neighbour, helping us to establish with everyone, without discrimination, relationships of respect, understanding, esteem and love.[18] Conversely, it is in struggling for enduring peace and greater social justice that the Church prepares to adore.

To say *source* means that from Eucharistic Adoration flows 'the whole Christian life' which necessarily includes the concerns and responsibilities of social justice. For 'action on behalf of justice and participation in the transformation of the world fully appear to us as a constitutive dimension of the preaching of the Gospel, or, in other words, of the Church's mission for the redemption of the human race'.[19] And to say *summit* means that Christian life culminates in, finds its supreme meaning and expression, in Eucharistic Adoration.

This reality invites us to consider the social implications of the Eucharistic mystery, to consider the food of truth and human life, and also the Church's social teaching and the sanctification of the world and the protection of creation.

Conclusion

Finally, the very use of physical elements of bread and wine 'which earth has given and human hands have made' can suggest the cosmic interdependence of all peoples today. In our mutual dependence on such elements, we are linked with one another and with all of creation. What is more, as Teilhard de Chardin tells us so eloquently,

---

[17]   Cf. Leigh, 'Toward a Sacrament of the World', pp. 33–46.
[18]   Cf. Blessed John Paul II, 'Believers United in Building Peace', Message for the 1992 World Day of Peace, p. 4.
[19]   Synod of Bishops, *Justice in the World*, 1971, p. 6.

this material world does communicate divine life in the Sacrament of Unity, for not only entire peoples but indeed the entire universe is to be transformed by Christ:

> As our humanity assimilates the material world, and as the Host assimilates our humanity, the Eucharistic transformation goes beyond and completes the trans-substantiation of the bread on the altar. Step by step it irresistibly invades the universe. It is the fire that sweeps over the heath; the stroke that vibrates through the bronze. In a secondary and generalized sense, but in a true sense, the sacramental Species are formed by the totality of the world, and the duration of the creation is the time needed for its consecration.[20]

---

[20] Pierre Teilhard de Chardin, S.J., *The Divine Milieu*, London: Collins, 1960, pp. 125–6, quoted by Leigh, op. cit.

Fourteen

From Adoration to Serving the Poor

Sister Joseph MC
Missionaries of Charity, Rome

Introduction

I wish to express how almost tangibly, and powerfully, our Eucharistic Adoration forces the very life giving power of Christ Himself into the fabric of our lives and work as Missionaries of Charity.

The Adoration of Jesus in the Eucharist, before all else, urges a purity of intention in our words and deeds. One hardly begins to face Him on the altar, and the sins and faults that need to be dealt with in our fraternal relationships present themselves. It is no wonder that priests who have perpetual Eucharistic Adoration in their parishes report increase in the number of confessions!

When we are in Adoration we become an open window for God to enter our world and flood it with His life and light and love. When we go out then, He goes with us and makes 'good things happen'!

This prayer 'Radiating Christ', was central to Mother Teresa's life and *is so* for all Missionaries of Charity.

> Dear Jesus, help me to spread your fragrance everywhere I go.
> Flood my soul with your spirit and life.
> Penetrate and possess my whole being, so utterly,
> that my life may only be a radiance of yours.
> Shine through me, and be so in me,
> that every soul I come in contact with may feel your presence in
>   my soul.
> Let them look up and see no longer me. But only Jesus!
> Stay with me, and then I shall begin to shine as you shine;
> so to shine as to be a light to others; the light,
> O Jesus will be all from you, none of it will be mine;
> It will be you, shining on others through me.

Let me thus praise you in the way you love best by shining on
   those around me.
Let me preach you without preaching,
not by words but by my example, by the catching force,
the sympathetic influence of what I do,
the evident fullness of the love my heart bears to you.
Amen.

One day, as our community emerged from the Church, a sister
greeted a man passing by very simply. Later we came to know who
he was and what that greeting meant to him. He was struggling with
addiction, trying to hang on to his recovery programme. One day,
near despair, as he walked down the street, he heaved a sigh and
cried from the depth of his being: 'My God help me!' In that moment,
he saw a sign on our gate: 'Missionaries of Charity Contemplative',
turned in and sat down in the chapel. The Blessed Sacrament was
exposed and he was immediately enveloped in peace. This incident
illustrates well the connection between the Eucharist, the Poor and
the Missionaries of Charity.

The Importance of the Eucharist in the Life of the Missionaries of Charity

Our congregation was founded to quench the infinite thirst of Jesus
on the cross for love and for souls. Our Lord actually pleaded with
Our Mother, Blessed Teresa of Calcutta, to bring Him to the Poor, to
bring the Poor to Him, to take Him into the dark holes of the Poor,
to make Him known to the Poor. He said: 'They don't know Me so
they don't want Me'.

As Jesus pleaded with Mother, she kept telling Him, 'I am too
weak, too sinful' and so on. Jesus said: 'Yes, I know, that is why I
chose you'. 'I will be with you'. And so it was.

Mother knew her powerlessness and relied totally on the power
of the Eucharist. She often repeated: 'I could not live one day without
the Eucharist'. So we begin each day with Holy Mass and fervent
Holy Communion which is our moment of greatest intimacy with
our Spouse. This time spent with Him is our preparation and power
for our work among the Poor.

The importance of Eucharistic Adoration grew in our congregation. Our Society was founded in 1950 and the work load was soon
overwhelming. Nevertheless in 1973, sisters felt the need for one
hour of daily Adoration. Mother prayed and agreed. She never for
a moment regretted it and often remarked: 'Not only did the work
not suffer but even though it increased, it was done more efficiently
and with greater love'.

In India following a big earthquake some years ago, relief teams came from all over the world. They asked that a few of our sisters be in each relief camp to organize the work. To their surprise the sisters insisted on beginning each day with prayer and Holy Mass and that there be times to withdraw for meals and prayers. Some did not agree but those who remained saw the wisdom of it. Because there was reliance on God, the teams could continue. Another proof that our strength comes from Him Who said it clearly: 'Without Me you can do nothing'.

I speak in the name of our sisters everywhere and from my own personal experience: without the strength provided by the Eucharist, it would not be possible to live our vocation.

The reflex of the sisters in any situation of extreme danger is to expose the Blessed Sacrament and to pray with the patients. Once in the midst of the war in Rwanda, rebels with guns in band ready to shoot burst into the chapel where the sisters were having Adoration. Seeing Jesus exposed on the altar, they stopped suddenly and marched backward out of the chapel. Years ago, a hurricane did a turn and by-passed Haiti in response to Adoration. And we have all experienced such miracles.

In her last years, when Our Mother became very ill, everywhere we would have Adoration 24 hours, taking turns. At first I thought, 'impossible, how can we manage our work and have every few hours another hour of Adoration?' But in fact we were strengthened and carried and experienced indescribable joy.

The development of this need for prayer resulted in the foundation of our contemplative branch where our fourth vow of whole-hearted and free service to the Poorest of the Poor is directed towards the spiritually Poorest of the Poor. We live it through Adoration and in going out in search of souls for two hours each day. Our Mother wanted the contemplative branch to be life blood for the society. Our life must be so lived that it involves us in a deeper and more meaningful way in the sufferings of the world.

Thus we go in search of souls, both actives and contemplatives; those who do not go physically go in spirit before the Blessed Sacrament. When we adore, we do not go alone, but we are there 'in the name of all who do not pray, who do not know how to pray, who do not want to pray, who do not dare to pray'. When the hours of prayer seem long and difficult, it helps to keep in mind that they are all with me, in my heart at His feet. No matter how I feel, I remain; God is at work.

It is a great comfort to tell the suffering persons we visit that we are taking them in our hearts to Jesus in the Blessed Sacrament. So we take Jesus out with us to the Poor, we find Jesus in the Poor, and we carry the Poor back to Jesus in our Adoration.

The Eucharist and the Poor

We might ask: Is it so easy to see Jesus in the Eucharist and in the Poor? Jesus can evade us; we need a pure heart to see God, and a pure heart is a Poor and humble heart. And a pure heart *can* see God.

Often we see that Jesus reveals Himself directly to the Poor. In Calcutta we have Adoration the whole day in a church near the largest train station and the biggest market in the city. People of all kinds and all religions enter the church and sit before the Blessed Sacrament. Asked why, nearly all say 'I get peace!' Not a few also receive healing and other graces.

A woman who was mentally disturbed would sit in the front row with a big bundle of all her belongings. She was a Hindu. When we needed the place for the sisters to say the Divine Office she wouldn't move – 'Leave me, I am talking to that big doctor'. No one had ever taught her about the Blessed Sacrament

In Washington DC, where we are, most of the children would not be Catholic, but the Sisters invite them to stop in and talk with Jesus. One day a little guy came in and ran right up in front of Jesus on the altar and said loudly, 'Jesus make my Mom stop going into the bathroom and taking drugs'. And she stopped!

Sometimes, we who are privileged to have the Eucharistic Jesus under the same roof risk getting used to Him and get a real wake-up when we see the reaction of others.

A woman phoned our convent in Vancouver and said 'I am a Witness of Jehovah and lately I am getting a strong interior message to go inside a Catholic Church; can I come to see you?' She came. As I walked into the Church ahead of her, towards the tabernacle, thinking of how to explain the red candle, etc. Suddenly she screamed loudly and ran out of the Church. I also ran to see what was happening and she shouted: 'God is in there! God is in there!'

In our work with AIDS patients, as we receive them into the house, we always stop by the chapel before going to their living area. I remember Kenneth, a strikingly handsome tall fellow exclaiming as soon as he put his head into the door of the chapel, 'Wow! The first thing I want to do in this house is to become a Catholic!' We never preached to these men; they preached to each other. Kenneth was a man of few words but very convinced and gave powerful witness to the others. When these men came to our home preparing to die, they actually began a whole new life. I can't remember them being afraid of dying.

We have noticed also, that youth who have powerfully experienced God's merciful love seem urged from within to spend time in Adoration. A young man in addiction recovery expressed it thus: 'You know, sometimes I feel there is someone inside of me, pulling me'.

Why then can Jesus in the Eucharist connect with the Poor like an explosion of Light? Perhaps it's because Jesus is the poorest of all in the Eucharist and those who have nothing to lose feel comfortable with Him. Jesus identifies Himself with them by His deliberate choice to be there, not forcing our attention, allowing anyone to receive, handle or even neglect Him. He can be thrown, insulted, whatever; and so also is the condition of the Poor of this world.

Somehow, in some way, it seems that the violation of the Precious Body and Blood of Christ goes hand in hand with the violation of His broken Body in the Poor, just as Christ has now on this earth no bands to do His work (He stoops to use us). In the same way, He can no longer suffer in His humanity on earth; so He suffers now in the Poor. That redeeming suffering goes on until the end of time. As if in fellowship with the suffering Poor, Jesus undergoes every possible insult and outrage in the Eucharist.

In our home for the dying in Calcutta, where we bathe our very sick patients, it is written on the wall in large letters 'THE BODY OF CHRIST', so that sisters and volunteers can remember that in touching the broken body of the Poor they are touching the broken Body of Christ. Our Mother preached everywhere her 'Gospel on Five Fingers' – 'You Did It To ME'. Whether we are serving the homeless Poor, the dying destitute, the unwed mother, the prostitute, the addict, the lonely or the abused child we are serving Christ who said, 'Whatsoever you do to the least of my brothers you do it to ME'.

Jesus told Our Mother how it hurt Him to see all these little children sullied by sin. What might He say now with the escalating sinful possibilities available everywhere?

While visiting a prison in Canada, we met a 22-year-old man who had repeatedly sexually abused young girls. One of the girls died as a result of his violence and he was imprisoned for life. He said: 'Sisters, I deserve to be here. I have done great evil. If only someone in my life had ever told me the beautiful things that you are teaching me now, my life could have been so different'.

Radiating Christ

After each Holy Communion, Our Mother prayed the beautiful prayer 'Radiating Christ'. For me, it is an x-ray of Our Mother's heart and soul. She allowed Jesus to do in her what she asked in this prayer. This prayer is also our daily plea. It is a bit like a set of instructions or a work manual.

Mother could truly say with St Paul, 'It is no longer I who live, but Christ who lives in me'. She united Jesus in the Eucharist and Jesus in the Poor. Again and again she repeated, 'It is the same Jesus', and she would follow that by saying, 'Jesus is God. Jesus cannot tell a lie'.

In fact, we came to know after her death that for many years, Jesus hid Himself from her in the Eucharist but showed Himself to her in the Poor. He led her in the darkness of faith and even filled her with a radiating joy which she did not feel but which others felt.

In my first weeks of religious life, I waited for Mother's visit, planning to tell her: 'I don't want to go home, but, to be honest I must tell you that perhaps I don't belong here because I don't *feel* this warm love for Jesus that I see in the other candidates'. When I sat down with Mother, before I could say a word, she looked me right into my eyes and said: 'The only one who wants you to go home is the devil'. 'But Mother I don't *feel* . . .' She then said: 'Love is in the will not in the feelings'. The whole world today needs to hear these words.

So Mother went forth, filled with Jesus, to serve Jesus. The fulfilment of this 'Radiating Christ's Prayer in Mother became visible and tangible. She *did* spread the fragrance of Jesus; she *did* shine His light everywhere. People in her presence sensed they were in the presence of God, even though Mother was in utter spiritual darkness. He was shining brightly through her. Mother became truly a channel for the Eucharistic Jesus in the Poor.

A young man came to our door and said: 'Coming up the walk to your chapel today, I met a young woman who greeted me. She was pretty yes, but sister, there was something else; I saw a kind of beauty which I have never seen before. It seemed to be something from within'. Then I said: 'Yes, she was coming from her hour of Adoration but she did not leave Jesus in the chapel; He came with her'. Would that we too come out of the chapel radiating Christ like that young woman!

We cannot all be Blessed Teresa of Calcutta. We cannot go to all the places of poverty, but we can do something. We can go to Jesus truly present in the Eucharist. He will use our presence there to shine Himself on us, in us, through us, because of us and on the whole world. Think of it! This is the only place on earth where we can touch directly eternity, heaven, and God Himself. Spending time before Him is essential because we cannot give what we do not have.

Blessed Teresa used to tell of a priest who said: 'Mother Teresa, since I left the priesthood, I have so much more time for the Poor and I can do so much more for them'. Mother said to us: 'I told him – "Yes, before, you were able to give them Jesus; now, you can give them only yourself."'

Our communities are meant to witness the brotherhood of all mankind. If we are living the Eucharist sincerely , this will overflow in fraternal love. Sr. Nirmala, co-founder with Mother Teresa of our contemplative branch, once defined the contemplation of Missionaries of Charity as 'To see Jesus in the other with the eyes of

Mary'. Seeing thus, we choose to become a little more blind to their faults, a little more understanding and merciful, and far more able to see the beauty in the other.

When I joined the Missionaries of Charity and heard that we have to be a healing touch, I thought, 'This is crazy. I do not have the gift of healing'. But now I know that if I give Jesus, He does the necessary healing, especially of aching and wounded hearts. No matter what the situation, our job is to bring Jesus into it. Jesus *is* the solution.

Though we cannot fix anything, the presence of Jesus lightens the burden of the Poor and gives them strength. We need the help of the Holy Spirit to approach the Poor with the gentleness, mercy and delicacy of Jesus Himself. We need humility to listen, lest we go to them with 'solutions', having no idea what pains and wounds are in each heart. Our every word or gesture can bring light and joy into a heart, or they can increase the darkness and pain. That's why we need Jesus!

We do fail, and I never stop placing all my failures into His Sacred Heart and plunging them into His precious wounds where He alone can redeem and make all things new.

Our Society belongs to Our Lady, and our Mother has told us: 'It was born at her pleading'. As Missionaries of Charity we pray the rosary daily before the Blessed Sacrament exposed and also on the streets. Our Lady always leads to Jesus. In our rule we have: 'We will inspire in the hearts of the Poor full confidence in Our Lady, Mother and Hope of the Poor, we will fly to her for help when the work for souls is hard. She will obtain for us the strength to open to Jesus hearts until then closed'.

One of Our Mother's favourite devotions to Our Lady was her 'Flying Novena' of nine *Memorares*. This novena can start a stalled car, obtain a visa, can stop the rain, and can open a heart. And Our Mother, who could be very mischievous, always prayed it in *thanksgiving* for what she was asking.

Long ago in Mexico, our Catholic people were being evangelized against devotion to Our Lady. One day we gathered a group of women being thus influenced and prayed the rosary with them. Upon reading St Luke's account of the Annunciation, at the words, 'He will be called the Son of the Most High' I experienced an interior 'bolt' which seemed to imprint in my soul 'Mary is truly the Mother of God'. Amazingly, everyone present felt something.

Also in Mexico, going out after Adoration, we met a woman weeping and desperate; she told us her husband was unfaithful and neglecting her and the children. We taught her to pray the rosary. Months later, we met her again: this time very happy. 'Did your husband change?' we asked. She answered, 'No, but ever since I began praying the rosary I have changed!'

Our Mother used to tell us: 'Teach them to pray the family rosary and they will be all right'. And she never added, 'if they are Catholic!'

In New York a sick man who was quite anti-Catholic came to spend his last days in our home. On entering his room, he saw the image of Our Lady of Guadalupe on the wall. He was amazed and said, 'Who is that? She is the one I saw in my dream and she told me, "go to my house in New York". I phoned my mother in New York and she said, "The lady surely must be speaking of the Mother Teresa House"'. He died a Catholic with his non-Catholic parents praying the rosary with him.

Some years ago, six of our sisters were hostages during a war and only two of them survived. Other survivors in the group said they all took courage from our sisters' continual praying of the rosary as they ran through gunfire and bloodshed.

We have a prayer in which we say: May this rosary be my weapon to sanctify me and to spread the Kingdom of the Immaculate Heart among the Poorest of the Poor.

According to our Rule, the fruitfulness of our apostolate depends on the use of simple, humble means. A sister of another congregation once wrote me: 'Since Vatican II, we sisters no longer go around giving out medals and scapulars and rosaries; we have much more to do'. I answered, 'We also have much to do; and medals and scapulars and rosaries are included'. Indeed, we have all seen many miracles connected with these articles.

One of our sisters affirms that she was converted in this way: being neither a believer nor one who prayed, she accepted to wear a Miraculous Medal out of trust. After a few months, she experienced a powerful light that changed her whole life and today she is a Missionary of Charity.

Donald, in his fifties, upon admission to our home for men with AIDS announced: 'Now I was raised a Catholic, but don't try to convert me because I belong to the devil'. 'Surely we won't: conversion is GOD's work. But would you do one thing: would you wear this scapular?' To my surprise he said, 'Yes! I had one of these when I made my First Communion'. He put it on.

When he became stronger and found our house and rules too constricting he left. Months later, at 2 p.m. on Good Friday, a nurse phoned from the hospital: 'Donald is here dying and asking for the sisters'. We found Donald breathing heavily and rapidly and there was the scapular bouncing up and down with every breath! We asked, 'Can we bring the priest for the Sacraments so you can go Home to Jesus?' He said 'Yes!' Monsignor was there within minutes and Donald died in the Hour of Mercy on Good Friday.

As she gave Miraculous Medals to everyone, everywhere, Blessed Teresa taught even kings and presidents to pray, 'Mary, Mother of Jesus be a mother to me now'. In our home for single mothers in one place, the young women would often get through their deliveries praying this prayer.

Our Mother often reminded us: We have every reason to be the happiest people in the world. We have the joy to be 24 hours with Jesus. Does that mean no sufferings? Surely not. All of us suffer misunderstandings, pain and failures: no one is exempt. Suffering is necessary. Like the Eucharistic Jesus and the Poor we serve, we too have to be broken.

Once when I arrived at a new mission, fresh from experience of painful and humiliating failure, feeling heavy and useless; on the first day my Superior introduced me to a man we were caring for. He immediately took my hand and led me to another, who was dying. He said; 'Norman, we have a new Sister and she understands us'. In that moment, I became aware of how my own personal sufferings bonded me to them in their suffering. I saw the cross as precious, a sign of greater love. Miracles happen in the times of our greatest sufferings. This is true even if we do not suffer well.

It pleases God to use 'our nothingness' to do great works. God alone knows what is success or failure in our works. Our Mother used to say to visitors: 'Look what God is doing with our nothingness'.

Years ago, Fr Benedict Groeschel shared with us that, feeling hesitant about undertaking the work he felt called to do, he confided to Our Mother that he was too weak. Mother encouraged him saying: 'Go ahead – God does not use weak instruments, He uses broken ones!'

Humbly acknowledged and given to Jesus, our misery is no obstacle in His way. And Jesus' love brings miracles of conversion and contrition.

We ourselves have to go before Jesus in Adoration because we have to bring His love to those who have never known it. To experience God's love results in desire to be forgiven. 'God loved us when we were yet sinners'. We experience His love and become aware of our sin.

One day a co-worker asked me, regarding a new patient in our home: 'Did you confront him with his sin?' I said: 'Certainly not!' A person imprisoned in darkness and sin ('dark holes') cannot be frightened or threatened or accused into life, but he can be loved into life. Who does not blossom when they are loved? 'Lord, shine through me. Let them feel Your presence – let them see You in me'.

One day, a gentleman suffering with AIDS appeared at the door and asked to speak to a sister. We sat down. He began:

> Some weeks ago while carousing in a nightclub, I had an incredible experience. Sometime after midnight, sitting drinking with my friends, I was suddenly aware of a tiny pin point of light piercing my being and in that instant I became aware of being bound in chains. As the light increased I began to struggle against the chains. The more I struggled the brighter the light became. The more the light increased, the more I struggled until the chains broke and I was flooded with light. *And I was free!* I went out into the street. Early morning I found a priest and made my confession after many years. I went to tell my friends 'We are all slaves.' They wanted no more to do with me. They said I had become mad. So now I go quietly to the infectious disease clinics and sit in waiting rooms and speak to people, one by one, about what Jesus has done for me. I will continue to do this until I die.

Someone, somewhere, obtained that light for this man. Perhaps it was a fruit of someone's Adoration in those hours of the night?

When one opens his heart to Jesus, no matter what his life has been, Jesus can transform him to the point of resembling Himself even physically, in a very short time. God can work fast!

And there was Joseph. He left our home because there were too many reminders of the faith he had abandoned, especially the praying of the rosary. At 10 p.m. one night, a call came that Joseph was in the hospital near death and he said that he had no one but the Mother Teresa Sisters.

We phoned a very elderly Jesuit priest known to be zealous for souls. He said: 'Pick me up on the way'. He got into the car and without another word began to lead us in prayer. As soon as we walked into the ward Joseph, with all the tubes everywhere, literally leapt to cling to the priest.

How many times we have all stood at the bedside of someone dying and really felt we were looking at Jesus – the sisters who are privileged to pick up the dying from the streets perhaps even more so.

I remember a young man in Mexico who was dying. Someone told us: 'Go to see Sally'. Sally was there in a tiny shack with earth for floor and logs for a bed. Wasting no time, we asked 'Would you like to receive Jesus in Confession, Anointing and Holy Communion?' When he said yes we quickly went for the priest. We sat outside while Sally made his confession and then joined in prayers for the

Anointing and Holy Communion. As soon as Sally received Holy Communion he began to rejoice, throwing up his arms and crying out: 'What Joy! What Joy! What Joy!'

Confession, Anointing and Holy Communion – a powerful package – in the hands of every priest – greater than any nuclear power!

The Poor Themselves Become Channels of Light

In our contact with the Poor, we discover many hidden saints; they in turn give us Jesus. We can lean much from them.

Larry was charming young man who had been brought up singing in the streets and was dying in our home. Only a couple of days before his death, he came, more tumbling than walking, down the stairs to our early morning Mass. At Holy Communion time, as Father was going to the back of the chapel towards Larry, he cried out: 'No Father, I can't receive Jesus! I could not find my nice rosary that the sisters gave me for my Baptism, and I was thinking in my mind that one of the guys took it, and then I found it in the pocket of my coat'. That was more than 20 years ago. I can't forget his words and his tender conscience. He would not receive Jesus after having suspected others of wrongdoing.

Father gave him absolution and Holy Communion. Larry died a couple of days later, with the whole gang, sisters, volunteers and other patients around his bed praying the rosary. As we finished the 'Hail Holy Queen', he took a big last breath and said triumphantly 'I'm going home!' As we finished the Immaculate Mary hymn, another man said; 'Sisters, promise me to do everything just the same way when my turn comes'.

When this same Larry had said: 'Sister, what do I have to do to become a Catholic?' we taught him the simple Catechism. He adhered to the truth, loved it and lived by it. When I returned from my retreat at one point, I noticed a sadness in Larry and a couple of the others. I asked 'What is wrong?' At first they did not want to tell me because they thought I would feel bad, then Larry said: 'That young university student who had been coming as a volunteer gathered some of us together and told us not to believe everything that the sisters taught us. Then he began to tell us that what we were doing before was ok and he spoke bad things to us and wanted us to join in. We told him he was wrong and he argued with us. Then I told him: 'I did not study like you but I know what is right and what is wrong. I know that what the sisters are teaching is true'. Those on the side of truth know Christ's voice.

Over the years, in the United States, I worked in our homes for men dying of AIDS. Deaths such as Larry's are not unusual. We all gather around and accompany them as they die, and they are very often with us in prayer. We would also go to them and tell them: 'Ask Jesus this . . . Ask Jesus that'.

We had a chart at the entrance of our chapel listing the names of those who had died in our home. The caption of this chart was 'Heaven is our true Home'. One young man was so happy when he came there to live, upon seeing the list of names he added his name to the list even before he died!

We Try to Help the Poor Find Meaning in Their Suffering

We went with a priest to bless a dying woman who was in great distress and fear. He did a wonderful thing. He took her face in his bands and said: 'Giuseppina, one day Jesus said 'Do you love Me?' You said 'yes!' Then He said, 'Giuseppina, I want you to help Me, you said 'yes!' Then He said: 'come up here on the cross with Me'. You said 'yes!' Now Giuseppina, you are on the cross with Jesus and you are helping Him to save souls'. A tremendous peace came over her. Sometimes *we* also have to believe in the meaning of their sufferings.

In a nursing home we visit, there is a woman with an illness that causes morbid twisting of her body and constant gasping and panting. This has been going on 24 hours a day for more than 15 years! She is unable to attend Holy Mass even in a wheelchair. It is heart rending to look at her. One day a sister in her powerlessness to help, was moved to pray for her in the Spirit. This sister, in her heart, heard the words: 'Through Him, with Him, in Him' and she understood that this woman was united to the sacrifice of Jesus in the Eucharist.

Conclusion

I would like to conclude by illustrating how those who are touched by grace are urged from within to evangelize others – they can't hold it back.

A young woman I know, since her conversion, is quietly bringing, one by one, her family members and her friends to Jesus. She guides them to Confession, frequent Holy Mass and Adoration. She evangelizes them by her example, her companionship, her direct simple words of truth and her joy. She uses a marvellous expression when she comes to share all this: 'Good things are happening Sister!'

Fifteen

Adoration as the Heart of Diocesan Life

Antonio Cardinal Cañizares Llovera
Prefect, Congregation for Divine Worship and the Discipline
of the Sacraments, Vatican City
Translated from Spanish by Mauricio Rafael Gonzalez Bustillos

Introduction: The Feast of *Corpus Christi*
Today the Church celebrates the feast of the most Blessed Sacrament and the Body of Christ; it is a day that with a special and with a particular intensity is dedicated to the Adoration of the Blessed Sacrament of the Altar.

There are few feasts, indeed, that are so beloved by the Christian people as the one we celebrate today; there are few feasts, that have such deep roots in many churches – I think of my country, Spain, and Latin America. We could say that *Corpus Christi* is the feast of Christian joy, because it is the perennial celebration of the mystery of Christ and thus also of the redemption of every creature who longs and yearns for the life of the sons of God. The Lord, we worship in the Eucharist and Him whom we joyously rend tribute to during the processions through our streets, is the same God who lived on earth, died and rose again and lives in eternity, everything that happens does so is in Him. Everything was made through Him and without Him nothing that exists is made, in Him is the life and its fullness that we have all received, grace and truth come through Him.

Today's feast is a public confession of faith. In these times when so many Christians hide or forget their convictions, or when powerful currents want to reduce it to the private sphere and turn off its impact on the life of society, we need these public demonstrations of faith. They, in turn, express how faith affects everything human and has a public dimension, just like a human person who also has an essentially social and public dimension. By going out into the street on this feast of *Corpus Christi*, as an extension of the Eucharistic sacrifice, showing in the public square before the gaze and contemplation of men the Eucharistic Mystery of our faith, Jesus Christ Himself in person, wholly, really and truly present here in His Body, Soul and Divinity, also reminds us that faith is not lived in hiding and in anonymity. Eucharistic Adoration is inseparable from the fate and lives of men and peoples. The faith we confess and the Adoration of the Blessed Sacrament we publically manifest during the feast of *Corpus Christi*, thus, revives in us the awareness that, at the present time, the Church faithful to the spiritual riches that animates it – Christ, the Eucharist – must be *the leaven of the Gospel for the animation and transformation of temporal realities.* This is wrought with the dynamism of hope and the power of Christian love, which comes from communion with the Body of Christ and from its deepest and most profound Adoration.

We must remember that the feast of *Corpus Christi* solemnly commemorates what we celebrate every day in the simple peace of our churches: the Mystery of the Body and Blood of Christ. The living Bread which came down from heaven ordains a greater and more splendid worship that we can adore and receive as Christians. God has given us Himself as promise and possession in simple and ordinary food, bread and wine. Under these earthly signs of everyday life, God gives Himself to us as food. However, this same simplicity can make us forget the infinity and the greatness of what we celebrate, and whom we celebrate. So we need a special day that that manifests this grandeur and rekindles and all the meaning and force of Eucharistic Adoration, which is by itself the heart and soul of the Church that subsists in each one of the particular churches, and it should be also in the consciousness and life of all Christians, and should with the passing of days have greater force in all communities.

We have become accustomed to it, and we may not have enough lucidity or insight to realize that what we celebrate on this day is nothing less than the real presence, in the fullest sense, of the Body and Blood of Christ in the Eucharist, that is, the substantial presence by which Christ, whole and complete, God and man, is present as the same One who took flesh and was born of the Virgin Mary, went about doing good, was crucified, died and was buried and now resurrected and victorious, lives forever with the Father, interceding for us, and carrying out His work of salvation through the Church, His historical and Mystical Body, which works, acts and remains.

With this we affirm that Christ, with all that He is, is truly the centre of the Church, of history, of the world. Christ is not a memory nor is His nearness due to or thanks to an icon of Him, or to a mere sign. He is with us and works His perennial redemption in the Eucharistic Sacrifice. Through communion and worship and the action of the Holy Spirit He forms one Body, that is the Church. This is what we celebrate and worship, not just today but every day in the Holy Eucharist, and this is extended outside Mass by Eucharistic Adoration. This causes awe and fascination, and fills us with joy. The joy of today's feast, the feast of Eucharistic Adoration, is the unspeakable joy with which the immense love of the Triune God fills us. We participate in the supreme gift that is the Eucharist, Christ made Eucharist, with our prostration and worship: this same gift contains everything that comes from God.

You cannot imagine the happiness and the joy that I experience before you, who are an important and noteworthy representation of the millions of men and women, adults, youth, elderly and children, families, priests and religious, who bear within you such a deep and lively Eucharistic Adoration. Without a doubt, as the Psalm says, God is being very good to us and we are glad for the grace of Adoration with which He has enriched the Church and is enriching the Church during these times. Without recognizing Him as the centre of everything, as when He is recognized in Eucharistic Adoration, without the same Eucharistic Adoration, the world perishes and closes itself to its future; but thanks to Him, thanks to the Holy Trinity, He has in recent years raised, around the world, an unstoppable and vivifying stream of Adoration of the Blessed Sacrament, of perpetual and permanent, Adoration throughout the day, Adoration during night vigils with youth, the formation of new Eucharistic groups and the formation of groups of children. This trend is unstoppable and a godsend; so I am – we are – very happy. There is no future for man without the Eucharist, nor without Adoration that is inherent in the Eucharistic celebration, and in its extension of Adoration in spirit and in truth.

Whoever looks back at the Magisterium on the Eucharist for the last fifty years, especially the last fifteen years, will be surprised by its extraordinary wealth. And not just at the Magisterium, but also at many of its acts: The Year of the Eucharist, the Synod on the Eucharist, the emergence and growth of groups of Perpetual Adoration, among others. Excepting the thirteenth century and the contributions of the Council of Trent, one might well say that the period between the beginning of the twentieth and early twenty-first century has been, if one looks at the whole the history of the Church, in doctrinal contributions, the most intensely Eucharistic. The post-conciliar Magisterium on the Eucharist has deepened, as it had not occurred before, the understanding of the Eucharistic Mystery and the deepest and most authentic sense of Adoration, not only in the act of Eucharistic piety, but in the actual faith present in the very mystery of the Eucharist, and, in a particular way, in the close relationship between the Eucharist and the Church, and, therefore, between the Adoration of the Eucharist and the Church.

The Eucharist and the Church

In a speech to the Tenth Ordinary Council of the General Secretariat of the Synod of Bishops (16 November 2004), Blessed John Paul II recalled the key importance of the Eucharist, crucial for the Church, in direct reference to the issue that would be dealt with during the next Synod. He said: 'The next XI Ordinary General Assembly of the Synod of Bishops, that with care you have been preparing for some time, will face a crucial issue for the Church: the Eucharist'. Indeed, the precise formulation of the theme of the Synod is: 'The Eucharist, source and summit of the life and mission of the Church'. The Church receives from the Eucharist the vital energy for her presence and action in the history of men. In the words of Blessed John Paul II, the Eucharist is presented as the 'crucial issue for the Church' because she receives 'vital energy for her presence and action'. The truth of the Church (for her nature and mission) is clarified in the light of the Eucharistic Mystery. The 'presence and action' of the Church in the world have in the Eucharist their vital principle. The being and acting of the Church are either Eucharistic or, strictly speaking, are not. The 'history of men' comes through the action of the Church, whose life and mission flow from the Eucharist.

Blessed John Paul II with his personal experience of faith and Eucharistic life and with his magisterial teaching about the Eucharistic has shown in a very concrete manner the relationship between the Eucharist and the Church, and between Eucharistic Adoration and the Church. It is only necessary to peer into his priestly biography *Gift and Mystery* and to see him in front of the Tabernacle, or to see him celebrating the Eucharist in his private chapel, or to see him during the *Corpus Christi* procession, or to see his great pastoral initiatives, such as the Jubilee Year of 2000, they are full of meaning or Eucharistic. You can also see the inseparable relationship between the Eucharist and the Church in his principle Eucharistic texts such as *Mane nobiscum Domine* and especially *Ecclesia de Eucharistia*. The depth and breadth of meaning of this relationship, as well as the inseparable relation that celebration of the Eucharist and Eucharistic Adoration have, is therefore, of critical importance in the life and mission of the Church who practices Eucharistic Adoration.

The teachings, the Magisterium and life of Blessed John Paul II are also evident in the Synod on the Eucharist, which was convoked by him as a continuation and culmination of some of his initiatives. These thoughts, experiences, proposals and conclusions are collected, confirmed and deepened by Pope Benedict XVI in his Apostolic Exhortation *Sacramentum caritatis*, which in its first part specifically addresses the relationship of Church and the Eucharist. 'The faith of the Church, before addressing the issue, is essentially a Eucharistic faith and is especially nourished at the table of the Eucharist' (6). The Church appears as the subject of a faith whose object is the Eucharist. Moreover, the Eucharist is not only the object of faith of the Church, but the 'compendium and summary of our faith' (*Catechism of the Catholic Church*, 1327). In the Eucharist everything that the Church believes is condensed. That is why, in the first part of the exhortation, the Pope offers a summary of the faith of the Church formulated from the Eucharistic Mystery. In doing so, the Holy Father knows that this contributes to the vitality of the faithful, because, 'the more lively the Eucharistic faith of the People of God is, the deeper its participation in ecclesial life through the steadfast commitment to the mission that Christ entrusted to His disciples' (*Sacramentum caritatis*, 6). That the relationship between the Church and the Eucharist is discussed here means that this relationship is essential to the profession of faith. The Church is not only the subject of Eucharistic faith, but she herself is a *mystery to be believed from the Eucharist*. The truth of the Church becomes clear from the Eucharistic Mystery, so that its nature and mission are found in Him as well the light that illuminates His truth.

Pope Benedict XVI favours the historical-salvific-trinitarian perspective and invites us to contemplate how 'the Eucharist reveals the loving plan that guides all of salvation history (cf. Eph. 1.10, 3.8–11; *Sacramentum caritatis*, 8). The Church is part of a story that comes from the eternal love of the Father, the Son and the Holy Spirit. Jesus Christ, by giving Himself in the Eucharist, through the Holy Spirit, grants us the divine life which He receives eternally from the Father. This is an absolutely free gift that the Church welcomes with faithful obedience, she celebrates and loves and uses it to enter into communion. The Church lives from this gift, which constitutes her a sacrament of communion. It is up to her to respond to the gift and live it sacramentally until He comes (cf. *Sacramentum caritatis*, 11). It is Jesus present in the Church, who has given the Church the task of participating in His hour, the mission of entering into communion with Him in His sacrificial act (cf. *Sacramentum caritatis*, 11).

It is important to speak about Jesus' hour as an offering of the Son, true sacrificial lamb, before treating the ecclesiological dimension or the relationship between the Eucharist and the Church. By affirming the incorporation of the faithful to the 'hour' of Jesus through the Sacrament of the Eucharist, the true meaning of the memorial applied to the Eucharistic Mystery is signalled. Partaking of the Bread and the Chalice supposes the real participation in Christ's sacrifice, in Christ's offering and total surrender to the Father by His obedience, in His union and total self-giving love, in His full consecration in obedience, in the unconditional affirmation of God the Father and of His love.

By this, objectively and really, the death of the Lord is proclaimed. The memorial is no longer understood simply as the memory of God's past actions that allows me to continue to recognize His presence and action, but rather it allows an existing participation, a communion, in what has happened once and for all (to be incorporated into the 'hour' of Jesus, united with Himself). In this Eucharist gift, 'Jesus Christ entrusted to his Church the perennial making present of the paschal Mystery. With it he brought about a mysterious 'oneness in time' between that Triduum and the passage of the centuries' (*Ecclesia de Eucharistia*, 5), a mysterious communion between Jesus Himself and His Church, His Ecclesial Body. This very 'oneness in time' has been made possible by the mystery of the Incarnation, in which He who is eternal has entered history, and through Easter, which He has lived in time, He has entered into eternity, turning time into a 'dimension of God' (cf. *Tertio millennio adveniente*, 10).

There is a 'causal influence of the Eucharist' in the very origins of the Church (*Ecclesia de Eucharistia*, 21). The Apostles, by accepting the invitation of Jesus in the Cenacle, entered for the first time into sacramental communion with Him. Since then and until the end of time, the Church is built up through sacramental communion with the Son of God delivered up for us. By joining with Christ, the people of the new covenant becomes a 'sacrament' for humanity, that is, a sign and instrument of salvation, precisely thanks to this participation and communion with Him. In this way, the Eucharist, by building the Church, creates specifically communion with God and community between men: 'the sacrament of intimate union with God and all mankind' (*Lumen gentium*, 1). It is a reality that is also fulfilled by the Adoration of the Eucharist outside Mass. The Eucharist is a priceless treasure, not only celebrating it but also by praying before it outside of Mass through Adoration. It gives us the possibility to reach the very wellspring of grace, the loving spring that gives life (there will be no another way to celebrate and to participate in the Eucharist that is not in Adoration, in communion with Christ offering Himself and uniting Himself to the Father in a reciprocal love without measure, that is Adoration). A Christian community who wants to better contemplate the face of Christ must also develop this aspect of Eucharistic Adoration, which prolongs and increases the fruits of the communion with the Body and Blood of the Lord (*Ecclesia de Eucharistia*, 25).

In *Sacramentum caritatis*, Pope Benedict XVI highlights not only the chronological precedence of the Eucharist for the Church but also its ontological precedence, based upon Christ having 'first loved us'. The causality of the Eucharist for the Church is explained in two moments. First one analyzes how Christ gave birth to the Church on the Cross and from there stems the causality of the Eucharist. After that one refers to the circular correlation between the two. In this order there is already an important teaching: if the Eucharist is the cause of the Church it is because it is born of Christ Himself. The influence that the Church receives from the Eucharist is not extrinsic, but intrinsic, that is, it belongs to its nature. There is no Church without the Eucharist, as there is no Church without Christ. The Pope recalls that 'Christ himself, in the sacrifice of the cross, has given birth to the Church as a wife and body' (*Sacramentum caritatis*, 14). Such has been the repeated testimony of the Fathers in their Christian commentary on the birth of Eve from Adam's side while he slept (cf. Gen. 2.21–23). The *Catechism of the Catholic Church* (766) summarizes this teaching that the Church is born from the total gift of Christ, anticipated by instituting the Eucharist and realized upon the cross. But the Church is born primarily from the total gift of Christ for our salvation, anticipated in the institution of the Eucharist and realized in His offering and consecration by the sacrifice of the Cross.

Contemplating *Him who was pierced* (cf. Jn 19.37), leads us to consider the causal link between Christ's sacrifice, the Eucharist, and the Church. Indeed, the Church 'lives from the Eucharist' (*Ecclesia de Eucharistia*, 1). Since in her is present the redeeming sacrifice of Christ, one must first recognize that 'there is a causal influence of the Eucharist in the very origins of the Church' (*Ecclesia de Eucharistia*, 1). The Eucharist is Christ who gives Himself to us in the offering He makes to the Father. He continually builds us up as His Body (*Sacramentum caritatis*, 14). Christ's offering that is an oblation and consecration to the Father builds the Church. From the offered up Body (Christ on the cross) the built up Body is born (the Church). The Eucharist by actualizing Christ's sacrificial offering, actualizes the building up of the Church.

One can then claim, as does the Pope, that in the correlation between the Eucharist that builds the Church and the Church that makes the Eucharist the first cause corresponds to the first statement: 'The Church is able to celebrate and adore the mystery of Christ present in the Eucharist precisely because Christ first gave himself to her in the sacrifice of the Cross' (*Sacramentum caritatis*, 14). The causal influence of the Eucharist at the origin of the Church discloses both the chronological and ontological priority of having been 'first loved' in compliance with the will of the Father and in total offering to His will. Because Christ 'first loved us' (cf. 1 Jn 4.19), the Church can 'make' the Eucharist. The Mass involves always, therefore, the primacy of Christ's gift: 'For all eternity he remains the one who loves us first' (*Sacramentum caritatis*, 14). Here we find the meaning and the deeper reason for Adoration. Because by the Eucharist we are united in such a manner with Christ and to Him, loved by Him, because He offers Himself to the Father for us through the same and singular sacrifice of the cross that is actualized in the Eucharist. It is where God occupies the first place and as such is recognized in the sacrificial offering. The Eucharist is Adoration: 'It is an encounter and unification of persons, but the person who comes to meet us and wants to join with us is the Son of God. This unification can only be brought about by the means of Adoration. To receive the Eucharist means to adore Him whom we receive. Just so, and only thus do we become one with him' (Benedict XVI, Address to the Roman Curia, 22 December 2005).

Eucharistic Adoration as the Heart of the Church

The core of the Eucharist is in the true Adoration of God. The principle is in Adoration because God is first. It is the celebration of the Eucharist where Adoration takes place primarily, indeed the Eucharistic celebration is Adoration. 'There is an intrinsic connection between celebration and Adoration'. Indeed, the Mass is itself the greatest act of Adoration of the Church: 'no one eats of this flesh', writes St Augustine, 'without first adoring it'. Adoration outside the Holy Mass prolongs and intensifies what has taken place in the liturgical celebration and renders a true and profound reception of Christ' (Benedict XVI, Address, 10 June 2007).

The Eucharist, therefore, must be lived as Adoration, and as the extension of the Eucharist in Adoration of the Blessed Sacrament of the altar. It is also about ensuring that the Holy Mass receives the full dimension of Adoration, and cultivating Eucharistic Adoration in order to truly celebrate the Eucharist and to participation in it actively and fruitfully as demanded by the Council. Without Adoration the great richness and truth of the Eucharist is lost. We should never forget that in the Eucharist, the Son of God comes to us and wants to join with us, so as to enter into communion with Him who offers Himself to the Father, in total obedience, loving us to the end so that we may live from His same love, as He has loved us, as God pleases. Eucharistic Adoration is simply the extension or the obvious continuation of the Eucharistic celebration, of the communion with the Lord in His sacrifice on the cross. The Eucharistic celebration is itself the greatest act of Adoration of the Church.

Participating in the Eucharist, receiving Holy Communion, receiving the Eucharist, means adoring Him Whom we receive. Precisely so, and only so, we become one with Him and, in some ways, it is a foretaste of the beauty of the heavenly liturgy. Adoration outside Holy Mass prolongs and intensifies what happened at the same celebration, it is inseparable from the celebration. The act of Adoration outside the Mass, closely linked to the celebration, is of great value for the life of the Church, and it tends towards both sacramental and spiritual communion. It is invaluable to take part in the Eucharist. So also a good and proper catechesis is necessary that explains to the faithful the importance of Eucharistic Adoration outside of Mass, which allows a deeper and more fruitful liturgical celebration of the Mass.

Only in Adoration can a profound and genuine reception of the Eucharist mature. And precisely in this personal act of encounter with the Lord can then the social mission contained in the Eucharist mature and where it is possible to break down the barriers not only between the Lord and us, but also and above all the barriers that separate us from each other. So that is why Eucharistic Adoration is so important, and also why it is so highly recommended and why it is so joyous to practice Eucharistic Adoration, both personal and communal.

Pope Benedict XVI was moved by the experience of Eucharistic Adoration during the World Day of Youth in Cologne, by observing the joy of Adoration that emerged and came forth with such force and grandeur. The theme for that World Youth Day was: 'Come, let us adore Him'. 'Before any activity and any change or transformation of the world Adoration must be practiced', the Pope said to the Roman Curia recalling that World Youth Day, 'only Adoration makes us truly free, it only gives us the criteria for our action. Precisely in a world which progressively loses its criteria for action and where the danger exist that each one becomes one's own criterion, it is essential to emphasize Adoration' (Address, 22 December 2005).

The Pope reminds us that:

The Latin word for adoration is 'ad-oratio', it is a going from mouth to mouth, a kiss, an embrace and, hence, ultimately it is love. Submission becomes union, because he to whom we submit is Love. In this way submission makes sense, because it do not impose anything strange, but liberates us from the depths of our being . . . The Greek word is *proskynesis*. It refers to the sign of submission, the recognition of God as our true measure, whose norm we accept to follow. It means that freedom is not simply about enjoying life in total autonomy, but to orient oneself according to the measure of the truth and the good, to become, thus, ourselves, true and good. This gesture is necessary even if initially our yearning for freedom is resists, at first, this perspective. (Homily, 21 August 2005)

With either meaning, the Latin or Greek, better yet with both because they are complementary, Eucharistic Adoration is an essential way of being with the Lord, to be one with Him, to simply be, just like Mary, the sister of Lazarus. This is a great experience, which can provide power, great comfort and firm support. You can only be before the tabernacle with a true and a real Adoration. The only true treasure of the Church is in the sanctuary. And as the Pope adds:

> In one of his parables, the Lord speaks of hidden treasure in the field, because the hidden treasure, the superior good to any other good, is the kingdom of God, it is Jesus himself, the Kingdom in person. In the Sacred Host he is present, the true treasure, always accessible to us. Only by adoring his presence do we learn to receive him properly, we learn to communicate, we learn this from within the Eucharistic celebration. (Homily, 11 September 2006)

No wonder the Holy Father feels moved by 'how everywhere in the Church there is an awakening to the joy of Eucharistic Adoration and its effects are manifested' (Address, 22 December 2005). Therefore it is necessary once again, as does Pope Benedict XVI in *Sacramentum caritatis*, to underline 'the intrinsic relationship between Eucharistic celebration and Eucharistic Adoration. A growing appreciation of this significant aspect of the Church's faith has been an important part of our experience in the years following the liturgical renewal desired by the Second Vatican Council.

During the early phases of the reform, the inherent relationship between Mass and Adoration of the Blessed Sacrament was not always perceived with sufficient clarity. For example, an objection that was widespread at the time argued that the Eucharistic bread was given to us not to be looked at, but to be eaten. In the light of the Church's experience of prayer, however, this was seen to be a false dichotomy. As Saint Augustine put it: 'nemo autem illam carnem manducat, nisi prius adoraverit; peccemus non adorando – no one eats that flesh without first adoring it; we should sin were we not to adore it'. In the Eucharist, the Son of God comes to meet us and desires to become one with us; Eucharistic Adoration is simply the natural consequence of the Eucharistic celebration, which is itself the Church's supreme act of Adoration' (*Sacramentum caritatis*, 66).

If the Eucharist is the heart of the Church, if it is the greatest act of Adoration, and Eucharistic Adoration is concomitant or the continuation of the celebration, we must point out with truth and joy that Eucharistic Adoration is the beating heart of the Church. The Eucharist is Adoration. There is no Church without the Eucharist. There is no Church without Adoration. God today is opening the roads and directing the steps of the Church in order to live Adoration every day more intensely and with greater fervour and breadth in so many different ways.

Let us give thanks to God Who gives us such a future. In this way the new, very urgent, and pressing evangelization, which is the joy and the deepest identity of the Church, can be brought about.

Sixteen

Spiritual Fruits of Adoration in Parishes

Father Florian Racine
Founder, of the Missionaries of the Most Holy Eucharist,
Fréjus-Toulon, France
Translated from French by David Nugent

O Sacrament Most Holy, O Sacrament Divine, all praise and all thanksgiving be at every moment thine!

It is with this prayer of praise that I wish to bless Our Lord Jesus, truly present in the Sacrament of His Love. The Eucharist is our treasure on earth. Nothing is more beautiful, nothing greater, nothing more admirable than this presence of the Risen One, who without leaving heaven, comes to set-up His tent in our midst, making His tabernacle among us, in order to enrich us with His Grace and to clothe us with His Glory. How many parishes, in kneeling before the King of kings and the Lord of lords, have not only experienced His love, which makes sense of our existence, but have also caused to come down upon the Church and the world the glorious light of the Risen Christ.

Pope Benedict XVI in his catechesis on St Juliana of Cornillon, affirmed his joy that 'today there is a 'Eucharistic springtime' in the Church: How many people pause in silence before the Tabernacle to engage in a loving conversation with Jesus! It is comforting to know that many groups of young people have rediscovered the beauty of praying in Adoration before the Most Blessed Sacrament . . . I pray that this Eucharistic 'springtime' may spread increasingly in every parish' (General Audience, 17 November 2010).

On the one hand, a growing number of parishes centre pastoral life on the Eucharist celebrated, and then continually adored. Adoration thus becomes an inexhaustible source of holiness for the faithful. On the other hand, as Blessed John Paul II recalled,

unfortunately, alongside these lights, there are also shadows. In some places the practice of Eucharistic adoration has been almost completely abandoned. In various parts of the Church abuses have occurred, leading to confusion with regard to sound faith and Catholic doctrine concerning this wonderful sacrament. At times one encounters an extremely reductive understanding of the Eucharistic mystery. Stripped of its sacrificial meaning, it is celebrated as if it were simply a fraternal banquet. (*Ecclesia de Eucharistia*, 10)

This is one of the reasons why Adoration of the Blessed Sacrament has fallen into disuse over several decades. At the time of the Council, many considered Eucharistic Adoration as a devotional exercise, while for liturgists, Adoration was viewed a something merely palliative to a liturgy that had become inaccessible to the faithful. They had thought that after the Council Adoration would simply have to disappear since, as a devotion, it would have to give way to a more authentic spirituality, and that the renewed Liturgy would permit a true participation of the faithful. But such views did not understand the proper role of Eucharistic Adoration and its continuity with the Holy Sacrifice of the Mass. Thanks to the pastoral contribution of Blessed John Paul II and the theological input of Pope Benedict XVI, the Church has not ceased to remind us that Eucharistic Adoration is neither a personal piety nor a private devotion, but is a prayer that enlarges the heart to the dimensions of the world. In touching the Heart of Christ, God touches all the hearts of mankind. In adoring the Holy Eucharist, 'we enter into this movement of love from which flows forth all interior progress and all apostolic fruitfulness' (Blessed John Paul II, Homily, Monmatre, 1 June 1980).

Let us develop some of the perceptible graces that flow from this contemplative prayer. However, let us not forget that we 'walk by faith, not by sight' (2 Cor. 5.7). Thus the visible graces flowing from the Eucharist are just the tip of the iceberg, in comparison with the invisible spiritual blessings that the Lord bestows upon His Church and the world. Since the Eucharist is the memorial of the Passion of Christ, the fruits of the Eucharist flow directly from the Cross: and while upsetting the interior reality, the visible world does not change radically, because we await 'a new heaven and a new earth' (Rev. 21.1).

But before speaking of the fruits flowing from Eucharistic Adoration, let us recall what is most essential: the Lord is worthy to be adored for His own sake, because He is our Creator, our Redeemer, our Sanctifier. The Servant of God Paul VI wrote: 'It is for us a very sweet duty to honour and adore in the Host that our eyes see, the Word Incarnate which they don't see, and Who, without leaving heaven, makes Himself present before us' (Credo of the People of God, 30 June 1968).

To adore God is therefore a 'sweet duty'. First of all 'a duty', because it is the first commandment: 'You must adore the Lord your God, with all your heart, with all your spirit, and with all your soul; this is the first commandment' (Mt. 22.36). However, this duty is 'sweet' because the blessings for the soul and for the world are innumerable:

> Anyone who approaches this august sacrament with special devotion and endeavours to return generous love for Christ's infinite love, experiences and fully understands, not without great spiritual joy and profit, how precious is the life hidden with Christ in God, and how great is the value of converse with Christ, for there is nothing more consoling on earth, nothing more efficacious for advancing along the road to holiness. (Paul VI, *Mysterium Fidei*)

Even if Adoration of the Blessed Sacrament seemed to be penitential, or if there seemed to be no real concrete fruit flowing from it, the Lord would still be worthy to be adored for His own sake. That which must motivate our walk of Adoration should not be the spiritual benefits that we will receive. To adore is the first act of justice where we acknowledge that God is first of all, the Giver of life. He is the Alpha and the Omega. All comes from Him, all subsists in Him, and all must return to Him.

Before sending His disciples on mission, the Risen Christ 'showed them His hands and His feet' (Lk. 24.40), with His glorious wounds, sources of grace for humanity. Because – From the glorious wounds of Christ flow spiritual fruits for the adorer, for the Church and for the world. All spiritual fruits flow from the sacrifice of Jesus on the Cross, made present in the Eucharist. These fruits are all profoundly linked: in renewing the heart of the faithful, the Lord edifies the community. Thereby, He gives to the Church vocations and to the world Apostles. Each life changed renews the Church and transforms the world.

Personal Graces

First of all, in prostrating oneself before the Blessed Sacrament, the adorer experiences the tenderness of God. Already, in Galilee, the crowds pressed around Jesus to hear and see Him perform signs and wonders. Think of the woman who touched Jesus by her faith, thus releasing His power. Jesus knowing that power had come out of Him said, 'Who touched me?' (Mt. 5.30). Our faith touches the Heart of Jesus and releases its healing power and love on us, our family and the world, whenever we go to Him in the Blessed Sacrament. In the silence of Adoration, we respond to the invitation of Jesus to the multitudes: 'Come to me . . . all you who are thirsty . . . all of you who are weary . . . repose in a deserted corner . . . Because from my heart shall flow rivers of living water'. He was speaking of the Holy Spirit. In the Blessed Sacrament, Jesus replenishes our strength and puts new hope in us when all seems lost. Blessed John Paul II said:

> It is good to spend time with Him, leaning on his breast like the Beloved Disciple, to be touched by the infinite love of His heart. If, in our epoch, Christianity is to be distinguished above all by the 'art of prayer,' how can we fail to feel a renewed need to spend time in spiritual converse, in silent Adoration, in heartfelt love before Christ present in the Blessed Sacrament? Many times I have experienced this, and I received strength, consolation and support! (*Ecclesia de Eucharistia*, 25)

To better evangelize the adorer must first be evangelized. He must let the merciful love of Christ heal him, liberate him, enlighten him, raise him. To the question 'What does Jesus do in the Blessed Sacrament? 'the Cure of Ars replied, 'He waits for us'. There, Jesus veils His majesty so that we might dare to go speak with Him, as one friend to another. He tempers the ardour of His Heart for us to experience its sweet tenderness. On the Cross, Jesus turns hate into love and death into life. Similarly, in the Eucharist, Jesus performs the same wonder in us: He changes evil into good, darkness into light, fear into confidence. Pauline-Marie Jaricot, an untiring Apostle of charity, living in Lyon in the nineteenth century, sums up this personal transformation that takes place in the heart of adorers who allow the Spirit to change their hearts of stone into hearts of flesh:

> It is at the foot of your holy tabernacles that my heart, withered by the severest trials, has consistently found the strength necessary to bear the rigour. It is there that my combats are turned into victories, my weakness to courage, my tepidness to enthusiasm, my uncertainties to lights, my sadness to joy, my obstacles to success, my desires into reality, my resentment against my neighbour into burning charity. All I know, I learned at your feet, Lord.[1]

Faithfully to adore the Blessed Sacrament, then, is a school of spiritual fervour and of fidelity in prayer. When a parish organizes Perpetual Adoration, each parishioner is invited to come regularly to adore one hour per week. This weekly commitment has a number

---

[1] Pauline-Marie Jaricot, *L'Amour Infini dans la Divine Eucharistie*, Impr., Lyon: St Joseph, 2001.

of advantages: it helps the parishioners to remain faithful to personal prayer time, despite the aridity, or spiritual dryness endured. As one Parish Priest has put it:

> The great spiritual teachers stress that all spiritual progress requires regularity, fidelity and asceticism. The rhythm of one hour of adoration permits us to enter into a weekly schedule that is convenient for everyone. It allows us to place Jesus before any activity, as in the gospel passage of Martha and Mary, where Jesus reminds us, through the testimony of Mary seated at Jesus' feet, that one thing alone is necessary; or in Gethsemane, when Jesus asks to Peter, 'Simon, do you sleep? Have you not the strength to watch one hour? (Mk 14.38)[2]

By making the commitment to worship one hour per week, the parishioner is free of an approach that is too sentimental, and gradually moves to adore 'in spirit and in truth' in an Adoration in the Church and for the Church. Often, after several months of Adoration, some adorers say, 'I will stop Adoration, because I do not feel anything'. But Jesus said that 'The Father seeks adorers who adore in spirit and in truth' (Jn 4.23), and not adorers who are motivated solely by sensible graces. Thus, an Adoration chapel welcoming the parishioners in turn, is a true school of fidelity, of fervour, where the encounter with Jesus becomes a true spiritual experience, independent of the consolations felt.

I would like to emphasize the importance of putting in place an organization in which each adorer is aware that he is a guardian of the Blessed Sacrament. If he can't get to this 'appointment of love' he must follow a simple procedure to find a replacement. A team helps to assist with this. It helps to underline the ecclesial dimension of this type of organization: the adorer takes the place of another and will leave, after an hour, to be replaced by a new adorer. This chain of Adoration encourages the adorers to remain faithful, because the presence of one adorer encourages the other in the changeover of the hour, day or night. In addition, the use of a traditional monstrance is strongly recommended, placed worthily on an altar, rather than using a tabernacle with closable doors or a monstrance placed behind a grill. Instead of elevating the real presence and making the process of Adoration of the Blessed Sacrament solemn, this form of exposition, despite not being recommended by the Church, pervades in so many parishes today, and has as a direct consequence of loss of the adorers. In seeking an easy solution that wishes to economize on the work of organization (whose sole purpose is to foster fidelity),

---

[2]   Testimony of Father Michel Pieron, Parish Priest of Vichy, 2005.

Adoration is reduced to a simple private devotion, and not an ecclesial prayer. It is no longer a prayer serving the needs of the world where each watch, is in turn, in the Church and for the Church. The adorers lose the sense of 'a guard of honour' or 'guard of love'. They will be demotivated very quickly and will have no reason to seek a replacement to address their absences. The chain of Adoration will be quickly broken and gradually wither and disappear. Finally, a parish that chooses one of these modes of exposition, to the detriment of the monstrance exposed day and night on an altar, does not offer the act of faith that the Lord waits for and through which He gives a very specific grace for our Church and our time! 'Do not be afraid, have only faith' (Mk 5.36).

Render 'love for love' to Jesus. St Peter Julian Eymard said,

> I have often reflected on the remedies to this universal indifference that takes hold in a terrifying manner of so many Catholics, and I can find only one: the Eucharist, the love of Jesus Eucharistic. Loss of faith comes from the loss of love.

The Eucharist is the gift of the Sacred Heart of Jesus that goes 'to the extreme of love' (Jn 13.1). Jesus shows His Heart to men, for, seeing them so poor in love, He would like to enrich them with the treasures of the Heart of God. For this reason, He institutes the Eucharist, invention of love. In the Eucharist Jesus is burning with the desire to be loved. His Heart is 'an inexhaustible source',[3] 'a fiery furnace'.[4] St Eymard also said:

> In the Blessed Sacrament, He cannot be more loving! And yet He is not loved. His love is not appreciated. It is not even known, and by only a few of His own. He has many good apostolic servants, and some pious adorers in His service. But He has very few spouses. Even out of His friends, who visit out of affection, who converse with Him from the heart, very few are dedicated purely for Him![5]

In coming to adore faithfully, the parishioner has a real and genuine encounter in faith with the Risen Christ. He becomes a disciple of

---

[3]   St Margaret-Mary, *Vie et Œuvres*, Ed. Gauthey, t. II, 3e édition, 1915, Paris, J. de Gigord, p. 335.

[4]   St Margaret-Mary, *Vie et Œuvres de Sainte Marguerite-Marie Alacoque, Tome II, Autobiographie*, 1920, Paris, J. de Gigord, no 55, 56.

[5]   St Peter Julian Eymard, *Œuvres complètes*, no. 44, 2008 Nouvelle Cité , Centro Eucharistico, p. 133.

Jesus, according to His invitation: 'Learn from Me, for I am meek and humble of heart' (Mt. 11.29). Today Jesus remains in the Blessed Sacrament not only so that we have the same privilege to meet Him in His Divine Person, like the Apostles who had the opportunity to be at His side every day. More importantly, in the Sacrament of His love, Jesus awaits from each of us the same impulses of love, the same affection, the same feelings, the same interior dispositions that He received from the holy women of the gospel or from His disciples who let themselves be formed by the Good Master. In the Eucharist, God gives Himself without measure. He invites us to reciprocity, that is, to love Him in return, with all our heart, our whole soul and with all our strength, Jesus in His Divine Person, who makes Himself corporeally present to us. He is the poorest of the poor, the first one that deserves our love, the only one who deserves all our heart.

As pointed out by Blessed John Paul II,

> the presence of Jesus in the tabernacle must act like a magnet for an increasing number of souls deeply in love with Him, capable of remaining a long time in order to hear His voice and almost hearing the beating of His heart. (*Mane nobiscum Domine*, 18)

To listen to this Heart is to seek God's will. In Eucharistic Adoration, the adorer learns to do, instead of 'his will for God', but 'the will of God'. Everyone must live this conversion of the will. Too often Christians spend themselves generously in many services they have chosen, but are quickly discouraged because they have made their own will, God's will. Before acting, we must kneel, to receive from God, not only the knowledge of His will but also the strength to accomplish it with perseverance. Moreover, the adorer learns to take his mind off himself and to focus on Christ and His Word. Silent Adoration is learning to say 'Speak Lord, your servant is listening' (1 Sam. 3.9) rather than 'listen Lord, your servant is speaking'! Also, prayer is a powerful protection against daily temptations: 'Watch and pray that you may not enter into temptation' (Mk. 14.38).

Among the personal fruits, it is good to highlight those which renew the interior dispositions for worthily approaching the sacraments enabling us to receive their maximum benefit. Pope Benedict XVI reminds us of the intrinsic link between the Mass and Eucharistic Adoration. He writes:

> Eucharistic Adoration is nothing more than the explicit development of the Eucharistic celebration, which is itself the greatest act of Adoration of the Church. Receiving the Eucharist means adoring Him whom we receive. It is then, and only then, that we become one with Him and that we taste in advance,

in some way, the beauty of the heavenly liturgy. The act of Adoration outside Mass prolongs and intensifies all that takes place during the liturgical celebration itself. In fact, it is only in Adoration that can mature a profound and true reception. And it is precisely this personal encounter with the Lord that then strengthens the social mission which is contained in the Eucharist and that wants to break down barriers not only between the Lord and us, but above all the barriers that separate us from each other. (*Sacramentum caritatis*, 66)

The experience of parishes which adore the Blessed Sacrament reveals that, in adoring, parishioners learn not only to discern, beyond the appearances of bread, the real presence of the Lord, but that they also grow in awareness of the efficient presence of the Sacrifice of the Cross, made present at every Mass. Thus, as a result of long periods before the Sacred Host, adorers will not approach Holy Communion without due reverence and profound Adoration. Also, their understanding of the Mass will not be reduced to a simple banquet. In other words, adoring the Blessed Sacrament permits us to live the Eucharist more intensely in all its dimensions. Bishop Ruben Profugo, Bishop of Lucena in the Philippines, has given the following testimony to Adoration:

> In my diocese, Mass attendance has increased visibly not only on Sundays but also during the week. Many have returned to the sacraments because of Perpetual Eucharist Adoration. There is a strong link between Adoration and the Mass. By means of their weekly Holy Hour parishioners are prepared to live the Sunday Mass or to give thanks for that which comes to be lived.

The Holy Father did not hesitate to say that 'Adoration is not a luxury but a priority' (Benedict XVI, Angelus, 28 August 2005), in the Church today.

A young Vietnamese priest who was ministering to a small parish in Singapore recounted:

> Celebrating the Mass one Sunday in Lent, I was struck by the large number of catechumens: eighty young people between 18 and 35. At the end of the Mass, I was speaking to the young priest who had invited to this parish when I noticed that next to the church, there was a small air-conditioned room filled with flowers. In this room the Blessed Sacrament is exposed day and night, as in the Basilica of the Sacred Heart of Montmartre, and there are always at least a dozen or so people. The young priest

then told me that the large number of catechumens was directly related to this Adoration chapel. Indeed, in questioning these young people who were preparing for Baptism, all replied that for several months, during the night, they had been coming to pray before the Blessed Sacrament, without knowing very well what they were doing, but just that they were drawn to this Presence. Yes, Adoration attracts, because every man has in him the desire to see God.[6]

'It is not only repentance that leads to the Eucharist, but also the Eucharist which leads to repentance' (Blessed John Paul II, *Dominicæ Cenæ*). As a parish priest who has Perpetual Adoration, I can testify to the growing demand for the sacrament of reconciliation as the fruit of Adoration. The progression is not only quantitative but also qualitative. One cannot remain in front of the Blessed Sacrament without the light of Christ profoundly illuminating the soul and enlightening the conscience.

Those who cannot have access to Holy Communion, those who are divorced and remarried are, however, strongly encouraged to participate in the Sacrifice of the Mass and to contemplate the face of Christ in Adoration. Recently, a parishioner told me that she was not progressing spiritually. After an exchange, she disclosed that she was divorced and remarried and that despite this, she received Holy Communion. I invited her, then, to continue coming to church faithfully, but without communicating. I also encouraged her to adore the Blessed Sacrament more faithfully. Despite the shock and grief suffered, she returned a few months later, to let me know that her spiritual life had finally found a new impetus. Blessed John Paul II wrote:

Contemplation prolongs communion and allows for a lasting encounter with the Christ, true God and true man, letting oneself to be looked at by Him and to experience His presence. When we contemplate Him present in the Blessed Sacrament of the Altar, Christ draws close to us and more intimately than we are to ourselves: He gives us a share in his divine life in a transforming union, and the Spirit provides us with access to the Father, as He Himself said to Philip, 'Who has seen Me has seen the Father' (Jn 14. 9). Contemplation, which is also a communion of desire, intimately associates us with Christ and unites in a spiritual manner those who are unable to receive Him in Holy Communion. (Letter, 28 June 1996)

---

[6]   Mgr Patrick Chauvet, *Il est là ! L'adoration eucharistique*, Saint-Maur: Parole et Silence, 2008, p. 92.

How many divorced and remarried people are now experiencing the unconditional love of Christ in the Blessed Sacrament by adoring Him faithfully! Through this spiritual communion, Christ gives them the graces necessary to continue to live the commandment of charity and to engage in the mission of the Church.

Graces for the Parish

By renewing the heart of the parishioners, Adoration leads people to become more involved in their parish community. A community is primarily made up of people who feed their baptismal life by means of an intense Eucharistic life.

One Parish Priest says that Adoration nourishes and strengthens faith: He says that the Lord has always answered the prayers of the adorers and continues to do so. The chapel of Adoration has become a real 'centre of prayer' for several years. His Christian community is full. He believes that Perpetual Eucharistic Adoration is the most noble and yet the easiest accomplishment of his life as a priest. The benefits, he says, are numerous and the effort on his part is minimal. Perpetual Adoration makes Jesus present for everyone, he asserts, because, He is really there in person for all.

Sometimes parishes can be like dry land in which it is difficult to launch new pastoral projects or to renew existing ones. Through continual Adoration, Jesus pours out His Spirit on all the various movements of the parish, like rivers of living water flowing from His Divine Heart (cf. Jn 7.37–39). This water gives life to the parish community, making it more available to the mission, and giving all pastoral activities a greater fecundity. Also, unlike a windmill which constantly changes direction, through Adoration, a parish is anchored on Christ, the Good Shepherd of souls, who blesses and gives fecundity to the pastoral initiatives, despite the inevitable changes in priests, parishioners, movements. Jesus celebrated and adored is the rock on which the parish rests. From His pierced Heart which throbs for love of us in the Blessed Sacrament, the Spirit from Whom springs spiritual water, irrigating the dry land of the parish so that it can produce abundant fruits of conversion, commitment, charity, etc.

Another Parish Priest gives the following testimony:

> The parish of St Louis-St Blaise has been experiencing graces of charity which are drawn from Eucharistic adoration: links are forged or tightened, the parishioners are more attentive to each other, more supportive. Jesus in the Blessed Sacrament overwhelms the heart of the parish and opens it gradually to the mission that we are trying to put in place. Thanks to this chain of uninterrupted prayer, all the groups of the parish are gathered in prayer. In the exercise of my ministry, I know that at each

moment, there is a parishioner who is praying for the parish and its priest. On the first anniversary of Perpetual Adoration, we had more than two hundred people attending the conference. This shows how the parishioners have truly gathered around Jesus in the Eucharist. I am touched by the loyalty of my parishioners and to their commitment to prayer. It is so beautiful![7]

Jesus said, 'I am the vine, ye are the branches, if you remain in me and I in you, you will bear much fruit, but apart from me you can do nothing' (Jn 15.5). Thus, any pastoral fertility stems from the union of the community with Christ. Since the Eucharist is the sacrament of communion with God and neighbour, the more we live the Eucharist, the more our communion with Christ is authentic and therefore the more our love of neighbour is concrete.

Although the Mass is the first place for gathering the parish together, it happens, however, that the parishioners often only attend 'their Sunday Mass', which does not always favour unity and communion. By contrast, if in addition to the Mass, Perpetual Adoration is proposed, new spiritual links are created between the adorers who succeed or replace each other. It can be noted that the parishioners of different spiritual sensibilities that do not meet at the Mass, have become friends through the chain of Adoration. Yes, 'the Eucharist builds the Church and the Church makes the Eucharist' (Blessed John Paul II, *Ecclesia de Eucharistia*, 26).

In living the Eucharist, that which is at the service of the Gospel walks in the love of God and neighbour. It helps to build the Church as communion. Eucharistic Love motivates and founds the vocational activity of the whole Church.

> In the intimacy of the Eucharist, some find they are called to the ministry of the altar, others to contemplate the beauty and depth of this mystery, others to make this momentum of love be pour out over the poor and weak, and others to reap the transforming power in the realities and gestures of everyday life. Every believer finds in the Eucharist not only the interpretative key of his life but the courage to carry it out so he can build up, through the diversity of charisms and of vocations, the one Body of Christ in history. (Blessed John Paul II, Letter to Priests, Holy Thursday 2000)

So many bishops testify that priestly vocations in their diocese have abounded ever since they introduced continual Adoration.

---

[7]   Testimony of Fr Pieron, Parish priest of St Louis-St Blaise, 2005.

Blessed Teresa of Calcutta said: 'It was not until 1973 when we began the daily holy hour, that our community began to grow and flourish'. Blessed Teresa distinguishes three graces received from Eucharistic Adoration. First, she learns to love her sisters with the love that flows from the Eucharist. Then, the recognition of Jesus under the appearance of bread helps her to better recognize Christ in the poorest of the poor. Finally Adoration allows her to give the people she serves, not just herself or what she possesses, but rather, Jesus who lives in her. In a letter she wrote:

> Every day we expose the Blessed Sacrament, and we have perceived a change in our lives. We felt a deeper love for Christ disguised in the poor. We were able to know ourselves better and to better know the poor as the concrete witness of God. Since we started this Adoration of the Blessed Sacrament, we have not reduced our work, we spend as much time as before, but with more understanding. People accept us better. They are hungry for God. They no longer need us, but Jesus . . . The Holy Hour before the Eucharist must direct us to the holy hour with the poor.[8]

In this sense, many parishes in France have organized a contact centre to listen or give support directly related to the chapel of Eucharistic Adoration. The parish of St Patrick's Soho, in London, offers a permanent hotline. The operators remain in prayer before the Blessed Sacrament in a chapel specially designed for that purpose. Blessed John Paul II wrote:

> Proximity to Christ, in the silence of contemplation, does not separate us from our contemporaries but, rather, makes us attentive and open to the joys and sorrows of men, and it enlarges the heart to the dimensions of the world. It gives us solidarity with our brothers in humanity, particularly the littlest, who are the beloved of the Lord. (Letter, 28 June 1996)

In order to foster holy religious and priestly vocations, the Congregation of the Clergy encourages the practice of Perpetual Adoration in dioceses. Cardinal Hummes wrote that there is an urgent need for:

> A movement of prayer, that places at its centre 24 hour continuous Eucharistic Adoration, so that from every corner of

---

[8]   Cf. Mother Teresa, *Tu m'apportes l'amour, Écrits spirituels*, Paris: Le Centurion, 1975.

the globe, the prayer of Adoration, thanksgiving, petition and reparation, will be raised to God, with the primary intention of awakening a sufficient number of holy vocations to the priesthood and, at the same time, spiritually uniting with a certain spiritual maternity – at the level of the Mystical Body – with all those already called to the ministerial priesthood. (Letter, 8 December 2007)

A parish that adores day and night obtains the graces of spiritual motherhood. It 'gives birth' to saintly vocations to the priesthood and religious life for the Church and obtains for them graces of sanctification. Through Perpetual Adoration, the parish becomes the bride who unites to her Bridegroom, Jesus in the Host. The Eucharist is the wedding banquet in which Christ gives to His Church the vocations they need in order to proclaim salvation to all nations. Yes, priestly vocations are obtained kneeling before the Lord in the Eucharist.

In the Gospel, 'Jesus went up the mountain and called to Him those He wanted. They came to Him, and He appointed twelve to be with Him and sent them out to preach' (Mk 3.13–14). Here Adoration is the 'come to him'. Evangelization is 'the being sent to'. Before 'going to' others in the name of Jesus, we must first 'come to' Jesus. Evangelizing without love is proselytizing. Adoration without evangelization is to escape. In his encyclical *Ecclesia de Eucharistia*, Blessed John Paul II said that:

> Every commitment to holiness, every activity aimed at fulfilling the mission of the Church, every implementation of pastoral planning, must draw from the Eucharistic mystery the necessary force and to be directed towards Him as towards the summit. In the Eucharist we have Jesus, we have His redemptive sacrifice, we have His resurrection, we have the gift of the Holy Spirit, we have adoration, obedience and love for the Father. If we disregard the Eucharist, how can we overcome our poverty. (60)

Here is the testimony of the priest who preceded me in my parish:

> It is already five years since our parish has had Perpetual Adoration. What a wonderful gift for a parish! This is the greatest grace there is because Jesus is loved in the Blessed Sacrament. Hour after hour, young people and adults of the parish come to the source of love and return to their day, filled

with strength, joy and peace. The Adoration of our parish has developed this great power of prayer and giving much perseverance in being faithful. Also, how can we think of evangelization if we do not first begin on our knees? Adoration and evangelization are two words that complement each other. It is for this reason that Adoration and the cells of evangelization, in place in our parish, form an inseparable link.[9]

'The sun of righteousness will shine with healing in his wings' (Mal. 3.20). In the Eucharist Jesus illuminates not only individuals but also groups, movements that come together to grow in zeal and ardour in proclaiming the Gospel. Don Macchioni, affirmed that for parish cells of evangelization:

> The community that does not know to make the choice (for Adoration) in faith will never see lasting fruit, which grow spiritually or increase in number of members, and this community will show laudably its initiatives but which are doomed to a fail. We can never repeat enough that this pastoral choice must precede and drive all the others. This praise and Adoration is a bulwark against the great temptations to which a growing community faces. Anyone who has spent his hour of Adoration at the service of the community, praying with love for the brothers that he is to evangelize, will emerge revitalized having received the vision of Jesus. In addition, he will gradually be cured of his inner wounds, because he has experienced God's love and will continue to do so.[10]

When a parish is made up of many small chapels or churches, Adoration without interruption is difficult to achieve. However, the chain of Adoration may be prolonged, making it a great source of grace for parishioners who do not have Mass every week in their own church or who are not very mobile. Many parishes are organized as follows. The main churches are chosen to become places of Adoration. Each local community is committed to providing a schedule of weekly Adoration. Everything is organized so that when the Adoration ends in one church, another church takes over, and so on. In this way, the Blessed Sacrament is still being adored in some church or chapel in the parish. This strengthens the unity of a parish with many smaller churches. Also, it 'gives life' to the different

---

[9] Testimony of Fr Bertrand Lorentz, Parish Priest of Sanary, 2004.
[10] Don Giuseppe Macchioni, *Evangéliser en Paroisse*, Nouan-Le-Fuzelier: Béatitudes, 2009, p. 76.

churches open for a several hours each week for Adoration. 'My house is a house of prayer' (Jn 2.17), and not a museum nor a place open only for a monthly Mass.

Also, several priests have borne witness to the fact that the Adoration Chapel open day and night helped prevent desecrations or damage. There are many examples where a devotee praying before the Blessed Sacrament, was able to prevent intrusion into the church or desecration. A lay journal in Brittany recently reported:

> They wanted to 'defend' the 'anti-clerical values' by attacking the Church of St Pius X in Vannes. They will eventually reflect on their actions here on the 1 June when they will appear before the Criminal Court of Vannes . . . After a drunken night spent at one of their houses, three students and one employee, equipped with red spray paint, went to the local church in Vannes with the intention of damaging the building with insulting graffiti. The police arrested them at around 1.30 a.m. when they were tipped off about the incident . . . It was the adorers who were in 'Perpetual Adoration' in a side chapel of this church who warned the police of the crimes being committed outside the building.[11]

Graces for the Church and the World

Blessed John Paul II wrote: 'To evangelize the world, we need experts in the celebration of, in the Adoration of and in the contemplation of the Eucharist' (World Day for the Missions, 2004). Through Adoration, parishioners are experiencing God's love. This leads them to become involved in their parish community, which gives them the Eucharist. In their mission, they are at the same time supporting the Church and interceding for the world. In other words, their Adoration becomes Trinitarian: in adoring the Son, they are led to the Father. In this dynamic, they receive a new outpouring of the Holy Spirit which leads them to involve themselves in the Church and the world.

In allowing the Spirit to act, the Adoration of the Blessed Eucharist urges the soul to truly develop a social love, for which the common good is preferred to the particular. For Paul VI, 'the Eucharist is of supreme efficacy for the transformation of the world into a world of justice, of holiness and peace' (Address, 15 June 1978).

Jesus presents His Heart to St Margaret Mary, sometimes like a sun of divine love, sometimes surrounded by a crown of thorns. It is both burning with love for men. On the other hand, He is offended

---

[11]   Le telegramme.com, Morbihan, 6 April 2011.

by their ingratitude. This dual consideration must move us, first, to render to Him love for love to the Heart of Jesus and second, to offer a compensation for the insult made to Him. To repair or to console the Heart of Jesus is to love Jesus with all your heart for those who reject or ignore Him. At Paray-le-Monial, Jesus said that this same Heart of flesh palpitates today in the Blessed Sacrament, for us who have not lived with Him 2000 years ago. 'Behold this Heart which has loved men so much, that has spared nothing in exhausting and consuming Itself in order to witness to them Its love. And in recognition, I receive from the most part nothing but ingratitude, by their irreverence and sacrilege, and the coldness and contempt they have for Me in this sacrament of love'. St Margaret Mary would pass all the time at her disposal to passionately love this Heart in the Blessed Sacrament, in reparation for those who do not know, ignore or despise It. Blessed John Paul II writes:

The encouragement and the deepening of Eucharistic devotion are proofs of that authentic renewal which the Council had fixed as its goal, and they are the central point. The Church and the world have great need of Eucharistic Adoration. Jesus awaits us in this sacrament of love. Let us not measure our time in going to meet Him in Adoration, in contemplation full of faith, ready to repair the great faults and great crimes of the world. May our Adoration never cease. (*Dominicæ Cenæ*)

Here is the testimony of one Texan night adorer:

Like a cruise ship, everyone can sense night and day the engine propelling the boat forward, likewise when a parish lives the grace of perpetual Adoration, at each hour of the day and night, a parishioner is united to the Heart of Jesus in the Eucharist, the true spiritual driving force of the parish. Then this Heart makes flow in abundance Its light and Its divine mercy on the Church and the world.

Blessed John Paul II presents Adoration as an eminent service to humanity:

By Adoration, the Christian mysteriously contributes to the radical transformation of the world and to the germination of the Gospel. Anyone who prays the Saviour brings in his train the world and elevates it to God. Those who stand before the Lord therefore fulfil an eminent service, they present to Christ all those who do not know Him or those who are far from Him, they watch before Him in their name. (Letter, 28 June 1996)

Thus, in adoring the Blessed Sacrament, we represent the person of our family, our parish, our world who has the greatest need of God's mercy. He receives the graces necessary to return to God the Father. In Exod. 17, when the Israelites fought against the Amalekites, Moses interceded before God by raising his hands to ask for the victory. As his arms grew heavy, he enlisted the help of Aaron and Hur to hold his arms raised up to God. And the Lord gave a complete victory to His people. In the same way, by Perpetual Adoration, an adorer is always present before the Lord in an unbroken chain of prayer and intercession. The heart of the parishioners is lifted up to God without cessation; and God gives victory to His people, His Church. He sends His mercy, His peace and light that chase the darkness from our hearts and the world. Also, in Isa. 62.4, it is written: 'On your walls, O Jerusalem, I have posted watchmen, day and night, they will never be silent'. When a parish is organizing Perpetual Adoration, the 'watchmen' are the adorers on the 'walls' that are 'never silent'. In other words, by their unceasing prayer, they are as if suspended between heaven and earth and to bring down on the humanity the outpouring of God's mercy. In the tabernacle, Jesus gives to His Church His great Adoration of the Father. He wants to associate us with it. The adorer is placed on the fractures of humanity. His supplication encompasses all situations where man has lost his dignity, his integrity, his resemblance to the Father. Adoration evangelizes by pouring out the graces of Redemption, through the Church, in all situations where man does not respond to his vocation as a child of the Father.

Blessed Charles de Foucauld adored the Blessed Sacrament in Tuareg country. He wrote: 'Sacred Heart of Jesus, radiate from the bottom of the tabernacle on the people who are around you without knowing you. Please advise, direct, save those souls that you love'. The Adoration Chapel is a beacon that illuminates, unites and protects the parish and the city. 'From His tabernacle, Jesus shines on these countries and attracts adorers to Him. My presence; does it do any good here? If mine does not, the presence of the Blessed Sacrament, in fact, certainly makes a lot of difference: Jesus cannot be in a place without shining on it'.

Blessed Teresa of Calcutta wrote: 'If people spent one hour a week in Eucharistic Adoration, abortion would cease'. Indeed, Perpetual Adoration of the Eucharist is a little piece of heaven on earth: Jesus is adored on this earth without interruption, as in heaven where the saints and angels adore Him continually. Divine life is spreading widely in hearts, protecting all human life from conception to natural death.

Speaking to St Faustina, Jesus said: 'Humanity will not find peace until it turns with trust to My Mercy'.[12] Further, we read: 'The Throne of Mercy is the Tabernacle'.[13] Thus, there can be no true peace in our hearts, families and the world without turning more toward the Eucharist, celebrated and adored. Bishop Ruben Profugo, Bishop of Lucena, the Philippines, said that

> Perpetual Eucharistic Adoration has protected my diocese from violence that threatened to tear it apart. Both priests and laity alike attribute to perpetual Eucharistic Adoration not only the protection of the diocese against communism, but also the establishment of peace and order.

The parish priest of Las Vegas wrote:

> We had prostitution in front of our church, there were people selling drugs. When we started perpetual Eucharistic adoration, it all stopped. When our Lord in the Blessed Sacrament has been exposed on the altar, crime has fallen significantly in the region. I am convinced.[14]

Mgr Josefino S. Ramirez, Vicar General and Chancellor of the Archdiocese of Manila in the Philippines, writes:

> Perpetual Eucharistic Adoration is the 'peace plan' of Our Lady. I am absolutely convinced that it will be through Adoration that peace will come upon our country and the world. When we do on earth what is done in heaven, that is, adore God continually, so we'll see 'the new earth and new heavens'. The only name, the only power, the only love that will bring eternal peace on the face of the earth, it is the Name, Power and Love of Jesus in the Blessed Sacrament.

It is God's love for man that created the world. It will be the love of man for God's Son in the Blessed Sacrament, which will recreate the world and will bring the promise of God's new creation. By His Incarnation the Son of God has united every man to Himself so that 'by His power to subject all things to Himself (Phil. 3.21), 'the world is created in order to be assumed into the Eucharist', where everything

---

12   St Faustina, *Petit Journal*, n. 300.
13   Ibid., n. 1484.
14   Testimony of Fr James Swenson, Parish of St. Brigid, Las Vegas, Nevada (n.d.).

and everyone will be perfected in the fire of divine love! (cf. Blessed John Paul II, Encyclical *Orientale Lumen*, 11).

Let us conclude with the words of St Peter Julian Eymard who, already in the nineteenth century, underlined the urgency of Eucharistic Adoration for the renewal of our parishes and of the world:

> Today solemn exposition of Jesus in the Blessed Sacrament is the grace and the need of our time. It is the sovereign grace. Exposition is the powerful weapon at the disposal of the Church and of the faithful . . . We are not afraid to say: the Worship and the Exposition of the Most Blessed Sacrament is the need of our time . . . This worship is necessary to save society. Society is dying because it has no centre of truth and charity, but it will be reborn in full force when all its members gather around the life of Jesus in the Eucharist. Go back to the source, to Jesus – especially to Jesus in the Eucharist . . . It is well known: a civilization grows or decreases according to its worship the Blessed Eucharist. This is its life and the measure of its faith, its love, its virtue. What the reign of the Eucharist will bring to pass! Impiety and ingratitude have reigned on earth for long enough. Thy kingdom come![15]

Pope Benedict XVI shows us the path to follow:

> The Eucharist is thus the source and summit not only of the Church's life, but also of her mission: 'an authentically Eucharistic Church is a missionary Church'. We too must be able to tell our brothers and sisters with conviction: 'That which we have seen and heard we proclaim also to you, so that you may have fellowship with us' (1 Jn 1.3). (*Sacramentum caritatis*, 84)

---

[15] Cf. Bernard Nodet, *Curé d'Ars : Pensées présentées par l'abbé Nodet*, Desclée, Paris: De Brouwer, 1989, p. 113.

Seventeen

Homily for the Solemn Mass of *Corpus Christi*

Pope Benedict XVI
Official Vatican translation from Italian

Dear Brothers and Sisters,

The Feast of *Corpus Christi* is inseparable from Holy Thursday, from the Mass *in Cœna Domini*, in which the Institution of the Eucharist is solemnly celebrated. Whereas on the evening of Holy Thursday we relive the mystery of Christ who offers Himself to us in the Bread broken and the Wine poured out, today, on the day of *Corpus Christi*, this same mystery is proposed for the Adoration and meditation of the People of God, and the Blessed Sacrament is carried in procession through the streets of the cities and villages, to show that the Risen Christ walks in our midst and guides us towards the Kingdom of Heaven.

What Jesus gave to us in the intimacy of the Upper Room today we express openly, because the love of Christ is not reserved for a few but is destined for all. In the Mass *in Cœna Domini* last Holy Thursday, I stressed that it is in the Eucharist that the transformation of the gifts of this earth takes place – the bread and wine – whose aim is to transform our life and thereby to inaugurate the transformation of the world. This evening I would like to focus on this perspective.

Everything begins, one might say, from the heart of Christ who, at the Last Supper, on the eve of His passion, thanked and praised God and by so doing, with the power of His Love, transformed the meaning of death which He was on His way to encounter. The fact that the Sacrament of the Altar acquired the name 'Eucharist' – 'thanksgiving' – expresses precisely this: that changing the substance of the bread and wine into the Body and Blood of Christ is the fruit of the gift that Christ made of Himself, the gift of a Love stronger than death, divine Love which raised Him from the dead. This is why the Eucharist is the food of eternal life, the Bread of Life. From Christ's heart, from His 'Eucharistic prayer' on the eve of His passion flows that dynamism which transforms reality in its cosmic, human and historical dimensions. All things proceed from God, from the omnipotence of His Triune Love, incarnate in Jesus. Christ's heart is steeped in this Love; therefore He can thank and praise God even in the face of betrayal and violence, and in this way changes things, people and the world.

This transformation is possible thanks to a communion stronger than division, the communion of God Himself. The word 'communion', which we also use to designate the Eucharist, in itself sums up the vertical and horizontal dimensions of Christ's gift.

The words 'to receive communion', referring to the act of eating the Bread of the Eucharist, are beautiful and very eloquent. In fact, when we do this act we enter into communion with the very life of Jesus, into the dynamism of this life which is given to us and for us. From God, through Jesus, to us, a unique communion is transmitted through the Blessed Eucharist.

We have just heard in the Second Reading the words of the Apostle Paul to the Christians of Corinth:

> The cup of blessing which we bless, is it not a participation in the Blood of Christ? The bread which we break, is it not a participation in the Body of Christ? Because there is one bread, we who are many are one body, for we all partake of the one bread. (1 Cor. 10.16–17)

St Augustine helps us to understand the dynamic of Eucharistic communion when he mentions a sort of vision that he had, in which Jesus said to him: 'I am the food of strong men; grow and you shall feed on me; nor shall you change me, like the food of your flesh into yourself, but you shall be changed into my likeness' (*Confessions*, VII, 10, 18).

Therefore whereas food for the body is assimilated by our organism and contributes to nourishing it, in the case of the Eucharist it is a different Bread: it is not we who assimilate it but it assimilates us in itself, so that we become conformed to Jesus Christ, a member of His Body, one with Him. This passage is crucial. In fact, precisely because it is Christ who, in Eucharistic communion changes us into Him, our individuality, in this encounter, is opened, liberated from its egocentrism and inserted into the Person of Jesus who in His turn is immersed in Trinitarian communion. The Eucharist, therefore, while it unites us to Christ also opens us to others, makes us members of one another: we are no longer divided but one in Him. Eucharistic communion not only unites me to the person I have beside me and with whom I may not even be on good terms, but also to our distant brethren in every part of the world.

Hence the profound sense of the Church's social presence derives from the Eucharist, as is testified by the great social saints who were always great Eucharistic souls. Those who recognize Jesus in the Sacred Host, recognize Him in their suffering brother or sister, in those who hunger and thirst, who are strangers, naked, sick or in prison; and they are attentive to every person, they work in practice for all who are in need.

Therefore our special responsibility as Christians for building a supportive, just and brotherly society comes from the gift of Christ's Love. Especially in our time, in which globalization makes us more and more dependent on each other, Christianity can and must ensure that this unity is not built without God, that is, without true Love, which would give way to confusion, individualism and the tyranny of each one seeking to oppress the others. The Gospel has always aimed at the unity of the human family, a unity that is neither imposed from the outside nor by ideological or economic interests but on the contrary is based on the sense of reciprocal responsibility, so that we may recognize each other as members of one and the same Body, the Body of Christ, because from the Sacrament of the Altar we have learned and are constantly learning that sharing, love, is the path to true justice.

Let us now return to Jesus' action at the Last Supper. What happened at that moment? When He said: 'this is My Body which is given for you, this is the cup of My Blood which is poured out for many', what happened? In this gesture Jesus was anticipating the event of Calvary. Out of love He accepted the whole passion, with its anguish and its violence, even to death on the cross. In accepting it in this manner He changed it into an act of giving. This is the transformation which the world needs most, to redeem it from within, to open it to the dimensions of the Kingdom of Heaven.

However, God always wishes to bring about this renewal of the world on the same path followed by Christ, that way which is indeed He Himself. There is nothing magical about Christianity. There are no short-cuts; everything passes through the humble and patient logic of the grain of wheat that broke open to give life, the logic of faith that moves mountains with the gentle power of God. For this reason God wishes to continue to renew humanity, history and the cosmos through this chain of transformations, of which the Eucharist is the Sacrament. Through the consecrated bread and wine, in which His Body and His Blood are really present, Christ transforms us, conforming us to Him: He involves us in His work of redemption, enabling us, through the grace of the Holy Spirit, to live in accordance with His own logic of self-giving, as grains of wheat united to Him and in Him. Thus are sown and continue to mature in the furrows of history unity and peace, which are the end for which we strive, in accordance with God's plan.

Let us walk with no illusions, with no utopian ideologies, on the highways of the world bearing within us the Body of the Lord, like the Virgin Mary in the mystery of the Visitation. With the humility of knowing that we are merely grains of wheat, let us preserve the firm certainty that the love of God, incarnate in Christ, is stronger than evil, violence and death. We know that God prepares for all men and women new heavens and a new earth, in which peace and justice reign – and in faith we perceive the new world which is our true homeland.

This evening too, let us start out: while the sun is setting on our beloved city of Rome: Jesus in the Eucharist is with us, the Risen One who said: 'I am with you always, to the close of the age' (Mt. 28.20). Thank you, Lord Jesus! Thank you for your faithfulness which sustains our hope. Stay with us because night is falling. 'Very Bread, Good Shepherd, tend us, Jesus, of your love befriend us, You refresh us, you defend us, Your eternal goodness send us in the land of life to see'. Amen.